The Policy of the Entente

The Policy of the Entente

Essays on the Determinants of
British Foreign Policy
1904–1914

KEITH M. WILSON
Lecturer in Modern History, University of Leeds

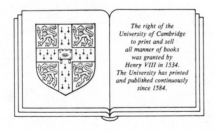

The right of the
University of Cambridge
to print and sell
all manner of books
was granted by
Henry VIII in 1534.
The University has printed
and published continuously
since 1584.

CAMBRIDGE UNIVERSITY PRESS

Cambridge
London   New York   New Rochelle
Melbourne   Sydney

Published by the Press Syndicate of the University of Cambridge
The Pitt Building, Trumpington Street, Cambridge CB2 1RP
32 East 57th Street, New York, NY 10022, USA
10 Stamford Road, Oakleigh, Melbourne 3166, Australia

First published 1985

Printed in Great Britain at the University Press, Cambridge

Library of Congress catalogue card number: 84–17038

British Library Cataloguing in Publication Data

Wilson, Keith M.
The policy of the entence: essays on the
determinants of British foreign policy 1904–1914.
1. Great Britain – Foreign relations –
1901–1910 2. Great Britain – Foreign relations
– 1910–1936
I. Title
327.41   DA570
ISBN 0 521 30195 5

When nations have gone down hill till they are at their last gasp their pride remains undiminished, if indeed it is not increased. It clings to them as Tacitus says the love of dissimulation clung to Tiberius at his last gasp.

Sir Edward Grey

TO GILL

Contents

Acknowledgements

The following institutions and individuals have given permission to use material which is in their keeping or on which they retain the copyright: the Controller of H.M.'s Stationery Office; the Bodleian Library; the British Library; Cambridge University Library; Lord Gainford; Lord Salisbury; Mark Bonham Carter; Elizabeth Cartwright Hignett; Major C. J. Wilson; the Trustees of the Imperial War Museum; the Trustees of the National Library of Scotland; Mrs D. M. Maxse; the West Sussex County Record Office; the Trevelyan family; Newcastle-upon-Tyne University Library; Times Newspapers Ltd; the *Guardian*; the holders of the copyright of Lord Murray of Elibank; the University of Birmingham; Admiral Sir Ian Hogg; Lord Simon.

The Longman Group, and Professor J. E. Spence, former editor of the *British Journal of International Studies*, where the original versions of chapters 7 and 8 first appeared in 1977 and 1975, have given permission for this work to be reprinted.

A grant towards the costs of publication was made by the Committee on Grants for Publications of the University of Leeds.

Introduction

Variations on the phrase 'the policy of entente' were applied without any great precision by British diplomatists in the years immediately before the Great War to describe the foreign policy of their country since the turn of the century. The questions of what that policy was, and of why it was what it was and not something else, are not made easier to answer by the fact that almost everyone involved in the making and executing of foreign policy had a view, not only of what the policy was, but of what it ought to be. Nevertheless, in its attempt to establish what were Britain's priorities in her relations with the Great Powers of Europe, those are the questions which this work addresses.

The existing interpretation of British foreign policy before the outbreak of war in 1914 has been encouraged by the following works: G. W. Monger, *The End of Isolation* (London, 1963); Z. S. Steiner, *The Foreign Office and Foreign Policy 1898–1914* (Cambridge, 1969), and *Britain and the Origins of the First World War* (London, 1977); K. Robbins, *Sir Edward Grey – a Biography* (London, 1971). F. H. Hinsley's *The Foreign Policy of Sir Edward Grey*, a collection of essays from many individuals working separately, commissioned in the mid-1960s but appearing only in 1977, and P. M. Kennedy's *The Rise of the Anglo-German Antagonism 1860–1914* (London, 1980) are the latest additions to this particular literature. This existing interpretation may be said to include the following elements: a large degree of continuity and the adherence by successive administrations to certain well-established traditions and well-defined principles of policy, in particular those of the balance of power and the free hand. On the whole, the impression given is that British foreign policy was as straightforward, honest and open as were supposed to be the ministers made responsible for it; that, if foreign policy was not actually made in the Foreign Office, by the officials there, and increasingly so after the implementation of the reforms of 1905, then it was at least the more or less exclusive preserve of the Foreign Secretary; that British foreign policy was to a large extent self-contained, and not a product of British domestic or

1

internal politics – not related so closely to movements in British politics generally or to developments in British society at large as, according to E. Kehr, F. Fischer, A. J. Mayer, V. R. Berghahn, the foreign policy of Germany in particular was related to trends within the body politic; that the maintenance and development of the Anglo-French Agreement of April 1904 which Sir Edward Grey inherited from Lord Lansdowne, and the making of the Anglo-Russian Conventions of August 1907 with which he complemented it, represented a change of orientation, an adjustment of priorities, a shift both in values and of emphasis, from the British Empire to the European continent; that this change was inspired by an accurate appreciation of the threat posed by Germany to Europe and to England; that Britain went to war in 1914 primarily out of concern for Belgium and for France, and that the British Expeditionary Force went where it did go in 1914 because the military conversations between the British and French General Staffs left no alternative.

In the formation of foreign policy very little is what it appears to be, and there is too much material, and too many nuances in this material, of which the received view does not take account, too many contradictions which the orthodox accounts neither resolve nor explain, or in some cases even notice – such is the extent to which certain ingrained assumptions have come to dominate the reading of the primary sources. The essays in this volume seek the actual content and real determinants of British foreign policy from a number of different angles. Using the full range of sources, some of which have only recently become available, each essay deals separately with some aspect or interpretation either of the period of the entente as a whole or the British decision for war itself. The conclusions arrived at mutually reinforce and support one another.

The policy of the Entente emerges as one in the interpretation of which due weight has to be given to domestic political considerations and constraints, especially upon the independence and freedom of action of the Foreign Secretary; allowance has to be made for the deliberate manufacture of myths; and room has to be found for the appreciation that the sources reflect several layers of reality – not only in the sense that some participants in the policy-making process had a firmer grasp than others of what the policy was, but also in the sense that cynicism lay below expressions of devoutness, despair behind confidence and bombast. Taken together, these essays maintain that the major principles of British foreign policy were not compatible; that so great was the scale of dislocation between means and the ends professed that it amounted to a difference in kind; that the makers of British foreign policy were less interested in Europe than in their Empire; that they regarded themselves on the whole as being less threatened by Germany than by Russia; that the achievement and maintenance of good relations with Russia as an end in itself was the main objective of British policy throughout these years; and that the entente with France, originally conceived and regarded as a stepping-stone to better Anglo-Russian relations, remained essentially subsidiary to these, and the necessity to support France something of an embarrassment, all the more so because of the lack of the means with which to do so, something which the French kept pointing out. It is further maintained that those responsible for conducting and executing British foreign policy, unable to admit openly the weakness of Britain's world position, unwilling to draw the logical conclusions from the unbridgeability of the gap between commitments and assets, resentful at the decline in their relative power and the consequent necessity for Britain to embroil herself in European affairs, pretended both to themselves and to others that she was still the force in the world that they liked to think she once had been. In so far as it is shown that severe limitations were imposed upon the pursuit of 'pure policy' by what was at the same time politically acceptable and financially possible, it is suggested that the primacy of *Innenpolitik*, even in the case of Great Britain, cannot lightly be set aside.

I have been asked to draw the attention of the reader to the fact that, in addition to some of the work of B. Williams, published in *Historical Journal* in 1966, and to some of the work of I. Klein, published in *Journal of British Studies* in 1971, and in addition to work more recently published, such as E. Ingram's article in *Militärgeschichtliche Mitteilungen* (1974), R. J. Crampton's *The Hollow Détente* (London, 1980), and S. Mahajan's article in *Journal of Imperial and Commonwealth History* (1982), there is also available now some work in the German language which indicates that there are yet other historians who, whilst this book was in course of preparation and publication, have been moving towards a similar view of the place of 'the Russian factor' in the formulation of British foreign policy during the period under consideration; these include E. Holzle, *Die Selbstentmachtung Europas* (Gottingen, 1975) and K. Wormer, *Grossbritannien, Russland und Deutschland: Studien zur Britischen Weltreichpolitik am Vorabend des ersten Weltkriegs* (Munich, 1980). The latest article on this particular aspect by the present writer is to be found in *Review of International Studies* (July, 1984). David E. Kaiser's article 'Germany and the Origins of the First World War' in *Journal of Modern History* (October 1983) is the latest piece of work convincingly to demonstrate that, at the very least, the makers of British foreign policy seriously misread the *Weltpolitik* of both Prince B. von Bulow and T. von Bethmann-Hollweg.

1

The Poverty of the Entente Policy

On 1 March 1893 Lord Rosebery addressed the members of the Colonial Institute in defence of policies of his which the leader of his party, Mr W. E. Gladstone, had described as 'imbued with the spirit of territorial grab':

It is said that our Empire is already large enough and does not need extension. That would be true enough if the world were elastic, but, unfortunately, it is not elastic, and we are engaged at the present moment, in the language of the mining camps, in 'pegging out claims for the future'. We have to consider, not what we want now, but what we shall want in the future ... we should, in my opinion, grossly fail in the task that has been laid upon us did we shrink from responsibilities and decline to take our share in a partition of the world which we have not forced on, but which has been forced upon us.[1]

By the turn of the century the British Empire was the largest and most widespread of all the empires acquired by the European Powers. In addition to safeguarding the territories of which this Empire consisted, the British had also to protect a volume of sea-borne trade amounting to an annual value of 1200 million pounds sterling, and 9 million tons of shipping upon which the British people depended, amongst other things, for the security of their food supply. In the twentieth century Britain faced what Lord Selborne called the 'terrific task' of remaining the greatest naval Power when naval Powers were increasing year by year in numbers and in strength and of being at the same time a military Power strong enough to meet the greatest military Power in Asia.[2]

A note of warning had already been sounded, by Joseph Chamberlain, in May 1898, when he pointed out that Britain was envied by everyone, and had interests which at one time or another conflicted with the interests of everyone else. This sentiment, and the solution Chamberlain suggested, was not at that time widely shared or well received. Leading members of the Liberal opposition had no wish to go 'touting for allies in the highways and byways of Europe', as H. H. Asquith put it.[3] The outbreak and early course of the Boer War, however, increased both the sentiment and the

4

degree to which Chamberlain's solution was acceptable. The views expressed in October 1900 and April 1901 by Lord George Hamilton to Lord Curzon were representative of his ministerial colleagues. On the latter occasion he wrote:

I am gradually coming round to the opinion that we must alter our foreign policy, and throw our lot in, for good or bad, with some other Power . . . As we now stand, we are an object of envy and of greed to all the other Powers. Our interests are so vast and ramified that we touch, in some shape or other, the interests of almost every great country in every continent. Our interests being so extended makes it almost impossible for us to concentrate sufficiently, in any one direction, the pressure and power of the Empire so as to deter foreign nations from trying to encroach upon our interests in that particular quarter.[4]

From the point of view of the development of the policy of the Entente, the significance of the Anglo-German negotiations of 1901 was that they established that a German alliance would be no solution to the problems facing the British Empire. The British wished to reduce the burden of their responsibilities, not to increase it. They wished to remain a World Power, not to become a European one. Lord Salisbury pointed out that the liability of having to defend the German and Austrian frontiers against Russia was heavier than that of having to defend the British Isles against France.[5] Sir F. Bertie, one of the officials at the Foreign Office, agreed that 'if once we bind ourselves by a formal defensive alliance and practically join the Triplice we shall never be on decent terms with France our neighbour in Europe and in many parts of the world, or with Russia whose frontiers are coterminous with ours or nearly so over a large portion of Asia'.[6] Lord Lansdowne listed as the second of five 'virtually insuperable' difficulties in the way of an Anglo-German alliance 'the certainty of alienating France and Russia'.[7] Salisbury had never believed that the Germans would ever stand by Britain against Russia, because of their long undefended frontier with Russia in Europe. The Germans had already justified Salisbury's lack of faith in them by interpreting the Anglo-German Agreement of October 1900 in such a way as to absolve them of any duty to consider Manchuria as an integral part of China.[8]

Chamberlain in 1898, Lansdowne in 1902, and Lord Haldane in retrospect, all invoked the existence of groups of Powers as the explanation for the end of English isolation.[9] Even in 1898, however, there was nothing new about these 'groups': they were a well-established feature of the international scene. The diplomatic remedies for the British condition that were taken were not due to the existence or formation of groups of Powers. They were due rather to something which Salisbury had included in an explanation to the Queen in 1886 of why it was the destiny of Her Majesty's servants in foreign affairs 'to be always making bricks without straw': 'Without money, without any strong land force, with an insecure tenure of power, and with an ineffective agency, they have to counterwork the efforts of three Empires, who labour under none of these disadvantages.'[10] Shortage of money was the chronic complaint which, in the early years of the twentieth century, became so acute as no longer to be tolerable.

In 1897 Salisbury had had to take the War Office to task for making proposals for the conduct of the Nile campaign which were, 'like many documents from the same source, defective in taking little or no account of money'. He went on: 'Money is our only serious difficulty. If we have money, the . . . power of the Khalifa's army matters little, for we can always bring up British regiments in sufficient force to defeat him. But if we have no money we cannot use the British army at all.'[11] In September 1901 he made the following pessimistic prediction to Curzon, the Viceroy of India:

Our main interest in the East (after China) has been the movements of the Persian Question. In the main it is a question of money. In the last generation we did much what we liked in the East by force or threats – by squadrons and tall-talk – but the day of individual coercive action is almost passed by. For some years to come Eastern advance must largely depend on payment, and I fear that in that race England will seldom win.[12]

Selborne, who echoed this prediction in January 1903, had in December 1900 been led to consider a formal alliance with Germany as 'possibly the only alternative to an ever-increasing Navy and ever-increasing Navy estimates'.[13] Considerations of economy were important in the making of the Anglo-Japanese Alliance of February 1902; it was on the same grounds that Grey argued for its extension in time in May 1911.[14] When Lord Cromer wrote to A. J. Balfour from Egypt in October 1903 suggesting that an understanding on all pending questions with France be regarded as 'possibly a stepping-stone to a general understanding with Russia', what he had further in mind was that the latter 'possibly, again, may prepare the ground for some reduction in our enormous military and naval expenditure'.[15] In a paper of July 1906 the secretary of the Committee of Imperial Defence, Sir George Clarke, took it for granted that the primary justification of negotiations with Russia was the removal of the mutual suspicions 'which have already cost us a heavy expenditure of life and treasure'. Looking back from the threshold of the signature of the Anglo-Russian Conventions of August 1907, and recalling that it had been the policy of all his successive Chiefs, Sir Thomas Sanderson, who had been Permanent Under-Secretary at the Foreign Office from 1895 to 1906, accounted for this in the following terms: 'The reason is an obvious one – the process of working in constant antagonism is too expensive . . . we could not pursue a really successful policy of antagonism to Russia without efforts and sacrifices which the public and Parliament would not agree to.'[16] Sir C. Hardinge, Sanderson's successor, declared to the Ambassador to St Petersburg in January 1909: 'We cannot afford to sacrifice in any way our entente with Russia'; Grey declared in the last week of July 1914: 'We cannot possibly afford to see the position of France weakened.'[17] These declarations have, in a real sense, to be taken literally.

In order to retain that command of the sea so vital to Britain, and in order at the same time to guard in arms against all comers every portion of the British Empire's land frontier, it would have been necessary to raise vast sums of money. This had even less appeal for a Liberal administration pledged to economise and to retrench, and whose programme of domestic reforms depended upon the savings to be made, than it had for their predecessors in office. At the beginning of 1909, facing the prospect of raising £38 million for the Navy Estimates alone, the Chancellor of the Exchequer D. Lloyd George reminded Asquith of 'the emphatic pledges given by all of us before and at the last general election to reduce the gigantic expenditure on armaments built up by the recklessness of our predecessors':

Scores of your most loyal supporters in the House of Commons take these pledges seriously and even a £3 million increase will chill their zeal for the Government and an assumed increase of £5–6 million for the next year will stagger them. There are millions of earnest Liberals in the country who are beginning rather to lose confidence in the Government for reasons we are not altogether responsible for. When the £38 million navy estimates are announced the disaffection of these good Liberals will break into open sedition and the usefulness of this Parliament will be at an end.[18]

Grey took the line that whilst he too had advocated retrenchment before the election, he had 'always excepted the Navy from my promises, and in any case promises must always be subordinate to national safety'.[19] Since Grey, Asquith, Sir R. McKenna and the Board of Admiralty were all prepared to resign over the matter, it was this line which prevailed.

It must be emphasised that this particular cabinet crisis was produced merely by the necessity of finding the money for the quite local purpose of the defence of the British Isles. A commensurately greater crisis would have been created by the necessity of finding the altogether larger sums of money to secure overall naval supremacy and to retain command of the sea as a whole. Command of the sea, moreover, would still have left the defence of the Empire to be provided for. Naval supremacy was no defence to India. The seas might still be regarded, with more than a pinch of salt, as all one, but this was increasingly irrelevant in an age when the development of railway communications rendered the greatest possession of the British Empire vulnerable to overland attack by a Great Power.[20]

Even as it was, in 1909 the Admiralty lowered still further the sights adjusted by Selborne in 1901. It decided that British needs would be met if the strength of the British Navy was maintained in a ratio of 16 to 10 with the German Navy.[21] The adoption of this 60% standard, which was not made public until 1912, effectively meant that the Admiralty had given up the struggle to retain command of the sea. They had retreated from the position they had taken up early in 1906, when they had said that the Board of Admiralty could not base its plans on the shifting sands of any temporary and unofficial international relationship, and when, on the grounds that ententes may vanish, that only battleships were substantial, they had declared that the existence of the entente with France was no reason to reduce the Navy estimates.[22] From 1909 'naval supremacy' meant only 'supremacy over Germany'. Britain's freedom of action was therefore still further reduced. Grey later observed in the House of Commons that it was at least as true that foreign policy depended upon armaments as that armaments depended upon policy:

If you are going to have an absolute standard superior to all the other European navies put together, it is clear that your foreign policy is comparatively simple. Supposing you find yourself at any given moment in such an unfortunate diplomatic situation that the whole of Europe is combined against you at once, you are still going to be able to defend yourself then. If you are not in that position, and if you are not going to have that kind of standard, your Foreign Secretary must adjust your foreign policy so that you will not at any given moment have combined against you navies which you are unequal to meet.[23]

Grey did maintain, in one moment of bravado, what Hardinge had been apt to maintain: that so long as Britain retained her sea power she could not be coerced even by a state which achieved European dominance;[24] but whilst the Navy might have been able to secure the British Isles, that was the only part of the British Empire that it would have been able to secure. Well might Grey have discouraged M. Briand in 1910 from spending on the French Navy money that could be spent on the French Army.[25] He had no wish to be a party to schemes for naval building which, if implemented, would have still further reduced Britain's 'naval supremacy' and increased her dependence on her 'friends'.

No doubt the sums of money, however vast, that would have been necessary in order to avoid diplomatic solutions and continue in isolation, could have been raised. Even if certain major components of the Empire, such as India, proved reluctant, as they had done in the past, to bear the charge for an Imperial war, even when the defence of Afghanistan was in question,[26]

Great Britain was a wealthy country. Income tax, before 1914, did not exceed one shilling in the pound.

Some Foreign Office figures were prepared to spend their way at least out of the potential trouble represented by the German Navy. The solution they offered to this problem was that of naval building. One of the Senior Clerks, E. A. Crowe, expressed the view in a memorandum of 1 January 1907 that 'nothing is more likely to produce in Germany the impression of the practical hopelessness of a never-ending succession of costly naval programmes than the conviction, based on ocular demonstration, that for every German ship England will inevitably lay down two, so maintaining the present relative British preponderance'.[27] The opinion of Sir F. Cartwright in Munich was that every shilling spent on maintaining the efficacy of the British Fleet was a shilling spent in the direction of the maintenance of the peace of Europe.[28] G. S. Spicer, one of the Junior Clerks, thought in 1908 that there was 'just a chance that were the German Government really and fully, once and for all, to realise that Great Britain meant to maintain at all costs her naval supremacy they might accept the fact and cease their challenge'; Captain P. W. Dumas, then Naval Attaché at Berlin, called for the specification of a real Two-Power Standard as often as possible and for Britain's adherence to it.[29] Sir E. Goschen, the Ambassador in Berlin from 1908, wrote to Hardinge in 1909:

the more determined we show ourselves to maintain our absolute supremacy at sea the more civil and anxious to come to terms the Germans will be . . . as I have often said, the best and only understanding we can have with them is to make them understand that we mean business and intend, whatever it may cost us, to maintain our maritime supremacy.[30]

Hardinge needed no encouragement. He always maintained that the best way of stopping, or of modifying, the German naval programme was through a declaration of intent to outdo it. He attributed an apparent slackening of the German programme in the winter of 1908 entirely to 'the firm declarations made by Mr Asquith of his adherence to the Two-Power Standard'. In 1910, he said that had the Government agreed to build by loan three years earlier, when he had urged strongly on Grey and the Cabinet that they should obtain authority for a loan of £100 million to be used as required, 'we might have dealt a very serious blow to the German naval programme, and possibly have knocked it out altogether'.[31]

There is no evidence that it occurred to these people, who were giving this advice at a time when they knew that Russia was quite unprepared for war, that if the German naval programme was terminated the German Government would have more money to concentrate on the German Army. There is no more evidence of this than there is that it occurred to the same individuals that closing abruptly the German option of expansion overseas, dashing prematurely her hopes in that area, might concentrate her mind and energies upon the continent of Europe and create a genuine German problem there both for Britain and for Europe. Yet this could well have been the result of the adoption of their arguments of 1911 against the acquisition by Germany of territory in Africa, as it could have been of the acceptance of their argument for an end to all negotiations with Germany because of the ambivalence their continuance implied – an argument that derived from fear that the British political pendulum would swing too far and stick in the German direction, and which betrayed the fact that its holders had less confidence in and less understanding of the internal political dynamics than had Grey himself.

Though Grey was determined to maintain naval supremacy over Germany in the North Sea, he was not prepared to go any further towards the solution of naval building. The scale of Hardinge's recommendations had no appeal for him. As recently as March 1904 he had recalled the example of Lord Goschen's Naval Defence Act of 1889: 'instead of discouraging the building of other Powers, this great effort on our part had increased the rivalry.'[32] Though by no means a free agent, though under pressure during the Agadir crisis and in the subsequent negotiations with Germany to act in the sense of the Cabinet as a whole, Grey also had no time for the idea of excluding Germany from Africa and other extra-European territories. He told Bertie in July 1911 that 'as to British interests it really doesn't matter to us who owns tropical territory that we do not want for ourselves'.[33] He forestalled the protest Crowe wanted Bertie to make against proposals that would bring Germany onto the Sudan frontier by stating bluntly: 'I do not think it matters very much whether we have Germany or France as a neighbour in Africa.'[34] He ignored in January 1912 Bertie's projection of Germany supplanting Belgium and Portugal in Africa and creating an empire across the black continent that would break at right-angles the all-red route from the Cape to Cairo.[35] But though he thus kept open and alive in the German mind the possibilities of expansion overseas, there is no evidence that it occurred to Grey any more than to his advisers that he was helping to spare Europe the strain she might otherwise have to endure.[36] The negotiations with Germany over the future of the Portuguese colonies were intended by him less to distract her from Europe than to distract those of his colleagues who wished to replace the policy of the Entente with a German policy from raising again the question of a political formula.

There is some evidence to account for why it was that, from the turn of the century, successive administrations should have been as reluctant as they were to contemplate large-scale expenditure on the defence of the British

Isles and British Empire. Overall annual expenditure had risen by almost 50% between 1895/6 and 1901/2: from £105 million to £147 million. The latter figures did not include expenditure arising from the Boer War. Between 1899 and 1902, £34 million was raised by special war taxes, but this was almost completely consumed by the £30 million rise in *ordinary* expenditure excluding non-recurring war costs. Sir Michael Hicks-Beach, the Chancellor, observed in October 1901 that it was 'undoubtedly a serious matter that even if we were free from any extra charge for South Africa our ordinary expenditure would still require the continuance at a war rate in time of peace of a tax which has always been considered our great reserve in time of war'. To raise income tax in peacetime to a figure higher than the wartime level of 1s 2d was, he said, out of the question: 'It could not be borne.'[37] His successor, C. T. Ritchie, faced with the problem of raising £34 million more than had been necessary only four years previously, revealed that he was aware that it would create 'difficulties' if the Government showed that it was prepared to reduce taxation which mainly affected the well-to-do, whilst leaving untouched the taxation which fell most heavily on the wage-earning classes. In his view, the outlook was grim: ' . . . one of the greatest dangers that I am afraid of is that, with one shilling income tax, and with bad times entailing want of employment, and perhaps an appreciably increased price of bread, there will be a violent reaction . . . '. This 'violent reaction' would compel sweeping and ill-considered reductions in defence expenditure. The only way of warding off the danger of ill-considered reductions was to anticipate the violent reaction and make an immediate reduction in the scale of expenditure. The present rate of expenditure, he said, 'cannot safely be continued'.[38]

Within a few years, the question of whether current rates of expenditure on naval armaments alone could safely be continued was exercising the Governments of both Britain and Germany. At the Foreign Office, Grey recognised that the pressure of taxation might alter the view of those elements in Germany who were in favour of a large Navy. He went so far, in April 1908, as to say that 'nothing but pressure of finance will bring the German naval expenditure down'.[39] It was, no doubt, encouraging to him to receive, from time to time, information to the effect that the financial situation in Germany was deteriorating. It was, no doubt, doubly pleasing to gather personally that the German Ambassador to London was 'depressed by the rapid growth of naval expenditure and would welcome a slackening of it . . . '.[40] Grey knew, however, that the Germans, for their part, were also hoping that England, or rather the people of England, would for financial reasons be the first to tire of the struggle of maintaining the superior Fleet.[41] His reluctance to force the pace, to increase the financial pressure on Germany, derived from his lack of confidence in the ability of the British taxpayer to sustain any greater pace and pressure. His pursuit of an agreement with Germany to limit naval expenditure, which was the one item in the whole complex of Anglo-German negotiations that he personally was eager to secure, also sprang from the feeling that there were limits to the patience of the British people. As he told James Bryce at the end of 1909: 'an arrangement based on the completion of the German naval programme would be comparatively easy, but then what a large naval expenditure we should still have to face!'.[42] His support of disarmament at the Hague Conference of 1907, which so amazed Crowe,[43] was another product of this unease. Even the spendthrift Hardinge was so shocked by his hosts on one visit to Germany that he exclaimed:

An end must be put to this ship-building competition; an arrangement must be arrived at for slowing it down. For our Government will have to bring in a big programme of fresh naval construction in the next five years, for which fresh taxes will have to be raised owing to lack of resources. It will be very unpopular, the people will grumble, and the Government may be turned out.[44]

Here Hardinge caught the mood that Rosebery expressed at the Imperial Press Conference of 1909 when, describing as 'a silent warfare' the competition in armaments between the European Powers, he wondered aloud 'where it will stop, or if it is nearly going to bring back Europe into a state of barbarism, or whether it will cause a catastrophe in which the working men of the world will say "We will have no more of this madness, this foolery which is grinding us to powder" '.[45] The difference between England and Germany was that in the former the challenge to authority was more likely to come from the left, in the latter it was more likely to come from the right.[46]

The diplomatic solutions devised by the British were not founded simply on the appreciation that the forward policies that it would be necessary to pursue just to stand still against Russia in Central Asia might actually provoke her into taking even more seriously than hitherto the development of a real design upon India. They were not based solely upon the possibility that a great effort to maintain naval supremacy might alienate other Powers and multiply the scale of the existing rivalry. The enemy was within as well as without. British Governments were as afraid of what their own people would do if asked to spend them out of trouble as they were of what foreign governments would do if they were not. The streets might become dark with something more than night.

In June 1911 Grey gave a lecture in a memorial series for a former colleague on the board of the North Eastern Railway. In it he said that the next country which had a great and successful war 'would be the first to have a social revolution'. The Agadir crisis, which was dealt with against a background of industrial and domestic troubles, bore out immediately his prediction that the industrial workers 'will not stand being played with, nor allow their problems of existence to be pushed on one side by international questions'.[47] A few months later, shortly before his Private Secretary noted that 'Grey is more anxious about strikes than about foreign affairs', he had written to one confidant:

This coal strike is the beginning of a revolution. We shall, I suppose, make it an orderly and gradual revolution, but labour intends to have a larger share and have laid hold of power. Power ... is passing from the House of Commons to the Trades Unions. It will have to be recognised that the millions of men employed in great industries have a stake in those industries and must share in control of them ... The Unions may of course like blind Samson with his arms round the pillars, pull down the house on themselves and everyone else, if they push things too far; or if the owners are too unyielding, there will be civil war ... There are unpleasant years before us; we shall work through to something better, though we who have been used to more than £500 a year may not think it better.[48]

It comes as no surprise, therefore, to find Grey agreeing with the German Ambassador in June 1912 'that, if there was a great European war, it was not likely to profit anyone, for even the Power which was successful in the war might, on being relieved from external pressure for a time, suffer to the extent of revolution from internal pressure'.[49] With war in sight, in July 1914, he told the Austrian Ambassador that it seemed to him 'that it must involve the expenditure of so vast a sum of money and such an interference with trade, that a war would be accompanied or followed by a complete collapse of European credit and industry'. That would mean, in the great industrial states, 'a state of things worse than that of 1848, and, irrespective of who were victors in the war, many things might be completely swept away'.[50] Morley was another minister who likened the times to the Year of Revolutions. The dislocation of industrial life that a war would produce must, he recalled saying at the end of July 1914, 'in the present temper of labour ... be fraught with public danger': 'The atmosphere of war cannot be friendly to order, in a democratic system that is verging on the humour of '48.'[51] As one of the great industrial states Britain was as vulnerable to these possibilities of disorder as either of the Central Powers. One of the statements that Grey is reputed to have made upon the outbreak of war was, after all: 'There will be Labour governments everywhere after this.'[52] The spectre of Labour Governments, of labour, and even of revolution whether as the product of war or the product of wartime levels of expenditure and taxation in peacetime, had been with the British ruling classes, by 1914, for a number of years, getting closer all the time. It was the ghost in the machine.

Early in 1906 Sir George Clarke, then secretary to the Committee of

Imperial Defence, expressed to Lord Esher the view that 'We are about to see a social upheaval, which may be swift or slow, but is certainly inevitable.' For this reason he wished to see the Volunteers which Haldane at the War Office proposed to raise dominated by 'the classes which are not likely to take up arms at the bidding of a Socialist County Council'.[53] At one extreme of the political spectrum F. S. Oliver wrote to Lord Milner on 3 March 1911: 'Nothing will save us except the sight of red blood running pretty freely; but whether British and German blood, or only British, I don't know – nor do I think it much matters . . . '; a Major Viburne, on the occasion of Haldane's visit to Berlin in February 1912, wrote:

Personally, I think there must be a war between this country and Germany sooner or later, and it had better come sooner. A good big war might do a lot of good in killing Socialist nonsense and would probably put a stop to all this labour unrest. We are within measurable distance of a coal strike which will cost quite as much as a big war, besides paralysing trade, and making stagnant the industries of the country . . .

The editor of the *Morning Post* wrote to his proprietor at the same time:

I must confess that I am still depressed about the strike, not because of the strike itself as of the altered state of mind that seems to animate the people. Up to the present I would have said that in any great crisis I would put my trust in the common sane 'horse-sense' of the masses. I have never believed in their ability to understand things but I have always had a feeling that they would never give their allegiance to out and out extremists. My faith in them has been sadly shaken.[54]

Towards the other extreme, C. P. Trevelyan, who was to resign from the Government in August 1914, wrote during the Agadir crisis of 1911 that 'we are now on the brink of a temporary overturn of society which may lead to very serious consequences'.[55]

   Background noise can be most obtrusive; and against the above background noise Asquith's adamance since at least October 1911 that, if ever the British Expeditionary Force were sent to the continent, a part of it would remain behind, becomes the easier to understand. At a War Council on 6 August 1914 he had his way. The question of the danger of German raids had been disposed of on the previous day, when Grey had raised the matter of how many men could be spared to go abroad. According to the First Lord of the Admiralty, there was no danger of such raids. The situation in this respect was even better than when a C.I.D. sub-committee on Attack on the British Isles from Overseas had reported the previous April. Lord Roberts and General Douglas, the C.I.G.S., pointed out that the Germans could hardly spare any men. Nevertheless, concluded Asquith, there was 'everything to be said for retaining two Divisions': 'The domestic situation might be grave, and Colonial troops or Territorials could not be called on to aid the civil power.'[56]

Those who conducted Britain's foreign policy had a strong sense of her identity as a Great Power. This sense of Great Power identity required the retention of the British Empire. The outlook of Lansdowne, a former Viceroy of India, and of Grey, who went abroad for the first time as Foreign Secretary after eight years in that office, was the same as that of Lord Curzon: 'as long as we rule India, we are the greatest power in the world. If we lose it, we shall drop straight away to a third-rate power.' To them and to their colleagues – even to most of those of Grey's colleagues who wished to abandon the entente with Russia – the idea of sacrificing the British position in Central and East-Central Asia was anathema, even though most contemporary collections of statistics would have revealed even India to be of little value except in psychological terms, to be still only 'a claim pegged out for the future', though the existing financial arrangements between London and the Raj did serve to conceal basic weaknesses in the home economy.[57] They did not dare to risk the consequences of asking the British people to assume the financial burdens and military anxieties of being a continental state in Central Asia. Nor were they convinced that their countrymen shared their opinion of the Empire's present value and future potential. As Balfour put it, when exploring in December 1903 as 'our only *permanent* security', given the difficulty of erecting and the drawbacks of operating any diplomatic barrier in front of the slowly creeping Russian tide, the laying down whenever possible of 'certain well-defined principles which, if broken, we should regard as a casus belli': it was not easy 'to find some definite ground of understanding at once so clear in itself, and of such obvious importance to our Imperial interests, that the British people would consent to make its attempted infraction at once regarded as a sufficient ground for putting forth their whole strength in its defence'.[58]

Compelled to become 'partisans du statu quo partout',[59] all the British really wanted was a quiet life. They would settle for being treated with 'ordinary diplomatic civility as a Great Power'. This defensive attitude left the initiative to those prepared to take it. The British could only hope that in the time they knew they were buying something would happen to improve their situation; that the evil day, if postponed long enough, would not come at all. The initiative was first taken not by Germany in Europe but by Russia in Asia. As, despite the deteriorating situation, Britain still retained India, it could be made out, by extension, that she remained a Great Power in European terms also. This ludicrous proposition, about which the British could not but be aware that the French, never mind the

Germans, had serious reservations,[60] became the consolation and compensation of some of the formulators, would-be formulators and agents of British foreign policy, who were themselves by no means sure that Britain deserved to be treated as a Great Power. As a result of this mechanism, of which this was not the first, and was not to be the last, example, Britain spoke with a double voice, maintaining the pretensions and language handed down from earlier periods. The squadrons were depleted, both relatively and absolutely. The battalions were not forthcoming. The tall-talk remained.

2

The Politics of Liberal
Foreign Policy I

In May 1905 Sir Edward Grey voiced the opinion that foreign affairs were not matters of party controversy.[1] The public treatment of foreign affairs in speeches delivered towards the end of that year and during the election campaign that followed the resignation of the Conservative Government would seem to confirm that opinion. On 6 November Lord Lansdowne welcomed a number of speeches by leading Liberals which had been 'almost without exception favourable to the general lines of foreign policy which [the Conservatives] have pursued'. He went on:

It is good that these questions of foreign policy should be lifted out of party politics and placed on a higher and different plane. It is of immense importance that our foreign policy in this country should be a continuous policy, and not be deflected from its course by the eddies of party political opinion.[2]

Sir H. Campbell-Bannerman, the leader of the Liberal Party, followed this on 16 November with a speech designed to counter any alarm 'lest on any change of hands there may be some breach of continuity in our foreign policy'. He assured his audience that 'there will be no breach in the consistency and continuity of your foreign policy so long as your foreign policy is sound'. He found no fault with the general tone, spirit and aim of Lord Lansdowne's foreign policy. Indeed, the foreign policy of the Conservative Government was 'the best thing about it'. In his first speech as Prime Minister he declared that he wished 'emphatically to re-affirm my adhesion to the policy of the entente cordiale'. His own election address in January 1906 contained the admission that 'the Unionist party have made it possible for us to pursue a substantial continuity of policy'. This was immediately seized on by Lansdowne, who repeated that the Conservatives had been told that in foreign policy things were to go on very much as before and that the policy which had been their policy would be the policy of the new Government also. There had been only one sour note: Balfour's anticipation that a shudder might run through the Chancelleries of Europe if the Liberals should come to power. Even this was easily turned

17

by Campbell-Bannerman into a joke: 'Sir Edward Grey tells me that foreign Ambassadors come to see him just as if nothing had happened.'[3]

Beneath this veneer of an easy transition from one administration to another without any fundamental alteration in the content or emphasis of foreign policy, the reality was very different. Participants and observers were well aware that the foreign policy of a new Liberal Government would not necessarily be the same as that of its Conservative predecessor. It was also clear that the Liberal Party itself was split in its approach to foreign policy. Louis Mallet, Lansdowne's Private Secretary, apprehensive in April 1905 as to what the next Government would be like – 'possibly all Socialists with Lady Warwick as their Egeria' – feared for the chances of renewing and extending the alliance with Japan if the 'little Englanders' were in a great majority.[4] Lord Rosebery, in the early summer, wrote: 'The next Government will be radical, perhaps extremely radical; it will not at any rate be Liberal Imperialist. It will contain a notable nucleus indeed of that description, but this will tend to drift away . . .'.[5] Valentine Chirol, foreign editor of The Times, who was keeping Hardinge, still in St Petersburg, informed of developments, wrote that 'of course if (Edward Grey) and his friends were certain to rule the roost when the other party comes in, there would not be much cause for anxiety'. On the other hand, 'You will have a jolly time if its radical tail wags the next administration.'[6] Lord Knollys, the King's Private Secretary, told Haldane in September that

a Cabinet of which Campbell-Bannerman were the head, without the moderates, would be disastrous both for the country and the party. The Government would be a weak one, which would probably lead it to adopt very radical measures, possibly to interrupt the continuity of the foreign policy of the present and former Governments . . . Yourself, Asquith and Edward Grey would be a desirable restraining influence.[7]

Following a speech of 3 September in which Asquith said that the Liberals regarded the Japanese Alliance as 'an integral part of our policy in the Far East', John Morley demurred. He forecast that 'if the line foreshadowed by Asquith's language about "alliance" and "integral policy" be adopted, I expect we shall have the risk of another split . . . the pro-Boer section of our party – so to call them for short – will be restive at any general acceptance of the (Japanese) Treaty in the sense adopted by the Jingo newspapers'.[8] In these circumstances, continuity of foreign policy could by no means be taken for granted.

There was little the Foreign Office could do to ensure the continuity of existing policies. Nevertheless, certain individuals did try. Mallet attempted to get Lansdowne, on the eve of departure, to commit the next Government in one regard at least: 'could not some statement be made to the effect that if any future Russian Government makes overtures, your Lordship is convinced that H.M.G. would consider them with sympathy although H.M.'s present advisers are on the point of leaving office?'.[9] Hardinge had already told the Tsar in October that 'complete unanimity prevailed in England on the subject of friendly relations with Russia, since it constitutes part of the policy not only of the Government but also of the Opposition'.[10] Beyond this, however, the professional advisers could merely wait, and hope that the man whom they considered most likely to ensure continuity – Sir Edward Grey – would be appointed to succeed Lansdowne. Hardinge claimed to have been diffident about accepting the Permanent Under Secretaryship because he didn't know at the time who his future chief would be.[11] The considerable relief at the eventual outcome revealed some of the reasons for their concern. Bertie, the Ambassador in Paris, for instance, congratulated Grey in a letter of 12 December, and added: 'French papers and government circles have been in fear of a Minister with pro-German leanings, and are greatly relieved that you who made a speech favourable to France are to be at the F.O.'; Mallet wrote to Sir A. Nicolson that German attempts to 'capture' the Liberals 'will I think fail, so long as we have Sir Edward'.[12]

Nor could the Conservatives do a great deal. Lansdowne, however, did single out for praise the speech on 20 October in which Grey had said it was 'important to emphasise the need for continuity of foreign policy'.[13] He also selected Hardinge, a tried friend of Russia, to succeed Sanderson, because he attached 'immense importance to the presence in Headquarters of a high official thoroughly conversant with the recent course of Anglo-Russian relations'.[14] And at the end of November, knowing his own party's resignation to be imminent, he paid a visit to Balmoral which was effectively to dash Lord Elgin's chances of becoming Foreign Secretary. For he was able to assure the King that it was quite in order for a Foreign Secretary to be in the House of Commons, despite the fact that Lord Stanley had been the most recent one to operate from there. L. Harcourt reported to Campbell-Bannerman after seeing Esher:

The King's first question to you, after asking if you are prepared to form a Government, will be who is to be your Foreign Secretary. He does not think Elgin will do – not known here, or abroad, does not carry guns etc. . . . Grey will be pressed on you probably. I said impossible in House of Commons; too poor for Peerage; the answer was not too poor as he has no children; not impossible to have Foreign Minister in House of Commons. (Lansdowne apparently said this at Balmoral.)[15]

After Grey's appointment Lansdowne wrote to him saying how glad he was 'that you are to take my place at the F.O.', and putting himself at Grey's service if the latter 'thought it worthwhile to ask me any questions about the Office and the subjects with which it is at this moment most occupied'.[16] The meeting took place on 11 December. On the next day Lansdowne wrote to Hardinge: 'I had a long talk with Grey yesterday, and I fancy he is inclined to make arrangements of which we should both approve.'[17]

It remained for the Liberal Imperialists themselves to try to determine the complexion and content of future Liberal policy. On 11 September 1905 Asquith, Haldane and Grey met at one of the latter's fishing lodges and produced what has come to be known as the Relugas Compact. The full Relugas programme consisted of a place for Rosebery in the Cabinet (if not as Prime Minister then as Foreign Secretary, if his interest could be engaged), Campbell-Bannerman if Prime Minister to go to the House of Lords, Asquith to be Leader of the House of Commons, Haldane to be Lord Chancellor, and Grey to be Foreign Secretary in the absence of Rosebery. To some extent this programme embodied the personal ambitions of Asquith and Haldane to occupy particular posts. There can be no doubt, however, that it was concerned with 'external policy' in general and with 'continuity' in particular to an extent that has not yet been fully appreciated. Haldane reported to Knollys (with whom he had made contact in July) after the meeting at Relugas that the Liberal Imperialists believed they must take 'a definite step in defence of our own policy, if it is to have a chance of success'. The trouble with Campbell-Bannerman was that during the South African war he had taken the line that the group represented by Rosebery outside the House of Commons and by Asquith, Grey and others inside it did not represent the mind of the party, and that he must look to the majority view. The Liberal Imperialists had never admitted that this was a sound judgement, and were afraid that it might be repeated. If Campbell-Bannerman did leave the situation as he found it, 'all might be well'; but as it was more likely that he would take 'a different course from ours' under pressure from those who would not allow him to acquiesce in Liberal Imperialist policies, it would be better for the latter if he went to the House of Lords immediately. Without such safeguards and conditions as this and as the presence of Liberal Imperialists in certain posts, 'we should have no sufficient basis from which to exercise real influence on the future of the Liberal party'. In short, Haldane considered it

doubtful whether a very large number of those who will sit as Liberals after the next election will really be of the mind of the Daily News party, and whether a Government which is undecided in its views on the external policy of the nation and on the necessity for continuity in it can really hold their confidence for long.

The beginning, he concluded, would make or mar everything: 'A decided lead in the right direction is what is essential. The necessity for it will probably arise before the new administration is many days old.'[18]

The men of Relugas went into action a few weeks later. The speeches delivered by Grey on 13 October, in which he declared that foreign affairs were not a subject on which the election should be fought, 'as an election must be fought on something on which the two parties differed and not upon what they were agreed', and on 20 October, in which he attacked those who hoped 'that the coming of a Liberal government would result in some revision or regrouping of our present relations with foreign powers',[19] were the first steps towards the implementation of the Relugas programme. They both declared an interest and staked a claim. At the same time, the dinners given by Grey for the French Ambassador, at which the guests were Haldane and J. A. Spender, the editor of the *Westminster Gazette*, and by Haldane for the German Ambassador, at which the guests were Grey, Asquith and Spender, did nothing to conceal the distinct identity of the group.[20] On 13 November Asquith went to see Campbell-Bannerman, and 'strongly urged' on him that Grey should be made Foreign Secretary. He came away with the impression that he had succeeded.[21] This was misleading. Throughout the second half of November Campbell-Bannerman's own candidate for the Foreign Secretaryship seems to have been Elgin.[22]

The matter was complicated by an unseasonable speech from Rosebery on 25 November at Bodmin, in which he declared that he would not serve under any flag which would imply Home Rule for Ireland. As Asquith and Grey had already settled with Campbell-Bannerman that they would follow his lead as regards Home Rule,[23] the speech had the effect of dividing Rosebery from his followers. It was clear that Rosebery would now be unable on any terms to enter a Liberal Government.[24] Herbert Gladstone, anxious to see the allegiance of the Liberal Imperialists formally transferred from Rosebery to Campbell-Bannerman, pressed the latter to be 'as friendly and forthcoming as possible as regards Berwick [Grey's constituency] and Fife [Asquith's]': they were now on the right side, and it was 'of enormous importance to keep them there'.[25] Another Campbell-Bannermanite, Morley, was confident that Asquith and Grey 'could not possibly afford to break away from Campbell-Bannerman', and his confidence appeared justified when on 3 December a particularly harmonious discussion on policy took place between Campbell-Bannerman, Asquith and Grey.[26] Lewis Harcourt, meanwhile, had indirectly acknowledged the strength of the bid being made by the remaining Liberal Imperialists by advising his leader of the great importance of his (Campbell-Bannerman's) being President of the Committee of Imperial Defence, for this was 'more than anything else the P.M.'s Bureau and makes him supreme over his colleagues'.[27]

On 4 December the Conservatives resigned. On the evening of the 4th

Grey shattered any illusion of harmony and faced Campbell-Bannerman with the real meaning for him of the absence of Rosebery in which the Bodmin speech had resulted. Until late on 7 December Grey stood out for those parts of the Relugas programme which were crucial for him. He would only take office on condition that the authoritative declarations of policy were in hands in which he had complete confidence – namely, 'in the hands of one of those with whom I have been most closely associated'. It was vital that Asquith should lead in the House of Commons. He was not prepared to cut his losses, as Asquith was. What Asquith pointed out, that with his own inclusion the Government was of more than one colour, made little difference to Grey. He had no confidence in Campbell-Bannerman, and Haldane had not been offered a cabinet post, never mind the Lord Chancellorship. Grey was not entranced by the prospect of the Foreign Secretaryship for himself. He would be content to see it in safe and sensible hands. But the safeguards which the Relugas programme had been drawn up to secure were no less necessary. It was a question of power to ensure the continuity of Lord Lansdowne's foreign policy.[28]

On 5 December Campbell-Bannerman offered the Foreign Secretary-ship to Cromer. Crippled by arthritis, he declined. The arguments between Liberal Imperialists and Campbell-Bannermanites resumed. Asquith revived an argument he had already dropped, and tried to induce the Prime Minister, after all, to go to the Lords. Harcourt was adamant that he should not – if he did, it 'would be regarded as the triumph of the Rosebery section'. Asquith urged that Grey was 'the obvious candidate', that his 'qualifications were unique'. Morley, on the other hand, described Grey as 'grossly overrated', and likely to be a 'doubtful diplomatist'. Other names were mentioned. In the limbo between Cairo's being definitely 'off' and Falloden's being firmly 'on', Harcourt thought Lord Fitzmaurice might be 'a *possible* solution', perhaps on the strength of his recently published and favourably received biography of Lord Granville. Lord Burghclere was heard of for the first time, never to be heard of again. Morley was his own candidate. On the assumption that Grey's decision was irrevocable, Asquith thought Lord Crewe might be the best man for the Foreign Office.[29]

It was Herbert Gladstone who saved the day, by persuading Campbell-Bannerman not to close his mind against Grey until Arthur Acland, reputedly second only to Rosebery in his influence upon Grey, had been allowed a chance to bring him round. Acland's appeal for the unity of the Liberals in the face of the Conservative threat to Free Trade was successful. Grey would join the Government if a place could be found for Haldane. On 8 December Grey became Foreign Secretary, Haldane went to the War Office.[30]

The appointment of Grey as Foreign Secretary was the only item of the Relugas programme to be adopted. Continuity of foreign policy, however, could still not be taken for granted. The Liberals might still be 'captured' by the Germans,[31] or by pro-German elements. Grey, who had not been allowed the Parliamentary Under Secretary of State for Foreign Affairs of his choice,[32] might be captured, or *roulé*, by his cabinet colleagues. Mallet, who had encouraged Hardinge to accept the Permanent Under Secretaryship at the Foreign Office on the grounds that 'the importance of having someone who will keep the Liberals straight is overwhelming', sounded the alarm again early in January 1906. He asked Bertie to prime Hardinge concerning the implications of the 'crucial question' asked by Paul Cambon on the 10th: 'he must, supposing he agrees, do everything he can to buck up these miserable creatures'.[33] At the end of January 1906 Bertie made no attempt to deny the French opinion that if Grey, Haldane and Asquith left the Cabinet then 'the foreign policy of the remainder might not be the same as with the late Government'.[34] Lord Esher reminded the King in April of the complaints to which Liberal Governments were peculiarly liable, owing to the presence of 'warring elements' within the Cabinet.[35] Hardinge predicted in May, on the basis of 'wobbliness' recently displayed by some members of the Cabinet in a confrontation with Turkey, that 'the great difficulty of the future will be when Grey finds himself face to face with the peace at any price section of the Cabinet headed by the Lord Chancellor'.[36] Vigilance had to be maintained.

On the eve of the next election the same fears manifested themselves. Chirol wrote in September 1909:

Many shrewd and experienced observers anticipate a more or less sweeping radical victory. The consequences would affect very seriously the foreign policy of this country and our position in the world. For the extreme section of the radicals are admittedly against every sound scheme of national defence and convinced that peace can be best assured by graceful concessions, especially to Germany.[37]

Sir W. Tyrrell, similarly, feared that the triumph of the Lloyd George– W. S. Churchill section 'might have a very prejudicial effect on our foreign policy. It might bring Lulu Harcourt as Foreign Secretary.'[38]

A split in the ranks of the Cabinet over the opening of General Staff talks with the French had been successfully avoided in January 1906 by collusion between Campbell-Bannerman, Lord Ripon and Grey. It has been stated that, as a result, 'the unity of the Liberal Government on foreign affairs did not come under strain until July 1914'.[39] This is not the case. When Morley wrote, in 1928, that in July 1914, 'For the very first time something of the old cleavage between the Liberal League and the faithful

Campbell-Bannerman, Harcourt and myself began to be very sensibly felt. Hitherto not a whisper of the old schism of the Boer War',[40] he was suffering from a severe loss of memory. The unity of the Liberal Government on foreign affairs was under constant strain. As had been anticipated before the Liberals came to power, there was a contest between the Liberal Imperialist and Radical elements. Each group remained concerned to avoid being 'bossed' by the other.[41]

Churchill later wrote in *The World Crisis* that the situation within the Liberal Government 'reproduced the balances and reserves of the external diplomatic situation':

The Ministers who were conducting the foreign policy of Britain . . . were drawn entirely from the Liberal Imperialist section of the Government. They were narrowly watched and kept in equipoise by the Radical element, which included the venerable figures of Lord Morley and Lord Loreburn, on whose side the Chancellor of the Exchequer and I had usually leaned. It was clear that this equipoise might easily make it impossible for Great Britain to speak with a decided voice either on one side or the other if certain dangerous conditions supervened.[42]

The impression given here that there was a balance, and that his own and and Lloyd George's defection from one side at the time of the Agadir crisis tipped that balance in favour of the Liberal Imperialists, is not unsupported. W. Runciman remarked to Harcourt at the time on the 'positive desire for a conflict of colleagues of ours on whom we had always relied for anti-war feeling', and concluded that 'the stability or balance of opinion of the Cabinet cannot now be relied on by us'.[43] Lord Loreburn in July 1911 advised C. P. Scott of the *Manchester Guardian* to 'Always remember that this is a Liberal League Government'; in September 1911 he held forth on the great weakening of the real Liberal Radical element in the Cabinet since the death of Campbell-Bannerman:

Besides the substitution of Asquith for Campbell-Bannerman there had been the loss of Bryce, Elgin, Ripon and Gladstone. In their places Churchill, Pease, Runciman and Samuel (men owing promotion to and dependent on Asquith, and Runciman at least an avowed Liberal Leaguer) – altogether an almost purely Liberal League Cabinet.[44]

Nevertheless, the impressions of Runciman, of Loreburn and of Churchill are all misleading. Despite the changes in personnel to which Loreburn referred, despite the change of allegiance on the part of Churchill and Lloyd George during the Agadir crisis, the scales were tipped throughout *against* the Liberal Imperialists.

The Government's determination to pursue the chimera of disarmament at The Hague in 1907, which Hardinge predicted would be a complete fiasco and would place Britain in a minority of one at the Conference, was an early tribute to the influence of the Radical element, though Grey personally supported this initiative.[45] The success of the policy of seeking an agreement with Russia – the hub of the whole policy of the entente – was heavily dependent upon the presence of Morley, anxious to reduce 'adventurism' and expenditure on the part of the Government of India, and equally anxious to lay the ghost of conscription, at the India Office. Grey admitted that 'without Morley we should have made no progress at all for the Government of India would have blocked every point and Morley has removed mountains in the path of the negotiations'. But Morley's value was greatest, as Grey also admitted, in that with his 'unimpeachable record' of anti-jingoism he warded off criticism from 'sentimental', anti-Imperialist liberals.[46] Eighteen months later criticism from within the Cabinet of the understanding with Russia raised its head. Nicolson in St Petersburg was told that the attention of the Secretary of State had been drawn to the use in official telegrams and despatches of the expression 'triple entente' when referring to the joint action of England, France and Russia, and found himself 'requested by Sir E. Grey . . . to avoid using it in future'. H. O'Beirne provided the explanation for the request:

I am told that the extremists in the Cabinet including L. Harcourt have of late been developing opposition to our entente with Russia. They do not like it, they are very sensitive to criticisms of it and questions asked about it by their supporters in the House and they would be glad of a pretext for dropping it as far as possible out of sight. This is the significance of objections raised in the Cabinet to the use of the term Triple Entente as to which I understand the F.O. are going to issue instructions to representatives abroad. The members of the Cabinet in question would gladly seize on the opportunity offered to them by a change in regime in Russia adverse to cooperation with us; and on the other hand they would make it difficult or impossible for the Govt. to entertain any suggestion for strengthening or developing our present understanding with Russia.

The instruction was ignored in practice. The day following his receipt of it, in fact, Nicolson embodied the offending phrase in a despatch, and Hardinge had to ask Grey how the telegram was to be dealt with in the printed sections: 'it contains the words to which objection has been taken and cannot make sense without them'. Hardinge himself protested to Sir G. Lowther at Constantinople that 'it is not a Foreign Office idea to prohibit the mention of the term "Triple Entente". It appears that some of the Cabinet Ministers are a little sensitive on the subject, and think it might offend Germany . . . '.[47] The criticism, however, remained. In 1912 S. Sazonov rightly suspected 'a certain section of the Cabinet' of being 'ill-disposed towards Russia'.[48] Indeed, Harcourt was to be found in January 1914 decrying to Grey the most recent use of this 'terminological inexactitude', as he called it:

You will remember that I have often protested to you against the use by our Ambassadors – mainly at St. Petersburg and Constantinople – of the phrase 'Triple Entente'. You have more than once promised me that you would draw the Ambassadors' attention to this inaccuracy. You can therefore imagine my horror when I find the phrase – in all the glories of capitals and italics – in your telegram no 440 of 31 December 1913 to Sir E. Goschen . . . I object to 'Triple Entente' because no such thing has ever been considered or approved by the Cabinet.

What Harcourt feared was that the frequent use of the expression since it was first coined in 1909 encouraged the assumption that a new Triple Alliance, opposed to that between Germany, Austria-Hungary and Italy, had come into being.[49]

It was the long drawn out series of negotiations with Germany over the limitation of naval armaments, for the exchange of naval information, and in particular the quest for some sort of political agreement, all of which the diplomats made it quite clear that *they* would never have entered into,[50] that bore more eloquent testimony to the influence of the Radicals in the Cabinet. The first German overtures arrived at a time when the departmentalism which had been such a feature of Campbell-Bannerman's administration was beginning to fade. Morley had begun to raise his head from his desk at the India Office to murmur imprecations against what he considered 'provocative' language and conduct towards Germany. In April 1907 Loreburn had persuaded him not to resign from the Government: 'The future colour of Liberal official policy largely depends on your presence and influence at a crisis which will get more pronounced before long.' He was now in a position to resume his campaign to restore to the Liberal Party its old Gladstonian soul, and to join with Loreburn and Harcourt against Conservatism, Liberal Imperialism, militarism and jingoism.[51] The German negotiations represented an opportunity to implement Radical alternatives. They provided the chance to halt the steady deterioration in the state of international morality, to end the worship of that 'horrible, bloodstained idol', the balance of power – by finding ways away from systems of alliances, from arrangements which resembled alliances, or were capable of being turned into alliances; by taking literally the sentiments expressed during the election of 1906 and equalising the entente with France by one with Germany which would remove from the former the point it might seem to have against Germany; by killing any German aggression with the kindness of concessions, assuaging through accommodation an *appétit* which the Foreign Office maintained *venait en mangeant*. Such a positive contribution to peace and retrenchment abroad would secure the time and resources to concentrate on reform at home, would convert the motto of the Liberal Party from slogan into reality.[52] In any such process, the policy of the entente would be entirely overthrown.

The negotiations with Germany persisted through two general elections. In January 1911 a Cabinet Committee was appointed to consider the questions involved. Nicolson at the Foreign Office at first welcomed this, on the grounds that it included 'One or two men whom it was desirable to convert.' Within a few weeks he had begun to doubt whether it did not in fact amount to 'putting the F.O. in commission and restricting the liberty of the Secretary of State'.[53] No records of the proceedings of this Committee have yet been found. Nicolson, however, was able to record in March that its views were 'not entirely harmonious'. This was not surprising, since it was composed of Asquith, Grey, Lloyd George, Morley, Crewe, and Runciman.[54] Nicolson also detected a tendency to fall in with the view of the German Government that a political arrangement was more important than the question of the exchange of naval information. In this he was correct. The Committee recommended that the basis of the negotiations should be extended so as to include a political agreement, and this recommendation was adopted by the Cabinet.[55]

If Runciman had been correct, later that year, in saying that the 'anti-war' section of the Cabinet, hitherto dominant, could no longer rely upon the balance of opinion in the Cabinet being in its favour, it would hardly have been necessary for the Liberal Imperialists, supplemented at this time by Churchill and Lloyd George, on two occasions in the course of the Agadir crisis to attempt to go behind the back of the Cabinet as a whole. The first of these occasions was the speech delivered by Lloyd George at the Mansion House on 21 July. This was the work of Lloyd George, Asquith and Grey.[56] Morley immediately protested as to its unauthorised nature, and went on to call Grey's defence of it in conversation with the German Ambassador on 25 July a provocation towards Germany. Loreburn on 27 July begged Grey to make it clear 'that we have no wish to interfere between France and Germany' and 'to undo the effect of Lloyd George's speech'.[57] The second occasion was the meeting of the Committee of Imperial Defence called for 23 August, from which Morley, Harcourt and Crewe, all members of that body, were omitted. Haldane proposed such a meeting at dinner on 14 August with Asquith, Grey, Churchill and McKenna, and there is nothing to contradict Harcourt's assertion subsequent to it that 'it was arranged some time ago for a date when it was supposed that we should all be out of London!'.[58] When they were told, by McKenna, what had transpired at the meeting, the Radicals immediately took steps to repair the damage. Morley, as the senior member of the group, was delegated to ask the Cabinet for a 'definite decision . . . that under no circumstances conceivable in the present Morocco controversy would we be prepared to land a single British soldier on the Continent'. So insistent were they upon demonstrating their strength that in November 1911 they pressed the Cabinet to a division upon two resolutions – the one that no communications should take place between the General Staff of Great Britain and those of other countries which could directly or indirectly commit Britain to military and naval intervention in a war, the other that such communications if they related to concerted action by land and sea should not be entered into without the previous approval of the Cabinet. Though Asquith tried to calm them by repeating that the constitutional position reserved all questions of policy for the decision of the Cabinet, the majority felt, as Pease recorded, that he had been a party to the rigging on 23 August of an arrangement to go to war – a feeling which his dismissal of McKenna from the Admiralty for refusing to implement measures to convey British troops to aid the French had done nothing to diminish. The division went in their favour by fifteen votes to five. Pease concluded: 'Asquith, Grey, Haldane, Lloyd George, Churchill thought they could boss the rest, but were mistaken.'[59]

Haldane was not so upset at the outcome as Grey. He wrote to his sister: 'I emerge unhampered in any material point . . . It was not very pleasant, but it is over.'[60] The episode may have been over. The serial was not. Loreburn, for one, certainly envisaged a sequel to the November Cabinets. In January 1912 he was contemplating following up the resolutions already made by asking the Cabinet to concur in and if necessary vote upon a statement to the effect that the country 'was not under any obligation direct or indirect, express or implied, to support France against Germany by force of arms'. The Liberal Imperialists were spared this particular ordeal only by Loreburn's illness and early retirement, for the other leading Radicals were not so disposed as he was to adopt extreme positions.[61] They were not spared further demonstrations of the fact that they were in a minority, the proportions of which had just been all too clearly revealed. If anything, that revelation increased the confidence of a majority whose vigilance had already been increased as a result of its discovery of the military conversations with France, and made the Liberal Imperialists' position even more uncomfortable. In January 1912 the Cabinet resumed what Tyrrell described as its 'curious hankering' of wishing to talk to Germany, and the permanent officials at the Foreign Office, for their part, renewed the fight against a formula which they had been conducting for the last five years.[62] But things were clearly out of the hands of the Foreign Office, and seemed to them to be distinctly out of hand. Nicolson told Henry Wilson in January that Grey 'was useless in this business and that only the other day he sat, with [Count P. W. von] Metternich, for an hour opposite the map of Africa wondering what we could give away to placate the Germans'. Crowe did not veil his sarcasm at what he called 'Mr Harcourt's own private negotiations with the German Embassy for exchanges of territory', at 'negotiations of which not even this office has any information'.[63] Those in favour of an agreement with Germany thought they saw an opportunity to intervene decisively in the struggle for power in Germany which they took to be raging between the 'good Chancellor' Bethmann-Hollweg and Admiral von Tirpitz. They had convinced themselves, or been convinced by Metternich, that there was a distinct possibility that 'a generous formula of friendship' would enable the proposed new German Navy Law to be 'almost withdrawn'. Harcourt, McKenna, Lloyd George, Loreburn and Pease were prepared so to extend the formula with Germany as to include a guarantee of British neutrality.[64]

As regards France, the majority in the Cabinet refused to be drawn into any commitment involving the immediate application of the arrangements made by the Military and Naval Staffs, and repeated the doctrine that 'anything which passed between experts . . . was not to be taken as prejudicing the freedom of decision of the Governments'.[65] Harcourt took it upon himself to stress in public that with regard to the Mediterranean, Britain's position would depend 'on no alliance or understanding, actual or implied, but upon our own and only our own needs, and to [sic] the tactical exigencies of our own unfettered policy and discretion'.[66] They also preferred mere letters to an exchange of notes, and in Nicolson's view watered down to some 'feeble expressions of goodwill' the more categorical assurances he had wanted to be given that all question of any political formulas with Germany had been definitely and finally abandoned. In 1913 they remained indisposed to going beyond the private letter of November 1912 to Cambon.[67]

In view of the sustained and serious challenge to it from within the ranks of the Government itself, how did the policy of the entente survive?

One thing that could always be relied upon by the Liberal Imperialists was the support of the Tory leadership. Six months after the Liberals came to power Balfour repaid Campbell-Bannerman's compliment of the election campaign by saying that foreign affairs was the one topic over which the Liberals had not spread a flood of calumny – he did not know 'where else to look either for success or for promise of success'.[68] In July 1911, when informed that the foreign outlook was critical, he responded to the appeal delivered by Lord Elibank, the Government Chief Whip, to show solidarity, by re-asserting the doctrine of the non-political character of foreign affairs. In November 1911 his successor Bonar Law announced his adhesion to this doctrine, and Lansdowne made it even clearer that the Conservatives had no quarrel with the manner in which their policy had been accepted and continued by their successors.[69] Grey, who according to Elibank 'frequently saw Balfour and had useful conversations with him', took advantage of an impending debate on the Government's foreign policy and of an initiative on the part of H. A. Gwynne, editor of the *Morning Post*, to place Tyrrell, his Private Secretary, who had acted as intermediary between himself and Balfour in the past, in touch with Bonar Law, so that the connection might be maintained into the future. Grey was prepared to see Bonar Law in person, if the latter so wished, in order to provide him with information which would 'prevent his falling into error',[70] and did in fact do so, in advance of his speech of 27 November to the House of Commons.

As regards Russia, the Liberal Party Whip Elibank, who made a visit to St Petersburg in January 1909, was able to tell his hosts that 'the regular opposition under Balfour had on the whole most disinterestedly supported the Government in its Russian policy'; he secured Isvolsky's agreement that it was 'a wonderful feature of our British Party System that we could sink our ordinary Party differences and unite on great national issues'.[71] Lord Stamfordham, the King's Private Secretary, wrote in 1912 to Nicolson, who was ever anxious that the Russian entente should be maintained: 'So long as the Opposition supports the Government's foreign policy in the loyal manner they have hitherto done all will be well so far as the Anglo-Russian entente goes, provided the Russians do not do such things as occupy Tehran!'[72] The Conservatives were in direct contact with the Russians in April 1912. Sazonov told Austen Chamberlain that 'Russian friendship was evidently very unpopular with the Liberal Party and its maintenance depended on the willingness of [the Conservative] Party to support it whole-heartedly.' Chamberlain reassured him that the Triple Entente was 'the only possible basis for our policy'.[73] After the visit of the Tsar and Sazonov to England in September 1912 Grey informed Bonar Law of what had transpired, secured his support, and then pointed out to the Russian Ambassador 'the importance of knowing that if anything happened to turn out the present Government it would make no difference to foreign policy'.[74] In 1913, over the complications in the Balkans, Chirol was able to remark:

It is lucky for Edward Grey that, in questions of foreign policy, the Tories are on the whole very reluctant to hamper the King's Government. One can imagine what would have been the language of the Radical press had it been a Unionist Minister who had been compelled to join in the coercion of Montenegro. They would have made the welkin ring with their appeals to the shade of Mr G.[75]

As regards Germany, the Foreign Office believed that the large German naval programme might not be adhered to if the Kaiser could be convinced 'that *all* parties likely to be in power in England will go on building to keep ahead of Germany and any other country together'.[76] In January 1910

Hardinge recorded that the German Ambassador had 'at last realised that it would be useless to come to terms with the present Government, unless the terms were such as would prove acceptable to the Opposition. This is a great safeguard for us, and it is fortunate that it has at last dawned on him.' No agreement with Germany, in Hardinge's view, would be worth the paper upon which it was written, unless both parties in England were in accord upon it – and 'Balfour would certainly not accept any agreement with Germany such as the Germans seem to desire.'[77] The point was further pressed upon Nicolson:

What the Germans do not understand is that an agreement, to be of any value whatsoever, must receive the assent not only of the Government in power but also of the Opposition. Thus it would be impossible to conclude a political agreement on the lines which the Germans desire, as no Unionist Government would listen to it for a moment . . .[78]

Conservative support was certainly a source of gratification to the Liberal Imperialists. It helped Grey, at several points, to disregard agitation on the part of the Radicals in the House of Commons directed against Russia.[79] It enabled Asquith to treat casually during the Agadir crisis a petition from the same quarter asking that every opportunity be taken to cooperate with Germany and that the Anglo-French entente not be allowed to stand in the way of such a rapprochement. The first thing Asquith wanted to know was whether there were any Conservatives amongst the signatories. (There was only one – Lord Henry Bentinck.)[80] At one time when the Government's foreign policy was being opposed by groups of Liberal M.P.s and when the Foreign Secretary was being attacked in organs of the Liberal press to such an extent that Asquith was led to consider the suppression or absorption of the 'pernicious' *Daily News*, it would no doubt have been some consolation to the Liberal Imperialists to know that certain elements in Conservative circles were trying to mobilise Unionist opinion against the efforts of what they referred to as 'gentlemen of German extraction' to undermine the Triple Entente, and were concerned lest preoccupation with domestic affairs divert Tory minds away from the problems of foreign policy.[81]

An even more important consideration was the Conservatives' knowledge and support of the 'military entente' with France. It was from the former Conservative Colonial Secretary, Alfred Lyttelton, that Loreburn heard for the first time in autumn 1911 that the Unionist leaders had been approached and asked if their support could be relied on in the event of war with Germany. This support was to be fully exploited in August 1914. The Agadir crisis was a dress rehearsal. It is of the utmost significance that the Conservative leadership was contacted on that occasion. The assurance Balfour gave to Grey and Lloyd George at Balmoral is contained in a letter of 21 September 1911 to his Private Secretary. This was just one of the secret conversations between Grey and Balfour which, as the Tory Chief Whip noted after talking with his opposite number on 22 November 1911, had produced a certain amount of apprehension amongst the Conservative rank and file.[82]

Crises such as Agadir, obviously, were the exception rather than the rule. They brought Conservative support into the foreground. For the most part it was of a background nature. However gratifying, it was to be found at a remove. It is doubtful, moreover, that Grey would have agreed with all the opinions expressed by the Tory Chief Whip who in a memorandum of 20 May 1912 on the Conservatives' Parliamentary Attitude on Foreign Affairs suggested that the Government be given a parliamentary opportunity to inform the country as to the progress of negotiations with Germany:

We have supported Grey for six years, on the assumption that he continues the Anglo-French Entente which Lord Lansdowne established, and the Anglo-Russian Entente which Lord Lansdowne began. We have kept Grey in office. Without our help he would have retired long ago. We are entitled to ask for assurances that he adheres to our jointly declared policy. We do not ask a quid pro quo for our support, but at a moment like this a renewed declaration is necessary . . . [83]

There was no doubt that if the Liberals left office a Conservative Government would continue to uphold the policy of the Entente. Grey's concern was that it should be upheld by a Liberal Government.

Grey also received the support of both the Prime Ministers under whom he served. Campbell-Bannerman, at the very outset, had no wish to expose the unhealed wound in the Liberal ranks and thereby lose the good relations with France so recently established. He might suggest friendly concessions to Germany, if these could be found, but like Grey he considered that 'France is another matter. We must stand by France.' Encouraged by Ripon, he was prepared to trust Grey's handling of foreign affairs. The personal loyalty to Campbell-Bannerman of such elements as Harcourt also helped ease the path of Grey's foreign policy in its early stages.[84]

Asquith's accession to the premiership actually improved on the conditions envisaged at Relugas. Grey's position, however, did not improve proportionally. The Radical section of the Cabinet had no loyalty towards Asquith. Almost immediately, in the summer of 1908, Lloyd George and Churchill made incursions into Grey's sphere by speaking about international affairs on the continent. The Foreign Secretary took such exception to this that he stated that if any harm was done 'I should have to insist on the Minister in question being disavowed, or on my resignation being accepted'. Asquith's reply was mild, to say the least: 'I cannot say that I think that any real harm has resulted from these indiscretions.' Grey had to take it upon himself to warn Churchill, who was due to go abroad again in December, that he deprecated his seeing important politicians in Paris, 'where the Prime Minister and Sir Edward Grey are regarded by those in authority as the exponents of the view of H.M. Govt. in questions of foreign policy . . .'. The following April Grey persuaded Churchill not to address the Chamber of Commerce in Paris, on the grounds that 'we want a little breathing time in foreign affairs now, and . . . the risk of a new departure is greater than its advantage at the moment'.[85]

Apart from the occasion when Asquith joined Grey, McKenna and the Sea Lords in threatening to resign unless the Navy Estimates were increased, to ensure a defeat in March 1909 for the economists within the Cabinet who wished to adhere to their pledges to reduce expenditure, his handling of the proponents of an alternative foreign policy was somewhat lax. With the appearance of the German overtures the Radical ministers took full advantage of their new freedom to discuss foreign affairs at length in Cabinet and to alter submissions from the Foreign Office.[86] Loreburn got the impression that it was useless to ask Asquith to wrestle with Grey – 'the fatal thing was that the Prime Minister who alone was in constant communication with Grey and alone could really influence him never attempted to influence him at all'.[87] He was evidently unaware of an exchange between Grey and Asquith in September 1911 when the latter, referring to a 'rather dangerous' conversation between the British Military Attaché in Paris and General Joffre in which the possibility of British assistance to France had been discussed, wrote that the French 'ought not to be encouraged in present circumstances to make their plans on any assumptions of this kind'. Grey's reply reflected the consternation that he predicted it would create if British military experts were forbidden to converse with the French: 'No doubt these conversations and our speeches have given an expectation of support. I do not see how that can be helped.'[88] It may be considered that Asquith made amends to Grey by removing McKenna from the Admiralty and replacing him with someone who would see that the necessary arrangements were made for the transportation of the British Expeditionary Force to the continent,[89] but the two were clearly not at one in the Cabinet held on 15 November 1911 so far as concerned the degree to which Britain was committed to cooperation with France – something which Charles Hobhouse, for one, detected.[90] Though Haldane considered that, on that occasion, 'the P.M. steered things through',[91] there was a certain ambivalence in Asquith's support of his Foreign Secretary.

This was necessarily so. Asquith had inherited a difficult position. He could not afford ostentatiously to take sides. Though he might fundamentally be at one with Grey on the policy of the Entente his support had to be pressed for. The circumstances had to require it. It could not be absolutely taken for granted.[92] There was, as the Cabinet's policy during the Agadir crisis and its behaviour in the aftermath of that crisis particularly well illustrates, such a thing as the 'sense' of the Cabinet. Asquith's record for the King of the Cabinet meeting of 4 July 1911 contains the remarks: 'the sudden discovery of German "subjects" and "threatened interests" in the immediate neighbourhood of the only place on the west coast of Morocco which can be developed into a naval and commercial base, facing the Atlantic, is an interesting illustration of "Realpolitik".' Another source suggests that he was rather more restrained than this, saying merely that 'the presence of a German gunboat at Agadir is no doubt reckoned to be sufficient as the starting point of a new diplomatic settlement of Morocco'. And it was the note of sympathy for German expansion that was sounded by the Cabinet at that meeting that was adopted as British policy for the next few weeks.[93] To some extent the Prime Minister was, to apply a phrase of Churchill's, 'the man in the howdah' – he had to go wherever the elephant went.[94] (In 1908 the Cabinet had overruled Asquith and Grey when they first suggested that Isvolsky's proposal that the rules governing the Straits be altered in a sense favourable to Russia, be adopted.)[95]

As the Conservatives occupied a position in reserve, Grey, until circumstances were such that in Asquith's view they required him to commit himself, was thrown back upon his own resources. In September 1908 he replied to the unsolicited advice proffered to him by Sanderson concerning the recent pronouncements on foreign affairs made by Lloyd George and Churchill. He wrote: 'One of the difficulties that exists with colleagues is to convince them that there are such things as brick walls; the most certain way of doing this is to let them run their own heads against them.'[96] He could not prevent Loreburn from injecting fresh life into the frequently interrupted discussions with Germany. Though he dwelt upon the difficulty of arranging a satisfactory formula, he could not stop his colleagues firing what they termed their 'range-finding shot' towards some political understanding.[97] He welcomed any development that made it easier for Britain to avoid being entangled in separate political negotiations with Germany to which other powers were not parties. His colleagues believed that a political formula sufficiently elastic to permit of its acceptance by France and Russia could be devised – and Grey let them believe. He himself shared Nicolson's view that to find such a formula was 'a task beyond the ingenuity of man'. His reaction to a proposal from A. von Kiderlen that was the same in all essentials as those from Bethmann-Hollweg, had been

that it was 'not going to meet with any response from us'.[98] Though he
stressed the dangers of a return to isolation, and the argument that 'the
Germans would obviously be at an advantage over us in a neutrality basis
subject to existing treaties, as they had a triple alliance and we had
nothing', he could not deny that the 'Peace party' had one point: that,
having clearly revealed a readiness to come to terms with Germany, 'in
case of future trouble we could then show we were not to blame'.[99] Nor
could he stop Colonial Secretary Harcourt from trying to give away
African territory that belonged to others in exchange for German goodwill. He appreciated that such negotiations served to prevent a return to
discussion of a neutrality formula, and hoped that they would lead some-
where for this reason alone.[100]

But Grey did have a sticking point. There was one thing he could do,
and he made this clear. Shortly after the Anglo-French Agreement was
signed he revealed how he regarded it. He wrote to one correspondent:
'But let us emphasise the fact that our recent agreement with France marks
a change of policy. I am not sure yet whether the Govt. realise that or
intend it. If they show signs of relapsing into German by-ways I shall
deplore and resent it.'[101] A little over a year later he wrote to R. Munro-
Ferguson that 'if any government drags us back into the German net I will
oppose it openly at all costs'. Before making his speech of 20 October 1905
he wrote to Spender:

I am afraid the impression has been spread with some success by those interested
in spreading it, that a Liberal Government would unsettle the understanding with
France in order to make up to Germany. I want to do what I can to combat this in
speaking tomorrow . . . I think we are running a real risk of losing France and not
gaining Germany, who won't want us if she can detach France from us.[102]

The speech itself encapsulated the policy which he was to develop,
especially the part in which he looked forward to the Agreement with
Russia, maintaining that the failure to renew the Alliance with Japan
would be regarded as an example of fickleness and folly which would
cause Britain to be distrusted in the world generally: 'We should not only
have lost a good friend . . . but we should, by the impression we had
created, have deprived ourselves of the power to make new friends.'[103]
Grey saw himself, by February 1906, as 'a Foreign Secretary who had
made it an object to maintain the entente with France'.[104] In September
1906 he told Haldane: 'I want to preserve the entente with France, but it
isn't easy, and if it is broken up I must go.'[105] His insistence that he could
not conduct relations with France unless he was able to assume that Britain
would land forces to help France, if Germany invaded her; the 'stiffness'
that Harcourt noticed in his reaction to Metternich's demand in March

1912 for a neutrality clause, and which Harcourt attributed, correctly, to fear of losing the entente with France; his chafing under the limitations imposed on the closeness of Anglo-French relations; his telling Harcourt in January 1914 that 'there may be difficulties' in the course of any Cabinet discussion of alternatives to letting things go on as they were[106] – these were all indications, more or less explicit, that there were limits beyond which he personally would not go. They were all threats, more or less veiled, to resign. As he told Bertie in July 1912, '*he* would not remain in the Cabinet if there was any question of abandoning the policy of the Entente with France'.[107] The assertion of George Monger, that towards the end of 1907 'there was a very real possibility of a change of policy', is highly dubious on much more than the immediate ground that Grey was at that very time writing to Lascelles that 'just now, we must give no colouring to the idea that we are wavering by a hair's breadth from our loyalty to the entente, and are contemplating a new departure in policy'.[108] When the sticking point was reached, Grey *was* the brick wall. In August 1914 the iron glove was taken off to reveal the iron fist.

It was the prospect of Grey's resignation that ensured the survival of his policy. His threats to resign were not lost on those against whom they were directed. Loreburn's appreciation was that 'the resignation of Grey would mean the break-up of the Cabinet as probably Lloyd George, Churchill and Haldane would go with him'.[109] In March 1909 G. L. Garvin, editor of *The Observer*, wrote of the 'notorious certainty' that Grey's resignation would break up the Government; Ramsay MacDonald in 1914 would say that Grey was 'indispensable' to the Liberal Party, which would be split in two if he were to leave the Government.[110] The Radical ministers were as indisposed as was Grey himself to handing back the country to the Conservatives. Loreburn, Harcourt, McKenna, Pease and others ceased their pressure for a British commitment to neutrality, and admitted they had gone 'as far as reasonable men should go' for the same reasons that Grey did not press for the conversion of the ententes into alliances – the break-up of the Cabinet and of the party.[111] Grey acknowledged that if he pushed for alliances, he might have to go;[112] they acknowledged that if they insisted on neutrality, he would certainly go. This basic stalemate was the real security for the policy of the entente.

3

<oooooooooooooooooooooooooooooooooooooooooooooooooooooooo>

The Politics of Liberal
Foreign Policy II

In February 1911, commenting on an article which had appeared in the French press, Crowe minuted:

The fundamental fact of course is that an Entente is not an alliance. For purposes of ultimate emergencies it *may* be found to have no substance at all. For an Entente is nothing more than a frame of mind, a view of general policy which is shared by the governments of the two countries, but which *may* be, or become, so vague as to lose all content. Some therefore of the faults criticised by the *Temps* are necessarily inherent in any system resting merely on 'Ententes'.[1]

Nicolson voiced a similar sort of dissatisfaction in 1914: 'Ententes are all very well for a certain time, but they are most unsatisfactory transactions as they have none of the benefits of an Alliance and are always liable to break down when there is the slightest friction or difference of opinion.'[2] Although the staff of the Foreign and Diplomatic Services were by no means unanimous on this score, there was a considerable body of opinion within them whose concern to remedy the deficiencies it considered inherent in ententes was manifested in support of their conversion into alliances.

Even before the formal signature of the Anglo-French Agreement Louis Mallet was hoping that it might be the prelude to a closer understanding. In the autumn of 1904 he expressed the wish that 'a nearer alliance' could be negotiated at once.[3] The following spring he lamented that

unfortunately we have no treaty, and no written engagement [with France]. If we had, there would be no need for anxiety and I believe that we should never be troubled with German ambitions again. It is the uncertainty attaching to the course we should take if war broke out which is at the bottom of the ceaseless intrigues of Germany ...

As things were, he advised the renewal and extension of the Alliance with Japan: this would have 'a tremendous effect in convincing Europe that we have a positive policy and that we mean to stick to it'. It would, moreover, increase Britain's strength and hence her value as an ally, and this would not be lost on the French. They were, after all, 'an intelligent people'.[4] Five months after his appointment as Private Secretary to Sir Edward Grey, he was writing: 'I shall never be happy until we have a defensive alliance with [France].'[5]

The Paris Embassy was of the same mind. On two occasions in 1905 Sir A. Lister, the Chargé d'Affaires, wondered if it wasn't the right policy to 'extend the scope of our understanding'.[6] Bertie, the Ambassador, agreed with Mallet that Britain should pursue 'a logical course', and return a positive answer to the French question of 10 January 1906 as to whether her armed support could be relied on in the event of 'agression brutale' on the part of Germany. In his letter in support of Mallet's position he warned Grey against simply assuring the French of the continuance of diplomatic support or of neutrality in the event of a war provoked by Germany.[7] Later, Bertie held that 'everything military and naval' ought to be arranged to meet the contingency of British and French forces having to act together. In 1912, believing that if Britain withdrew her naval forces from the Mediterranean the French would ask for a quid pro quo, he suggested an exchange of notes which Grey described as 'going much further than anything hitherto done and . . . something like an alliance'.[8]

Nicolson was even more persistent and categorical. He made three separate attempts upon the citadel. The first came in the spring of 1909, the events of which, Nicolson considered, presaged a critical period in which a regrouping of the Powers might take place. He would not be surprised, he wrote to Grey,

if we were to find both France and Russia gravitating rapidly towards the Central Powers, as neither of the former, distrustful of each other, feels that she can stand alone against the power of the central combination. Our entente, I fear, will languish, and possibly die. If it were possible to extend and strengthen it by bringing it nearer to the nature of an alliance, it would then be possible to deter Russia from moving towards Berlin . . . and if we could contract some kind of an alliance with Russia, we should probably also steady France and prevent her from deserting to the Central Powers.[9]

He considered that Hardinge was right to ask, in a letter of 30 March, 'will the Russians say to themselves "Is it not better for us to come to terms with Germany and Austria and leave France and England alone?" ', and replied:

If we wish to make sure that Russia will not eventually detach herself from us, we must, I submit, extend and consolidate our 'entente' in such manner and form as will enable her to rely with assurance on our support being really available in moments of need and danger. I admit that this is mighty like forming an alliance . . . I think that we should be more comfortable if it were made, and it would be well if it could include France and Japan.[10]

At the back of his mind, he revealed in June, was 'the idea of some assurance being given that if the equilibrium of Europe were endangered we should be prepared to afford help to re-establish it'.[11]

Nicolson's second bid for an alliance, this time with France, was made in May 1912. On this occasion he was strongly supported by Crowe, whose attitude towards an alliance may be surmised from his minute of 2 February 1911 and who, according to Sir Henry Wilson, the Director of Military Operations, told Grey on 1 May 1912 'that unless he [Grey] did something and buckled to we would lose all our friends and by Dec. 31 of this year we would be standing *alone*'.[12] On 2 May Crowe took advantage of the issue of the French treatment of British missionaries in Madagascar to minute:

I am afraid there can be little doubt that the French Govt. are under the impression that H.M.G.'s policy in its most recent phase is rather to minimise the obligations which a wider and more generous view of the Entente has hitherto been thought to rest upon them as regards cooperation with France in the defence of vital common interests . . .

I have no doubt myself that our obviously proper course is to uphold the spirit of the Entente in every possible way, and if possible to render our general understanding with France both wider and more definite . . . [13]

At this time Crowe was preparing a memorandum on the effect of a British evacuation of the Mediterranean on British foreign policy, in which he took the line that a large number of adverse effects would be incurred. These could only be averted if the place of the British Mediterranean Squadron were effectively taken by a powerful French fleet. The future attitudes of Spain, Turkey and Italy all depended, he maintained, on that of France, which in turn depended on French certainty about Britain:

unless France . . . can definitely rely on British assistance in case she herself is attacked by Germany, it will be impossible for her to concentrate an overwhelming naval force in the Mediterranean after providing for the defence of her Atlantic coast against the German fleet. The question therefore whether Italy and Austria can be kept in check by the French navy, is seen to depend on there being some definite naval understanding between England and France, amounting in practice to an agreement for mutual assistance in case either is attacked by the Triple Alliance.[14]

Nicolson, who seemed to Henry Wilson 'as much alive to the present dangerous state of affairs' as he himself, and 'just as anxious to clinch the present Entente with France and Russia by an Alliance', forwarded Crowe's memorandum to Grey on 6 May. He added a covering note to the effect that it would be well worth Britain's while to give France the reciprocal engagements she would naturally ask for if she agreed to safeguard

British interests in the Mediterranean in the early period of a war and until such time as vessels could be spared from British home waters to perform the task. This pressure was maintained throughout May, Crowe insisting on 'the necessity of an Alliance', Nicolson hoping to 'fix it up with France' before the arrival of Marschall von Bieberstein as German Ambassador.[15]

Nicolson continued to believe that 'the right policy would be . . . to form an alliance with France'. The time was approaching, he told O'Beirne in November 1913, when the Conventions with Russia would have to be revised. He hoped this would be done 'in a favourable sense so that if possible our relations should become even closer and more firmly established than they are at the present moment'. In the late winter and early spring of 1914 he deluged his correspondents with the opinion that 'the ideal undoubtedly would be that we should convert our understanding into an alliance'.[16] The fullest justification for this was embodied in a letter to Sir M. de Bunsen in April:

As matters at present stand, with the exceedingly loose ties which bind us to France and Russia, we always run the risk of being severed by some unexpected event. The uncertainty of our attitude creates misgivings in the minds of our friends, but encourages also in the minds of other parties the hope that they may be able to break up so fragile a combination as that of the Triple Entente.[17]

One recipient of these views, who also shared them, was Sir G. Buchanan, Nicolson's successor as Ambassador in St Petersburg. Early in February 1914 the Russian Foreign Minister, Sazonov, outlined to him a scheme for the conversion of the Triple Entente into a regular Alliance, which once proclaimed would remove fears of new coups on the part of Germany. It would be of a purely defensive character. Should England, France or Russia be attacked by any single Power the other two would remain neutral and only come to the assistance of their ally if another Power joined in the war on the other side. Though Buchanan parried this overture, he wrote to Grey that there was 'a good deal of truth in Sazonov's contention that, if Germany knew beforehand that France and Russia could count on England's support, she would never face the risks such a war would entail'. At the end of March he dwelt on Russian concern over the 'uncertainty' of British action as showing 'how difficult we may find it in the long run to maintain our understanding with Russia unless its basis can be enlarged'.[18] His Annual Report for 1913, which arrived in London in March 1914, contained the sentence: 'it is useless for us to blind our eyes to the fact that, if we are to remain friends with Russia, we must be prepared to give her our material as well as our moral support in any conflict in which she becomes involved in Europe'. Sazonov was certainly convinced that Buchanan was of his persuasion.[19]

The information that A. Benckendorff transmitted in February 1914, to the effect that at the Foreign Office Nicolson and Buchanan, Mallet and Crowe made little mystery of their conviction that alliance was the natural outcome of entente, would appear to be substantially correct. Only with regard to Hardinge, whom Benckendorff also listed, is this picture askew. Yet even Hardinge had written in a memorandum of May 1909: 'Were England the ally of either France or Russia the political equilibrium and peace of the Continent would probably be maintained . . . '.[20]

It was a possibility that particularly exercised Bertie that, unless the French were given 'something definite to rely on', unless they could be sure of British support, they would come to terms with Germany that would be extremely detrimental to the interests of the British Empire. This would result in Britain's being 'stranded in splendid isolation', a position which 'nowadays would be highly dangerous'.[21] It was a conviction particularly strongly held by British diplomats at St Petersburg, where it was perhaps most easily, and most understandably, arrived at, that Britain's understanding with Russia was, as Nicolson put it, 'in reality of far more importance to us than it is to her'.[22] This derived, in Nicolson's case, from his appreciation at the time of the signing of the Anglo-Russian Conventions, that Britain would in the long run be the loser in any protracted Imperial struggle with Russia, and that it was 'simple prudence to come to terms with her now, and not wait until she is in a position to be disagreeable and exacting'.[23] A contribution to the alliance debate from Balfour, in the form of a memorandum passed on to Grey in June 1912, was that 'an "entente" is a natural prey of every diplomatic intriguer. It must be the object of every German Foreign Minister to drive a wedge between France and Britain, to aggravate every misunderstanding, to foster every suspicion . . . '.[24]

Why – when the chances of the success of German 'intrigues' would have been much reduced, even if the policy itself were not discontinued, by the conclusion of an alliance with France, or Russia, or both; when thereby the nervousness of the French, which was much in evidence in 1905–6, in 1908–9, and in 1911, would have been overcome;[25] and when the disposition of the Russians to lean towards Berlin, which in the spring of 1909 the disgrace of Isvolsky and in the spring of 1914 the appointment of Goryemkin as President of the Council were thought likely to encourage,[26] would thereby have been countered – was no alliance ever concluded? Opportunities were frequently presented. Why were they not taken when the stakes were so high, the benefits so obvious, and when the Foreign Secretary was on record as dreading 'splendid isolation' no less than did his Ambassador to Paris?[27] Why did the risks continue to be taken? What was it that proved more powerful than the logic and positivism of those who wished to cease 'sitting on the fence' and 'dancing on a tightrope', who wished to substitute 'a definite line' of policy for 'evasive and uncertain answers', 'ambiguous and procrastinating statements'? Why was there not the 'departure' in British foreign policy for which they called?[28]

A considerable number, and variety, of arguments was advanced against the conclusion of specific alliances and against the conclusion of alliances in general. The very number of arguments is somewhat suspicious. Their diversity of type does not produce the impression of their lending support one to another. Conviction in them is still further reduced by the inconsistency in their employment. For sometimes quite different arguments against alliances are to be found in the hands of the most persistent advocates of alliances. In this situation it is not the easiest of tasks to determine which, if indeed any, particular argument or group of arguments really carried the day.

The first straw clutched at by Sir Edward Grey, on 15 January 1906, was that 'alliances, especially continental alliances, are not in accordance with our traditions'.[29] In the only work which so far has set out to test the 'principles' of British foreign policy against their practice C. H. D. Howard has concluded that the transactions – in his view only three in number – made by British Governments between 1822 and 1902 which placed Britain under an explicit, unequivocal and new obligation to go to war on the continent of Europe in a hypothetical contingency and in circumstances that were not merely temporary, 'do not constitute an impressive series of commitments'.[30] In 1822, however, G. Canning did inherit both the Alliance with Portugal, renewed on 22 January 1815, and the Quadruple Alliance concluded by Lord Castlereagh on 20 November 1815. When the occasions are considered on which British Foreign Secretaries were prepared to undertake towards continental Powers obligations involving a *casus belli*, albeit in the hope that these would be temporary expedients but in the absence of any guarantee of their short duration – as they were to France in 1863 and to Germany in 1885, and as they actually did to France and Prussia in August 1870 over Belgium – it cannot be maintained that 'continental alliances' were quite without precedent. Moreover, as far as 'tradition' alone is concerned there was, despite the 'precedent' of the Anglo-Siamese Convention of 6 April 1897,[31] certainly no tradition of alliances with small Asiatic Powers before the conclusion of the Alliance with Japan of February 1902. Even if there had been no examples of continental alliances, which was not the case, this should not, going at least by the Far Eastern example, have made any difference.

On 27 April 1909 Hardinge wrote to Nicolson: 'The fact that we cannot strengthen our agreement by an alliance is due to our Constitution, and we cannot help it.'[32] This cryptic statement was an echo of the position taken up by Salisbury in 1887 and adhered to in public until his retirement in 1902. In February 1887 he wrote to Queen Victoria: 'No English Government can give definite pledges of military or naval cooperation in a future contingency, because it cannot be sure that Parliament would make such a promise good.' In February 1896 he told Sir E. Monson, then the Ambassador to Paris, that 'in this country it was impossible to take any engagement involving an obligation to go to war'. This was because

no one can foresee or predict what in any future contingency a democratic Parliament will do. Tell me what is the casus belli and I may be able to give a guess at the conduct which England will pursue. But without such information we not only cannot guess what England will do, but we cannot determine her course beforehand by any pledges or any arguments derived from general interests.[33]

It is worth remarking in this context that the prospects of the British Parliament's refusing to ratify such instruments, and of such promises already made being repudiated at the last minute because they were for purposes of which the British electorate turned out not to approve,[34] whilst they tended to depress the Germans, did not deter the Germans or, at a later date, the French or the Russians, from continuing to press for their conclusion. Furthermore, whilst some members of the Foreign Office acknowledged that there was 'considerable hesitation here to binding ourselves to any definite course of action in view of possible eventualities', whilst they admitted, even though 'it went against the grain' to do so, that the Government would not be *disposed* to make such commitments, they made distinctions between 'this' and 'any' Government, between the present and the future.[35] In April 1909 Hardinge wrote of how impossible it was to hope for any step forward '*by this Government*' towards a closer entente or even an alliance with Russia: 'When Balfour comes into office it may be different, but we must hope that it may not be too late.' He repeated in May his feeling 'that with this Government in office we can do no more than we have done so far . . . When the next Government comes in we can take fresh stock of our position, and they would probably be ready to go further than the present Government would go.' This being so, his 'sole aim' was 'to keep things going on the present lines so long as this Government remains in office'. Nicolson took the point. 'I shall', he wrote to his wife, 'be glad of a change of Government. I am afraid we are not likely with the present people to have a well-defined firm foreign policy.'[36] Clearly there were different views as to what the Constitution did, and did not, permit. The confidence placed by Hardinge in Balfour personally was justified in 1912. Then, it was revealed that in The Constitution According to Balfour there was room for a defensive alliance with France,[37] just as there had been for an alliance with Japan in 1901. The views of Salisbury, with which Balfour perhaps more than anyone else had been favoured, had not carried the day with him on that occasion, any more than they had with the majority of Salisbury's colleagues at the time. Balfour recognised that the arguments used of late to reject the advances of Germany could, after the conclusion of the Alliance with Japan, no longer be employed: 'We have proved in our own persons that a Ministry can promise to go to war in remote contingencies and over quarrels at present unforeseen.'[38] If such obligations could be undertaken towards Japan, they could be undertaken towards any Great Power. Alliances could be made. Britain's 'democratic institutions', however often the contrary was maintained,[39] *did* permit of their contraction.

Alliances were 'impossible' only in so far as no Government could venture to propose them 'owing to the ingrained dislike of the British public of what they term "foreign entanglements" '. They were 'out of the question' only 'so long as the public in England remain in their present mood'. It was an ignorant and unreceptive public opinion which converted what Nicolson wished to see – the transformation of both ententes into definite alliances – into 'a matter of pure policy'.[40] Yet Sir Edward Grey, in October 1902, would not have been surprised if the Conservative Government had committed the country to an alliance with Germany, despite the public feeling against Germany prevailing at the time.[41] That Government, between August 1901 and February 1902, had made no efforts to ascertain the opinion of the country as a whole towards its projected alliance with Japan. Sir Edward Hamilton recorded on 13 February 1902: 'an Agreement signed and sealed with Japan – practically an offensive and defensive alliance – has transpired today and taken everybody by surprise'.[42] They had pursued that object, just as they pursued its renewal and extension in 1905,[43] well aware that there were quarters in which it would not be favourably received. In this case, the opposition came from the Opposition. Because of this, and because of the political circumstances of the time, it was the more easily ignored. It was less easily ignored, *faits accomplis* (criticisms of which, said Nicolson, referring to the Anglo-Russian Agreement, were not very serious)[44] were less easily presented, and less easily still after the elections of 1910, when opposition came from the supporters of the Liberal Government. For it was pre-eminently from the Liberal side that what Lansdowne called 'the suspicion with which any entanglement in foreign alliances was regarded by a large part of the British public'[45] emanated. In 1891, at a time when Gladstone was quite convinced that Salisbury *had* committed the country to a continental alliance, he ascertained that John Morley and Sir William Harcourt, like himself, held 'in the strongest form the doctrine that it is the business of

England to stand absolutely aloof from these prospective engagements. And such we believe to be the general or universal view of the Liberal party.' The following year he revealed that his dislike of the Triple and Dual Alliances was based on the misconception that their ultimate design and scope was not a peaceful one.[46] The making of alliances, especially continental alliances, was not a principle of Liberal foreign policy. It was not a practice Liberals were anxious to establish as a tradition of British foreign policy.

Other arguments, of a predominantly foreign political character, were also advanced against the conclusion of alliances. They were held to be provocative in nature, if not actually aggressive in intent. Lansdowne tried to take the sting out of this occupational hazard in regard to the second alliance with Japan. He asked Hardinge to try to convince the Russian Government that it was not directed against Russia:

I do not of course mean to say that the new Agreement is not from the force of circumstances aimed at Russia more than at any other Power, but this is inevitable. All measures of precaution, whether military and naval preparations or Alliances, must be directed against somebody, and no country has, it seems to me, the right to take offence because another country raises the wall of its back garden high enough to prevent an over-adventurous neighbour or its agents from attempting to climb over it.[47]

It was held, in particular, that Germany might take offence at a British alliance with either France or Russia. This was the argument used by Grey in September 1906:

The difficulty of making an alliance with France now is that Germany might attack France at once, while Russia is helpless, fearing lest when Russia recovered she [Germany] should be crushed by a new Triple Alliance against her. She might make an alliance between us and France a pretext for doing this as her only chance of securing her future.[48]

This was repeated by Hardinge in May 1909, following closely on the heels of his contention that it was the Constitution that stood in the way of an alliance. Writing to Nicolson, who had already admitted that Germany would regard an Anglo-Russian alliance 'with the highest displeasure', he said that a closer agreement than already existed between the Triple Entente Powers would result 'in the very thing which we wish at present to avoid, and that is a general war. Germany would be certain to regard an alliance . . . as a direct menace to herself, and it is not unlikely that she would at once begin preparations to provoke war in the near future.'[49] Of proposals made by the French Ambassador in April 1912 Nicolson wrote that they 'would be regarded by many as offering umbrage and a challenge to Germany'. In this case, it was 'wiser to leave matters as they were, and not to strain an understanding . . . which . . . did not by itself afford the slightest reason to any other country to resent or demur to it'. By the end of the following month, throughout which he had exerted all his force in the opposite direction, Nicolson was writing to O'Beirne: 'there is the danger that if at this moment we were to emphasise the closeness of our relations with France (by rendering our Entente a little more permanent and positive in character – i.e. developing it into an Alliance and some precise convention embodying our mutual obligations) Germany might become alarmed and perhaps precipitate a conflict'.[50] Later the same year Grey noted that the publication of any notes would 'at this time . . . have a very exciting effect in Europe'.[51] So solicitous was the Foreign Secretary on this score that in 1913 he decried the making of a public alliance between France and Spain. It would, he claimed, be presumed to be directed against Germany, and 'as long as her policy was unaggressive it would be a great pity to make any new alliance or agreement that would give Germany provocation or reason to depart from her present policy'.[52] Goschen's opinion, in 1914, was that the real question was

whether the advantage of being the intimate friend of Russia is greater in the inverse ratio than the disadvantage of being on our former cold terms with Germany . . . I doubt – no I am sure that we can't have it both ways: i.e. form a defensive alliance with Russia and France and at the same time be on cordial terms with Germany. One can imagine the German reaction if we did join France and Russia.[53]

The complement of the idea that Germany might take offence was that France might take advantage. Mallet, who in 1905 would not have hesitated to let the French know that Britain would back them up to the extent of going to war, nevertheless admitted that 'all appearance of egging them on' must be avoided.[54] In April 1907 Bertie remarked that whilst the danger of causing the French to lose confidence in British support had to be avoided, 'at the same time we must not encourage (them) to rely on our material land support to the extent of making them beard the Germans'.[55] In 1913 he told Grey that he realised that an alliance with France 'might encourage the French to be too defiant towards Germany'.[56] Grey himself was suspicious in June 1914 that Isvolsky, then Russian Ambassador in Paris, and R. Poincaré were leading the Germans to believe in the existence of an Anglo-Russian naval alliance, and reinforced the point that he wanted to discourage France from provoking Germany.[57] The same consideration was present at the outbreak of war the following month, Bertie writing on 30 July that 'if we gave an assurance of armed assistance to France and Russia now, Russia would become more exacting and France would follow in her wake'; Crowe minuting that 'what must weigh with H.M.G. is the consideration that they should not by a declaration of unconditional solidarity with France and Russia *induce* and *determine* these two powers to choose the path of war'.[58]

These foreign political arguments against the conclusion of alliances, both as they stand and as coming from the particular quarters from which they came, are no more convincing at first sight than those from tradition and the Constitution. Nor do they improve upon closer scrutiny. Hardinge on one occasion countered the view that alliances were instruments of war by claiming that 'a system of alliances' had preserved the peace of Europe for the past thirty years.[59] So far as the possibility of Germany's treating an Anglo-French-Russian alliance as a pretext for war is concerned, Grey may have been influenced by some information which reached him in April 1906 to the effect that in June 1905 the German Ambassador in Paris had threatened Rouvier with military action as a result of a belief that a convention or agreement between Britain and France was impending.[60] On the eve of the signing of the Agreement with Russia, following as it did the Agreement with France, Goschen expressed the hope that the British were not rubbing in Germany's comparative isolation too much, and the fear 'that Wilhelm II will feel we are driving him into a corner and that he may get sick of it'.[61] Alliances, it might be inferred, would have the same effect, only more so, particularly in the aftermath of the German failure to break up the Franco-Russian Alliance in 1904 and 1905. But what practical difference would alliances have made to the Germans, in most of the years before 1914? The calculation of William II and of Holstein of mid-1905 was passed on to Bertie by a French intermediary in the negotiation with Germany and transmitted by him to Lansdowne. It was that as nothing could be done against Germany from the sea, except the stopping of her commerce, and as a quick victory over France was expected, which would allow any damage to German colonies and commerce to be made good at the expense of the French, there was no reason to fear a war even if it did entail fighting against England at the same time.[62] The Germans persisted in their calculation: Baron Stumm told Bertie in 1913 that even if the British Navy destroyed the German Navy 'this would not advance matters for England'.[63] Nor did the Germans make any secret of their opinion of the British Army. As the Kaiser put it in March 1911, 'Excuse my saying so, but the few divisions you could put into the field could make no appreciable difference.'[64] Alliances, in themselves, only increased obligations, not strength. If it were maintained that the transformation of ententes into alliances automatically increased the power at their disposal, and we know that the German overtures for a neutrality agreement were interpreted in London as a tribute to British strength, it is difficult to understand why the Germans should be thought more likely to attack a stronger unit than to be deterred from so doing. The warning that Bethmann-Hollweg issued to Grey in June 1914 against the conclusion of an Anglo-Russian naval convention must not be taken out of context.[65] The growth of Russian power worried the Germans seriously only from the late summer of 1912.[66] Had an Anglo-Russian alliance been in existence in 1914 the German Chancellor's threat might well not have been uttered. Had one been made, say, in 1909, the actual response made to it might have been different from that projected at the later date. Certainly there was no likelihood of either the French or the Russians being inspired by an alliance with England to square up to Germany in the years before 1912. The *douche* administered to what French military ardour there was in 1907 by Campbell-Bannerman's stressing the reluctance of Britain to send her Army abroad was not called for. As Bertie reported at the time, the French Government was 'anything but bellicose'.[67] The French knew – and the British knew that they knew – that neither H. O. Arnold-Foster's nor Haldane's armies could defend Paris.[68] Their opinion of the value of Britain as an ally was the same in 1912 as in 1905: the French Military Attaché in Berlin wrote that if the French refused to be constrained by Germany they would find themselves embroiled 'in a war in which England will be but of very little assistance to us'. A copy of this letter was circulated by Grey to Asquith, Haldane and Churchill.[69] When in February 1912 Bertie said that if England bound herself not to join any combination to attack Germany she might tie her hands very inconveniently as regards France, Grey was clearly taken aback. He asked Bertie: 'Do you mean it is possible that France will attack Germany?' Bertie did not improve the matter by replying that the first attacker was not necessarily the real aggressor.[70] But though reports of a revival in French confidence began to arrive from Paris – the most alarming at the end of 1912 to the effect that if the Germans were ever in difficulties and an adventurous ministry were in power in Paris 'France may one day surprise us all' – Bertie remained confident that 'there need be no fear of the French *creating* a war with Germany'. In June 1913 he told Grey that he 'felt sure that France would not provoke a war without the *certainty* of having England as well as Russia with her in arms'.[71] The growth in French confidence and the revival of revanchist feeling was due to the recovery of Russia, not to the prospect of a British alliance.

It might, of course, be argued that it was beyond the draughtsmanship of the British Foreign Office to produce a purely defensive alliance. Balfour, however, who like Bertie recognised that the Power firing the first shot might not be the real aggressor, and who included himself amongst the many in England who would do all they could to save France from destruction but had no wish to be dragged at her heels into a war to recover Alsace and Lorraine, offered a solution to this. He at least thought that such fears could be allayed, and the advantages which a treaty, but never an entente, could confer, be obtained 'by requiring the Power which calls on its ally for assistance to express or have expressed its readiness to submit the points in dispute to arbitration'.[72]

Whilst the foreign political arguments against the conclusion of alliances were not always appropriate at the times when the propositions were put forward, no one could be absolutely certain of the severity of either the immediate or the longer-term repercussions. The points being argued, as to whether Europe would have been brought closer to war or rendered more secure, whether divisions and tensions would have been widened and increased or narrowed and reduced, whether the Germans would have been driven into a corner and the French encouraged to come out of theirs were, in the nature of things, debatable.

What was *not* debatable was that the impression, of increased commitment by Britain and greater division between the Powers, which the signing of an alliance would have produced in Britain would have resulted, in turn, in the end of certain illusions, the exclusion of certain possibilities. Britain could no longer have been portrayed as the Power 'balancing' between the two groups of Powers. It would not have been possible for Grey to maintain that he wanted Britain to be 'a connecting link' between Germany and the Triple Entente; or that Britain belonged to the Triple Entente not in order to exacerbate difficulties between the two groups 'but on the contrary . . . to prevent questions throwing the groups as such into opposition'. It would have meant an end to the claim Buchanan made without believing it himself that as 'a friend who might be converted into an ally', Britain could play the role of mediator to better purpose at Berlin and Vienna.[73]

In welcoming the Anglo-French Agreement Grey had expressed the hope that it would serve as a 'working model' for other cases.[74] As Foreign Secretary, he appeared to pursue the objective of making it a model for an agreement with Germany. He said of the North Sea Agreement of 1907, for instance:

If Germany wishes to make Agreements . . . which are in themselves harmless, I do not want to make a grievance with her about it . . . It may very well be that all Germany desires is to ratify her amour propre by appearing before the world as a party to some Agreements of the kind which are in vogue, and so demonstrating that she is not isolated . . . [75]

To the disgust of some of his advisers, such as Crowe, who maintained that all talk of an 'understanding' between Britain and Germany had 'an air of unreality', who even went so far as to say that 'with Germany we have no differences whatever', and Bertie, who was unable to believe that 'by a paper Agreement the fundamentally opposing interests of the British and German peoples can be reconciled', Grey continued to hold out the prospect of an agreement for the exchange of naval information or the limitation of naval building, observing in February 1912: 'France had made her Agreement with Germany as to Morocco; Russia had made hers as to the Baghdad Railway; but so far since I had been in office we had not made any Agreement with Germany as to any of the difficulties between us.'[76] The prospects, however slim, for a German entente would hardly have been improved by an alliance with anyone else.

Still less would Grey have been able to elaborate the idea of bringing France and Russia into an agreement between England and Germany. This was first broached in August 1909, when Grey wrote that he was 'not without hope that [an Anglo-German Agreement] may result in something of a generally reassuring character to which France and Russia might become parties'.[77] It surfaced again, to the increasing mystification of his advisers, in each of the three succeeding years. The fullest account of it was given by Grey to Goschen in October 1910. Welcoming a German suggestion that France and Russia ought to be parties to any naval agreement, the Foreign Secretary said that this

opens the way for our saying, at an opportune moment, what I have always thought to be the only possible solution, that France and Russia must be parties to a political agreement.

We may also have to say that a naval agreement is of no use unless Austria and Italy are in it. That would bring into the naval and political understanding all the six powers of Europe. Five would desire such an agreement, and a diminution of naval expenditure, but on Germany's part such an agreement would mean the renunciation of ambitions for the hegemony of Europe. The way in which she receives the proposal, if made, will be a test of whether she really desires peace and security from all attack for herself, or whether she has ambitions which can be gratified only at the expense of other Powers.[78]

Haldane was to recall, in 1922, that in 1912 Grey 'was willing to try – if Germany would check her shipbuilding – so to enlarge the Entente as to bring it to the form of a real concert of the Great Powers, and so secure Germany as well as France and Russia'.[79] Nicolson, at least, had a significantly different approach to the 'collecting' of Powers: his collection was not intended to include Germany.[80]

It is less certain that Grey believed, in the first instances, that this was how things were, or, in the last instances, that this was how they might be, than that he knew that this was the language which a substantial proportion of his colleagues wished to hear, that such schemes were policies which the majority of the Cabinet wished to see implemented. He had to reckon with those who had retained, or inherited, the outlook and principles and rhetoric of the Grand Old Man. John Burns' watchwords were 'Splendid Isolation; No Balance of Power; No Incorporation in the Continental System.'[81] Loreburn's policy consisted of no military or naval conversations, strict neutrality and the non-intervention in European affairs of the Expeditionary Force. He considered 'the old policy of non-interference in European combinations and intrigues', which he claimed to have been the policy of Disraeli and Salisbury and Gladstone, 'essentially right'. From the summer of 1911 he pressed for the French to be told that they must not in future rely on Britain's military or naval support. So far as he was concerned, the original friendly understanding had been 'perverted' into an alliance.[82] Exclamation marks fell like notes of horror from the pen of Harcourt whenever anything that might be construed as bringing the Anglo-French relationship closer to an alliance was raised. When in June 1912 Churchill wrote that the situation in the Mediterranean would become entirely favourable if France were taken into account, Harcourt's immediate reaction was 'Alliance'. When Churchill concluded that 'a definite naval arrangement should be made with France without delay', Harcourt wrote in the margin: 'Military also?'. And when Churchill claimed that such an arrangement would not decide the question of whether the two Powers should become allies or not Harcourt minuted 'Of course it would.'[83] Morley, when Nicolson suggested to him that the Mediterranean could be made safe by an alliance with France, 'threw up his hands and walked out of the room'.[84] It was to these quarters that Grey was referring when he said that 'the feeling here about definite commitment to a continental war on unforeseeable conditions would be too dubious to permit us to make an alliance'.[85] The lees of Gladstone still fouled the cup. Campbell-Bannerman, who believed as did Grey that 'We must stand by France', did not shrink from dwelling on British reluctance to undertake 'obligations which would commit them to a continental war'.[86]

Arguing in Cabinet in June 1912 against what one observer took to be Haldane's and Churchill's advocation of alliance with France, Grey said that no one knew what the position would be between France and Britain in two years' time.[87] This was a curious argument, but inasmuch as an alliance *would* have helped to determine the future, this was just the trouble.

That alliances were in some way demeaning was one thing. This was a sentiment not altogether absent from Foreign Office circles. Both

Hardinge and MacDonald, the Ambassador to Tokyo, referred in 1905 to British 'decadence' – 'twiddling our thumbs and paying other people to fight for us'. Tyrrell in 1907, with the Anglo-Russian Conventions in prospect, took up a remark made by Sir C. Spring-Rice concerning the 'policy of alliances' which both believed the current negotiations were promoting: 'Alliances can never be a substitute for a sound army and navy or in other words we cannot relieve ourselves of our duties of defence by relying on other nations to fight our battles. It is a stupid and demoralising policy.' He rather regretted the renunciation of 'the policy of splendid isolation in which Goschen gloried not so many years ago'. De Bunsen, in 1912, wrote that it was 'Better to depend on ourselves than on positive alliances with anybody.'[88]

Being 'driven by our weakness into dependence on an alliance with any European Power', as McKenna put it, however, was not as fundamental an objection as what appeared to accompany this, namely, the 'obligation to fight in a war not of our own making'.[89] What was really feared, what really had to be avoided, was that control of one's own destiny would not only be lost but be seen to be lost. The Conservative Government had faced this danger in the course of their negotiations with Japan. Lansdowne had been unwilling to give the Japanese a free hand to make a *casus foederis* out of any Russian encroachment in Corea, for they would then be 'free to embark upon hostilities in which we may become involved over some comparatively insignificant local question'.[90] Salisbury put it even more strongly: Japan's claim that she had the right 'to take without our permission measures which we might regard as provocative' would impose on Britain the liability of being committed against her will to a dangerous policy. It would involve

a pledge on our part to defend Japanese action in Corea and in all China against France and Russia, no matter what the casus belli may be. There is no limit: and no escape. We are pledged to war, though the conduct of our ally may have been followed in spite of our strongest remonstrances and may be avowedly regarded by us with clear disapprobation.

There was no justification, he continued, 'for surrendering without reserve into the hands of another Power the right of deciding whether we shall or shall not stake the resources of the Empire on the issue of a mighty conflict'.[91] It was such fears and susceptibilities as these that Grey had either reflected or been pandering to when in October 1905 he said: 'An alliance which appears a source of strength today might, under future conditions, become a matter of embarrassment. Were the policy of alliances rashly entered upon, I quite admit that there would be a danger that this country might be led into undesirable entanglements.'[92] Their remaining alive throughout the following decade placed him in the position of saying to the French Ambassador on 1 August 1914: 'France did not wish to join in the war that seemed about to break out, but she was obliged to join in it, because of her alliance. We had purposely kept clear of all alliances, in order that we might not be involved in difficulties in this way.'[93] This was, as was not uncommon with him, to make a virtue of necessity.

The central danger could be avoided. In the case of the Anglo-Japanese Alliance it had been avoided, at least to the satisfaction of Lansdowne. Nevertheless, the impression that it was insurmountable could not be eradicated. So great did fear of it remain that the point Churchill borrowed from Balfour's memorandum of June 1912 and made in August, that as things stood 'we have the obligations of an alliance without its advantages and above all without its precise definitions', implying that British commitments might actually be reduced by the conclusion of an alliance, was completely overlooked. The cast of mind of one of Tyrrell's correspondents was too widespread and deeply ingrained: 'It is easy to get into an alliance but devilishly hard to get out of one . . . I think we are much better as we are.'[94]

In addition to this impression and these preferences, the prospects for an alliance were not improved by what were widely regarded as its corollaries. These were – conscription, and the adoption by Britain of a 'continental' strategy. Esher, preferring in 1912 a solution of the Mediterranean problem through increased naval building, remarked: 'Whatever the cost may be it is cheaper than a conscript army and any entangling alliance.'[95] Esher's solution was that preferred by the *Manchester Guardian* and the *Westminster Gazette*. The former, having described an alliance with France as an 'absurdly disproportionate remedy', went on to say that 'the project of alliance with France would make us a Continental power in Europe . . . our army . . . would have to be such as to insure France against Germany by land'.[96] From within the Cabinet, as part of the pressure for an understanding with Germany parallel to that with France, and for it to be made absolutely clear to the French that no obligation to give military support existed, Loreburn had already made the point that 'If war came we could not prevent [France] from being overrun. If we are to continue the present policy we shall need to send not 150,000 men but at least half a million to be any good.'[97] Harcourt's reaction to Churchill's proposals of June 1912 – 'Alliance' – was followed immediately by his 'Our Army on the Meuse!', as if there were no distinction between the two.[98]

Conscription would not have been easy to defend against the charge of being a provocative measure. Grey put it this way: 'Conscription is imposed by the Continental countries to *defend* their own countries – it does not entail an obligation to serve abroad. We are defended by the navy; for us to impose conscription as continental nations do, would be to impose it for a purpose already provided for at great cost.'[99] McKenna agreed with Metternich in December 1908 that a big army was not needed to protect England 'and was bound, therefore, to be regarded on the Continent as a step towards aggression'.[100] In the summer of 1908, in fact, Metternich issued the following warning to Grey and Lloyd George: 'If we see Britain introducing national conscription with a view to Germany and to become worthy of an alliance with France, I do not believe that we would quietly wait for the conclusion of the development.' His point was that with such support from England revanche might really one day come to life again in France.[101] As the French made no secret of their unhappiness about the size of Britain's military establishment there was force in this. It was not diminished with the passage of time and such reports as Tyrrell received from Paris in 1912: 'They always say that we must have *conscription* if we want to make [an alliance]'; 'They are dying for us to have conscription. Why? Because they want an English, as well as a Russian army, at their back when the day of reckoning comes.'[102] The foreign political arguments against an alliance on the grounds that it would provoke or actually incite stand up rather better with the support afforded by conscription.

So far as British opinion was concerned, one Foreign Office official noted in May 1908 that conscription was so distasteful that there was 'no possible chance' of it.[103] The attitude of the principal organs of the Liberal press has already been noted. Campbell-Bannerman, according to G. Clemenceau, had 'nearly fainted' when told in 1907 that Britain should adopt some form of national military service. Haldane argued for his military reforms in terms of their being an alternative to military service: 'the more the plan succeeds, the more deeply is conscription buried in the grave'; Sir Henry Wilson believed the opposition of the former Secretary of State for War to a French alliance in May 1912 was because 'he sees it would probably mean conscription'. McKenna in December 1908 said there was 'not the least prospect' of England's having an army of a million men.[104] Though Lord Crewe told the German Chancellor in February 1909 that 'sooner or later England would come over to universal service' it was certain that no Liberal Government would be responsible for this. Out of the 105 Members of Parliament who allowed the journal of the National Service League to reveal in March 1910 their support for it only three were Liberals.[105] Lord Milner, in mid-1909, was afraid of the effect on the public if the Committee of Imperial Defence Invasion Enquiry should conclude that any substantial period of military training was necessary.[106] Lloyd George, who had hinted in German company in 1908 at the possibility of a strong army based on conscription, recognised in August 1910 that no party dare take up the matter, 'because of the violent prejudices which would be excited even if it were suspected that a Government contemplated the possibility of establishing anything of the kind'.[107] Lloyd George became a less and less secret conscriptionist as time went on. In February 1912 he denounced Haldane's army schemes as a failure and presented the Tory Die-Hards with what the editor of the *Morning Post* called 'the biggest thing going – the fulfilment of our dreams and the achievement of our efforts' by telling them: 'If we cannot get the men by a voluntary system and Haldane has proved that we cannot, why not *force* people to serve? To do this, he acknowledges that the Liberals must have the help of the Conservatives.' It would appear that a visit to him by Lord Roberts, engineered by H. A. Gwynne in autumn 1911, had strengthened his existing disposition to seek common ground with the Tories, and that he too had seen Lord Roberts' writing on the wall.[108] Even so, and although some prominent figures in the Conservative Party, including Lansdowne and F. E. Smith, were sympathetic, and Curzon Vice President of the National Service league, Balfour (twice) and his successor Bonar Law both turned down appeals from Lord Roberts to adopt conscription as a plank in the Tory platform. In February 1913 a Unionist Committee composed of Midleton, Salisbury, G. Wyndham and Sir A. Lee concluded that 'any proposal to institute Compulsory Service, if made by one political party would almost certainly lead to the defeat at the polls of the party that proposed it . . . '. The editor of *The Times*, who was engaged in supporting Lord Roberts' movement, noted the opposition to 'the idea that we want to enrol a vast citizen army for service on the Continent' and the likelihood that a display of aggressive jingoism on the part of the French, by giving colour to that notion, would alienate Great Britain altogether.[109]

These corollaries of an alliance were grist to the mill of the 'anti-alliance or commitment' side of the Cabinet whose desire for a sort of self-imposed isolation caused it to decry 'entanglements'.[110] Conscription would have meant the loss of the argument that Britain could not take part in a continental war because she had not the means to do so. And this would have appeared to bring that involvement closer, would have seemed, to some, equivalent to a declaration of intent. This would not necessarily have been the case, any more than a strictly defensive alliance would necessarily have involved Britain in a war. As its reception had indicated, however, Grey's argument in relation to the holding of military and naval Staffs talks, that being prepared provided Britain with a choice which she would not otherwise have had, had only a limited amount of mileage in it.

Basically, this was another case where the shadow was more important than the substance. What was important was that there should appear to be steps still to be taken, and a degree of doubt both at home and abroad as to what course Britain would pursue. In this way they could remain the masters of their fate. There may have been advantages in this situation from the Foreign Secretary's point of view, sometimes. Fundamentally, however, he had no choice.

The Cabinet contained men who preferred Britain to fight her own wars rather than those of other peoples not of her making, and to enter them under her own volition. It contained others who would enter a continental war only up to a point – Runciman, for instance, who drew 'a sharp distinction between action by sea and the certain destruction of British troops in Belgium or France'.[111] It contained still others who refused to contemplate British participation in a continental war under any circumstances whatever – who were prepared to look for, and who when the time came did look for, loopholes through which to escape existing treaty obligations. At the outbreak of the war neither Harcourt nor Sir J. Simon would regard the obligation to Belgium as binding on account of its age. (It was in this context that the architect of the Japanese Alliance consoled Austen Chamberlain on 1 August 1914 with the reflection that 'an entente is stronger than an alliance, because it is not defined'.[112]) Whether the country as a whole shared these views and opinions, as Grey was sometimes assured that he would find out that it did,[113] did not really matter, when they were so well represented in the Cabinet itself.

The ententes never became alliances for domestic political reasons. In the final analysis, alliances and conscription were both avoided because either would have split the Liberal Cabinet and raised the question of the future of the Liberal Party. On 31 January 1906, when Paul Cambon finally received the reply composed by Grey, Haldane and Campbell-Bannerman to his enquiry of the 10th, he noticed that the Foreign Secretary was 'évidemment préoccupé des dispositions d'une fraction importante du Cabinet et des tendances de la nouvelle majorité libérale'. He treated with the scepticism it deserved Sanderson's attempt to persuade him that bringing the matter before the Cabinet was dangerous because 'jamais un Gouvernement anglais quel qu'il soit ne s'engagera sur un hypothèse'. His own confidential information as to what passed between the Prime Minister and Foreign Secretary at Windsor was that the identity of British and French interests in the event of an attack by Germany had been recognised,

mais on est tombé d'accord sur ce point qu'une extension de nos accords devrait donner lieu à une discussion au sein du Cabinet et qu'à l'heure actuelle cette consultation aurait des inconvénients, car certains Ministres s'étonneraient de l'ouverture de pourparlers officieux entre les administrations militaires des deux pays et des études auxquelles se livrent en commun.[114]

That such a discussion 'aurait des inconvénients' was putting it mildly. How much of an understatement this was was indicated in August 1911 when, discussion of such matters having been carefully avoided in the meantime,[115] Loreburn let Grey know that if he tried to give military and naval support in what was 'a purely French quarrel', he would be unable to carry it in the present House of Commons, 'except by a majority very very largely composed of Conservatives and with a very large number of the Ministerial side against you. And this would mean that the present Government could not carry on.'[116] In May 1912 Nicolson told Austen Chamberlain, who had asked why the Government did not take up the question of an alliance with France, that 'They couldn't hold together if they tried it.' At the same time Sir Henry Wilson recorded Crowe's information that 'Grey seems to be coming to believe (the necessity for an alliance) but says such a step would break up the Cabinet.'[117] Wilson's own reaction to this prospect was: 'So best.' This reaction was not shared by Grey. In July of the same year, when Bertie observed in connection with an exchange of notes between France and Britain which he was advocating that 'the Cabinet could not afford to lose (Grey) and that if the Prime Minister was with him it would be the Dissenting Ministers who would have to drop out and they would not be a loss', Grey replied that he 'did not wish to break up the Cabinet and that it would be he that would go . . .'. In June 1913 Grey told Bertie that the Cabinet would not consent to go beyond the private letter written to the French Ambassador in November 1912: 'To do so would certainly cause some resignations'. Bertie felt it unnecessary to record Grey's response to his second attempt to get him to agree that the Cabinet 'contained so many members that some might be spared'.[118] Liberal unity became all the more important a consideration as the great parliamentary majority of 1906 disappeared in subsequent general elections. In 1912 Grey was reported by Haldane as taking 'a gloomy view of the future of the Liberal Party – if the Government goes out, there will be serious cleavages in the Party. Lloyd George will go off on Land Reform . . . Also that the differences on Foreign Affairs cut rather deep . . .'. As for conscription, C. F. G. Masterman is on record as saying that if the Liberal Government supported a scheme for compulsory service, 'the result would be to split the Liberal Party'.[119] For a Liberal Foreign Secretary in the decade before the Great War, the translation of ententes into formal alliances was not within the art of the possible.

The arguments for and against alliances were academic in more senses than one. The decision against alliances represented shutting the stable door after the free hand had bolted, however strenuously they tried to hide this from themselves. That interests determined actions was admitted, albeit after the last moment, even by Harcourt.[120] One consequence of the refusal to make formal alliances, however, was that it made it more difficult for the British to refuse other things. As Bertie put it when Clemenceau told him that the proposal for communications between British and French military and naval experts had come from Great Britain: 'if so, it was in the stead of something more definite which had been suggested by Cambon'.[121] In this connection it is ironic that the extension of the naval consultations in 1914 to include Russia deprived Bethmann-Hollweg of his main argument against a preventive war. With the 'secret intelligence' indicating the forging of the last link in the chain of German encirclement, and suggesting that Britain was on the point of joining forces with France and Russia, it was impossible to maintain any longer, against those who wished to fight the 'inevitable' war sooner rather than later, that the British Government, with which relations seemed to be improving, would be able to help in restraining the Russians in any way.[122] Thus did one set of domestic circumstances affect another, and rebound upon itself.

4

∽∽∽∽∽∽∽∽∽∽∽∽∽∽∽∽∽∽∽∽∽∽∽∽∽∽∽∽∽∽∽∽∽∽∽∽∽∽∽

The Dissimulation of the Balance of Power

At the beginning of 1907 Sir Eyre Crowe, then a Senior Clerk in the Foreign Office, provided the following description of the operation of the mechanism of the balance of power in Europe:

History shows that the danger threatening the independence of this or that nation has generally arisen, at least in part, out of the momentary predominance of a neighbouring State at once militarily powerful, economically efficient, and ambitious to extend its frontiers or spread its influence, the danger being directly proportionate to the degree of its power and efficiency, and to the spontaneity or 'inevitableness' of its ambitions. The only check on the abuse of political predominance derived from such a position has always consisted in the opposition of an equally formidable rival, or of a combination of several countries forming leagues of defence. The equilibrium established by such a grouping of forces is technically known as the balance of power, and it has become almost an historical truism to identify England's secular policy with the maintenance of this balance by throwing her weight now in this scale and now in that, but ever on the side opposed to the political dictatorship of the strongest single State or group at a given time.[1]

That Great Britain was pursuing such a policy at the time, and throughout the years 1906 to 1914, is a view that has come to be generally accepted. In this view, the beginning of this policy is commonly identified with the Anglo-French Agreement of April 1904, though Gibson Bowles was the only Member of Parliament to greet it as 'a return to the older, simpler and ... better system of the balance of power'.[2] The force of this interpretation is not diminished by the fact that officials, who enjoyed in the reformed Foreign Office a greater freedom to express their opinions, constantly and consistently employed the concept of the balance of power in their correspondence and advice. Their Chief, the Foreign Secretary himself, Sir Edward Grey, was less keen on the use of the phrase 'the balance of power'. He was anxious not to offend the sensibilities of several of his ministerial colleagues and of a large group of Liberal M.P.s, who held that a balance of power was not a suitable end for a Liberal Foreign Secretary to pursue. Nevertheless, it is clear that his foreign policy was discussed in cabinet meetings in terms of the 'equilibrium' of Europe and that it was understood by his colleagues to be a balance of power policy. Lord Loreburn, one of the Radical ministers, who was not at first an assiduous attender at cabinet meetings, was ultimately convinced that Grey's policy was a revival of 'the old Palmerstonian policy of the balance of power', and it was in all probability from Grey's own description and defence of his policy in Cabinet that this impression was derived.[3] With his representatives abroad and with the representatives in London of foreign Powers Grey could afford to be rather more forthcoming. He told Cartwright, the Ambassador to Vienna, in January 1909, that 'the balance of power in Europe was preserved by the present grouping, and I should not think of wishing to disturb it'; in June 1909, when the German Ambassador remarked that some organs of the British press were saying that friendship with Russia and France was necessary to keep Germany in check, Grey observed that 'it was a question of preventing the balance of power from being destroyed'.[4] When defending in November 1911 against attacks mainly from his own side of the House the policy he had pursued during the Agadir crisis of that summer Grey told the House of Commons:

The ideal of splendid isolation contemplated a balance of power in Europe to which we were not to be a party, and from which we were to be able to stand aside in the happy position of having no obligations and being able to take advantage of any difficulties which arose in Europe from friction between opposing Powers. That policy is not a possible one now.[5]

A year later, after the outcome of the first Balkan War had produced from the German Government striking declarations of future support for Austria-Hungary, Haldane was sent to tell the German Ambassador that 'the theory of the balance of power forms an axiom of English foreign policy and has led to the English leaning towards France and Russia'.[6] There can be no doubt that, on the eve of the outbreak of war in 1914, Crowe was correct in saying that the balance of power was 'the general principle on which our whole foreign policy has hitherto been declared to rest'.[7]

That, between 1906 and 1914, Great Britain leant, as it were, towards one of the two groups of Powers in Europe – towards France and Russia rather than towards the Triple Alliance of Germany, Austria-Hungary and Italy – is not in dispute here. What is in dispute is whether this British leaning towards France and Russia can really be accounted for, as many people both at the time and subsequently have accounted for it, in terms of considerations to do with the balance of power in Europe. Were British motives really as high-minded as they were high-sounding? Were they really concerned to preserve the liberties and independence of the States of Europe? Did those responsible for the policy of associating with France and Russia really consider Britain to be a party to the balance of power in Europe? Did they really believe that Britain was a factor in that balance, that she was making such a contribution to it as to entitle them to claim that it was she who was responsible for deterring Imperial Germany from embarking upon a bid of Napoleonic proportions to secure the hegemony of the continent?

The balance of power, again according to Crowe, consisted of 'a balance of force, actual or latent'.[8] If Great Britain was to take a hand in the European game, if she was to intervene to prevent the continent from being dominated by a single Power or by a certain group of Powers, if she was to interfere with the plans so frequently ascribed to Germany, how was this to be done? What force, what might, did she have, that could be thrown into the scales? What was it that was considered to constitute the British deterrent?

In 1907 a critic of the draft of the official General Staff memorandum on the ability of the British Army to support France or Belgium against German attack complained that it had failed clearly to point out 'that our army is not big enough for the job'. Captain Ommanney added that the most important work of the General Staff in the next generation would be 'resolutely and continuously to demand that the strength of the army be fixed according to the task in front of it. This will undoubtedly require an increase in its size, and an alteration in the method by which it is raised.'[9] Though the General Staff did not fail to raise these matters, neither of Ommanney's requirements was to be met. In March 1909 the Director of Military Operations, General Ewart, composed a memorandum on 'The Value to a Foreign Power of an Alliance with the British Empire'. This revealed that that value was much more 'latent' than 'actual'. Ewart wrote:

the British Empire has over a million men under arms, and if they could all be utilised for a common purpose we should indeed be a considerable military power. Limitations, however, imposed by the composition of these forces, by their varying conditions of service, and by their want of organisation, neutralise the value of the greater portion of this large army. When we come to analyse its composition we find that, in any sudden emergency, at the present moment, we could not hope, at the utmost, to mobilise and put into the field at short notice for service in Europe a larger force than one Cavalry division and six divisions of all arms, with a total strength of 170,000 men.

The Territorial Force is only organised for home defence; in existing circumstances it would be impossible to withdraw British troops from India; our naval stations must be held; proposals to employ our Native troops would in all probability provoke heated controversy; whilst the governments of our self-governing Dominions show as yet no disposition to guarantee the provision of contingents for Imperial service. Above and beyond all this an Imperial General Staff capable of organising and directing our vast undeveloped strength has only just been initiated.

Ewart gallantly saw 'no reason for discouragement' at the distance still to be travelled before more than a seventh of the Empire's peace establishment could be made available for common action. Many conditions, however, had to be met: 'If in the future we can all hold together; if the General Staff can work out some acceptable scheme of mutual assistance; and if our Navy can maintain our ability to cooperate; then, indeed, will our alliance be coveted by all.' As it was, the value of Great Britain as an ally in Europe, defined as he defined it – as depending on 'the strength and efficiency of the troops which we can make available for expeditionary action' – was highly problematical. When he wrote that he was satisfied that the establishment contemplated for the Expeditionary Force was the minimum compatible with a continuance of what he believed to be the policy of the British Government in Europe, namely the maintenance of the balance of power, he was making the best of a very bad job. This is clear from the Diary he kept, in which he deplored the size of the Expeditionary Force and held that if the entente with France and Russia was to last Britain must put her military house in order, perfect her mobilisation arrangements and increase her offensive striking power. A draft of his memorandum of March 1909 was forwarded to the Foreign Secretary.[10]

Ewart's successor as D.M.O., Sir Henry Wilson, had essentially the same difficulties to surmount over two years later when endeavouring to persuade a meeting of certain members of the Committee of Imperial Defence on 23 August 1911 that the whole of the British Expeditionary Force should be sent to France immediately upon the outbreak of hostilities between France and Germany. In a memorandum prepared for the meeting he admitted that England 'can only assist France to a very limited extent in promptly resisting a German invasion'. Nevertheless, the numbers of the opposing forces might be rendered so nearly equal, he contended, during the opening and early actions of a war that it was 'quite possible for the allies to win some initial successes which might prove invaluable'.[11] This was pitched rather higher at the meeting itself, at which Grey was present. 'It was quite likely', said the D.M.O., 'that our six divisions might prove to be the decisive factor.' This conclusion was based on his calculation of the number of through roads between Verdun and Maubeuge and the extent of front upon which a division could fight, which yielded 40 German divisions against an estimated 37/39 French divisions.[12] Initial successes were all the more vital in view of Wilson's belief that it will tax our resources to the utmost to put and keep 6 Divisions in the field during the first six or eight weeks. After that we might be able to add some troops from India and some improvised formations from home or the Dominions, but there would not be any marked addition to our forces in France for three or four months at the earliest and even then it would not be a very serious increase.[13]

Even though, the previous December, the journalist Valentine Chirol had found the War Minister, Haldane, 'altogether lucid and convincing' in arguing that the forces of the Triple Entente and the Dual Alliance were so equally balanced that three British Army Corps would just turn the balance in favour of France,[14] it was stretching Britain's military capability to the limit to imagine that the number of divisions she would send met the General Staff's own criterion of 'decisive force at the decisive place at the decisive time'. Such a belief posited a tremendous faith in the fortunes of war. This, moreover, was not the whole story. Wilson, who was an advocate of conscription for its own sake, nevertheless privately believed that six divisions were in all probability 'fifty too few' to take to a continental war.[15] The calculations involved in reducing the disparity between 84 German and 66 French divisions to proportions that would make the British contingent decisive included the counting of the four Belgian divisions as the equivalent of four French or German divisions, and the assumptions that Austria would be half-hearted and that Russia could immobilise the whole of the Austrian Army plus 27 divisions of the German Army. Wilson also allocated ten German divisions to the guarding of their coasts.

The picture is still not complete. It was only following a memorandum of January 1911 to the C.I.G.S. in which he pointed out 'the danger which existed owing to the entire absence up to date of those elemental measures necessary for the methodical mobilisation, entrainment and embarkation of the Expeditionary Force' that Wilson secured the permission of the Secretaries of State for War and for Foreign Affairs to consult the railway companies. It was only on 8 May 1911 that Wilson handed to the D.N.I., Admiral Bethell, a complete set of tables showing the shipping requirements of the Expeditionary Force. It was only on 20 July 1911 that Wilson met the French General Staff for the first time in order to confirm the main principles of coordination before working them out in detail. Not until September 1911 was he told 'where the French General Staff want us to go and what their plans are'.[16] (According to Haldane, General French had been instructed that he was 'on no account' to see the French military plans, even if the French wanted to take him into their confidence during his visit to their manoeuvres in 1910.)[17]

Moreover, the Committee of Imperial Defence meeting of 23 August 1911 had revealed that the Admiralty had deliberately ignored both the possibility that they might be called upon to transport the Expeditionary Force across the Channel, and their explicit instructions to arrange to do so. An uninitialled note on one file records that because the tables Wilson gave to Bethell 'were not sent *officially* the Admiralty denied any knowledge of having seen them when the crisis of August 1911 arose – '. McKenna, who on 3 December 1908 had given a guarantee on the Admiralty's behalf that British troops could be safely transported to either French or Belgian ports, claimed in August 1911 to be hearing of this scheme for the first time, and not to have realised that the dispatch of the Army was to take place simultaneously with the mobilisation of the Fleet, which he now maintained was not possible.[18] This 'terminological inexactitude', together with his dereliction of a duty he had found it distasteful to fulfil, secured McKenna the Home Office in October 1911.

Well might Sir Henry Wilson write at the end of December 1911:

When the crisis came on us in last July–September it found us unprepared for war.
Whether we consider war from the point of view of an Expeditionary Force on the Continent of Europe, or anywhere over the seas, or whether from the point of view of the Territorial Force and Home Defence, *we are still unprepared.*[19]

It took the Balkan War scare of November 1912 to bring to a head the General Staff's 'long outstanding difficulties' in respect of the general question of the provision of ships for the transportation of the Expeditionary Force. On hearing from Sir J. Cowans, the Quartermaster-General, that the Admiralty were saying they could not ship the Army in time, Wilson called this 'disgraceful' and issued an ultimatum: 'either the Admiralty must ship us or we must make the arrangements ourselves'. Though an Admiralty scheme was 'vetted' at a meeting on 1 December 1912, almost a year later the Admiralty had still not finalised the arrangements to be adopted for the admission of British transports to French ports – something the General Staff had by then been 'shouting for for a long time'; and that the Admiralty War Staff should be 'getting well forward with the question of taking up transport on mobilisation' was still 'one of the chief anxieties of the D.M.O.'.[20] It was thus by no means a straightforward business even to arrange for the nut to be presented to the sledgehammer.

Not even Sir Henry Wilson's skill with figures could conceal what in fact he readily admitted, that the Army in its present size and configuration could only constitute 'moral support' for the French, however important moral support might be.[21] If Grey, like Chirol, had been submitted, as is most probable, to Haldane's expositions of the worth of the B.E.F., and even found them 'lucid and convincing', then he had also been in a position to inform himself of the slow progress of the essential preliminaries. Grey himself had written in January 1906: 'I am told that 80,000 men with good guns is all we can put into the field in Europe to meet first class troops; that won't save France unless she can save herself.'[22] One wonders if the increase of 70,000 supplied by Haldane was really enough, especially as Asquith personally made it quite clear that he would allow no more than four divisions to leave Britain's shores, to cause Grey to revise this first estimate of the British Army as the prospect of conjunction with the Belgian Army caused Churchill to revise his earlier and rather sounder estimate of 1908 in 1911.[23] Certainly there is no evidence that he did.

As for the British Navy, it was widely held in both British and foreign diplomatic and political circles in the summer of 1905, during the crisis over Morocco involving France and Germany, to be incapable of restoring the equilibrium between the land forces of those two countries. On 6 June the French Cabinet looked askance at what T. Delcassé maintained was the wish of the English to make common cause with France 'pour détruire la marine et ruiner le commerce allemands': as the French Prime Minister put it: 'Nos flottes réunies auraient raison de la flotte allemande, et les ports de commerce allemands seraient à coup sûr détruits, mais pendant ce temps, le territoire français serait envahi, et la lutte sur terre, contre l'Allemagne, serait très inégale à notre détriment sinon désastreuse.' Sir F. Lascelles blithely told F. von Holstein that he 'did not understand how an offensive and defensive alliance with us could be of much advantage to France': 'We should no doubt be able to pick up some German ships and do enormous harm to her commerce but we could not come to France's assistance on land . . .'.[24] The sentiments expressed subsequently by even the Navy's most ardent champions would have provided cold comfort to the French. The opinion given by Admiral Sir A.K. Wilson, C-in-C Channel Fleet, in his 'Remarks on War Plans' of May 1907, that 'the stoppage of German trade or the capture of their ships would have little or no effect on the result (of a war between Germany and France and England combined) and if France was defeated, compensation for any injury that we had done would be extorted from our allies as one of the conditions of peace', was actually endorsed by the First Sea Lord, Sir J. Fisher, than whom there was no greater navalist, unless it were Esher, in December 1908.[25] Sir Charles Ottley, a former Director of Naval Intelligence, wrote in December 1908 that since 1905 the Admiralty had held that '(in a protracted war) the mills of our sea-power (though they would grind the German industrial population slowly perhaps) would grind them "exceedingly small" – grass would sooner or later grow in the streets of Hamburg and widespread dearth and ruin would be inflicted'.[26] The inhabitants of Hamburg would well before then have taken up residence in Paris. Lord Esher stoutly maintained that 'the French would not be likely to deny that fear of British naval supremacy restrained and still restrains Germany from precipitating a war with France; and that naval pressure upon German trade, German commerce, and the German food supply, would be certain to influence the result of prolonged military conflict ashore'. He went on, in the course of a memorandum prepared for the consideration of a C.I.D. sub-committee on the Military Needs of the Empire, to suggest

that the pressure which can be brought to bear upon Germany by the threat . . . of seizing her mercantile fleet . . . , by the deadly injury to her commerce, and the fear of raids, as well as by the freedom of action and moral support afforded to France, might be held to be a sufficient fulfilment of our share in the partnership between us and the French nation. In that case the British Navy might be counted as equivalent to the French Army, and if the dominating factor in preserving peace between France and Germany has been and is, not the strength of the French armies but fear of the British fleet, the Government and the country might hold that this represents to France the value of the *entente* in peace, whilst the fact that France would fight free from all apprehension of coastal attack, with certain use of a sea base, if required, and with complete conviction that whatever the fate of battles ashore, time and patience, even under unlikely crushing defeat, would mean – thanks to sea command – ultimate victory, is the value of the *entente* to France in war.[27]

The General Staff made short work of this in their replies, delivered the following March. They pointed out that the improvement in land communications and the enormous growth of modern European armies had greatly lessened the advantages once conferred by sea power. In their view, Germany was no more likely to withdraw any portion of her Army from the decisive point on land to cope with raids than she had done in 1870 when, as Esher himself had admitted, French preponderance at sea had had no influence whatever on the fate of her Armies. They concluded that 'it is a mistake to suppose that command of the sea must necessarily influence the immediate issue of a great land struggle. The battle of Trafalgar did not prevent Napoleon from winning the battles of Austerlitz and Jena and crushing Prussia and Austria.' Moreover, in their opinion, as in that of Fisher and Sir A. K. Wilson:

If Germany is able in the future rapidly to secure a decisive victory by land, she will be in a position to impose an indemnity calculated to compensate her at the expense of France for any losses which we may have inflicted on her maritime and commercial interests. In fact, the greater the industrial stake which she has at sea in a struggle with the United Kingdom the more she will exact in reprisal from those who have the misfortune to be unsuccessful as our allies on land.[28]

Despite the impressive tables of statistics of Admiral Slade, the D.N.I., regarding the economic effect of war on German trade, credit, inflation and unemployment, the sub-committee as a whole preferred the arguments of the General Staff to the effect that reliance upon the Navy would actually do more harm than good! Having considered three methods by which armed assistance could be given by Britain to France if she were attacked by Germany, these being a) by means of the Navy alone, b) by means of the Navy and a mounted force of 12,000 men and c) by means of the Navy and the Expeditionary Force of four divisions and a cavalry division, they concluded in their Report:

From the evidence that we have had, we are of the opinion that a serious situation would be created in Germany owing to the blockade of her ports, and that the longer the duration of the war the more serious the situation would become. *We do not, however, consider that such pressure as could be exerted by means of naval force alone would be felt sufficiently soon to save France in the event of that country being attacked in overwhelming force.* We therefore recognise the possibility that Great Brtain's success at sea might only cause greater pressure to be brought to bear on France on land, and the latter country might have to make terms with Germany which would not be less stringent owing to the losses suffered by her opponent at sea.[29]

The ministers who sat on this committee and signed its Report were the Prime Minister, Asquith (Chairman), Lord Crewe, Haldane and McKenna; Sir Charles Hardinge, the Permanent Under Secretary, represented the Foreign Office.

This verdict on the relative weight of the Navy as against that of an Army for whose transportation facilities did not at the time exist, which at the time was ignorant of the plan of campaign of the country to whose rescue it therefore could go only with difficulty, and which at any time would be able only on the most optimistic construction to make even a putative contribution to the outcome of the struggle, was repeated in August 1911. It only remained for Admiral G. A. Ballard, under whose chairmanship the Admiralty War Plans had been drawn up in 1906–7, to point out in October 1911 that this work had been done by a 'very small committee of officers chiefly serving outside the Admiralty altogether, none of whom had received anything approaching to a sufficient training in the subject'; that their work had then been opened to criticism from some of the officers whose duty it would have been to carry out the plans in war, 'but whose alternative suggestions were based upon no better opportunities for studying the subject, and lacked any appearance of a better understanding of the situation' – something that was perfectly obvious from Admiral Wilson's schemes for 'make-believe floating armies' – the end result being a state of 'indecision and chaos that would have been disastrous in war'.[30]

As instruments with which to deter a bid on the part of another Power for the hegemony of Europe, both the British Army and the British Navy left much to be desired. What is striking is that ministers and high officials who knew the true state of Britain's preparedness and capability to fight in a continental war continued to insist that Britain was still successfully pursuing a balance of power policy. Hardinge, for instance, had expressed in February 1906 the opinion that 'If it is understood by Germany that England is absolutely "solidaire" with France, such knowledge would almost certainly deter Germany from provoking a conflict by which Germany must lose her entire mercantile marine and almost her whole foreign trade.'[31] In May 1909 he was still holding such views as that Britain was 'the only Power that in the end would be able to support France and Russia in an independent position and to enforce peace', provided she maintained her absolute supremacy at sea and was consequently 'able to destroy in time of war German sea-borne trade',[32] despite the General Staff's demolition of them in March 1909 in the course of the proceedings of the C.I.D. sub-committee of which Hardinge was himself a member. His successor Sir Arthur Nicolson, who rapidly became a confidant of Sir Henry Wilson, wrote in January 1911:

I do not think that people quite recognise that, if we are to assist in preserving the balance of power in Europe and consequently the peace and the status quo, it is necessary for us to acknowledge our responsibilities, and to be prepared to afford our friends or allies, in case of necessity, some assistance of a more material and efficient kind than we are at present in a position to offer them.[33]

In May 1911, a month in which Nicolson expressed doubts as to 'whether a concerted plan of action will ever be settled', he was nevertheless maintaining that it was Britain's policy to preserve the equilibrium in Europe and that this policy must not be reversed.[34] In April 1912, after numerous conversations with Sir Henry Wilson over the previous months, he was still maintaining that 'in fact, England is really a factor of great weight either for or against peace'.[35] Goschen, the Ambassador to Berlin, forwarded in March 1910 a report on the dependence of Germany on overseas traffic for supplies in time of war compiled by his Counsellor of Embassy and by the Military and Naval Attachés, the first paragraph of which read: 'We can find no evidence that the cessation of import and export by German ports would in any reasonable probability result in a shortage of the necessary articles of food for the population of Germany.' Yet in October of that year he maintained that the only thing which had prevented the Germans securing the hegemony of Europe was England's naval strength.[36] These officials would appear to have been engaged in transforming an axiom into a shibboleth or even a fetish. Indeed Goschen wrote to Grey in March 1911 that he had told the Kaiser that 'the balance of power was a fetish worshipped by the British nation and a principle which in the past it had made great sacrifices to uphold and for which it had always fought'.[37] 'The theory of the balance of power', which they complained did not appeal to the German mind, had an irresistible appeal for them.[38] The power of the theory of the balance goes far to explain what otherwise would seem at the very least remiss: that no one in the British Foreign Office should have thought the Germans perfectly capable of coming to the same conclusions regarding the effectiveness of the British Navy as those to which the C.I.D. came in 1909 and 1911 (and to which, in fact, the Germans did come);[39] and that they should not have added these to their chronic reservations about British military strength, which they well knew were shared by the French, whom they equally well knew had serious reservations about the ability of the British Navy to save them from the German Army.[40]

Even the Radical ministers discerned the discrepancy between the proclaimed and professed ends of British foreign policy and the means of meeting them that were at her disposal. Morley, who frequently took charge of the Foreign Office during Grey's fishing expeditions, and who had the same facility as a chameleon for assuming the colouring of the background against which he operated, on one of these occasions quickly gained the impression that 'Friends and foes are beginning to ask themselves whether we are of much account in either capacity.' Loreburn clearly had his doubts. He maintained that: 'If war came we could not prevent (France) from being overrun. If we are to continue the present policy we shall need to send not 150,000 men but at least half a million to be any good.'[41] His recognition that only conscription, however much he opposed it, would remedy the situation, was a comment not only upon the British Army but also upon the Navy.

What the Radical ministers did not discern was that what they took from Grey and Haldane in particular to be the ends of British policy might only be ostensible ends. Though they called 'absurd' what they gathered to be the premises on which Grey's foreign policy was based, it did not occur to them that the premises might be false in more senses than one. Such was the gap between means and ends, however, that it does bring these ends themselves into question. There is, moreover, a body of evidence that cannot satisfactorily be absorbed by or accommodated in the view that Britain, during the years when Sir Edward Grey was responsible for her foreign policy, was pursuing a policy designed to maintain the balance of power in Europe. It is my contention here that Grey, those of his colleagues who shared his knowledge and certain members of the Foreign Office Staff were dissimulating: that they wished merely to give the impression that Britain was pursuing a balance of power policy, for which they knew she had not the means, but which, in several cases, they also had no intention that *she* should pursue; that the reasoning behind Britain's association with France and Russia – behind the policy of the Entente – had little to do, fundamentally, with the much-vaunted preservation of the liberties and independence of the States of Europe. If this interpretation is correct, then the least one can say is that Grey, who knew of the shortcomings of the British Army, who was familiar with the unmistakable verdicts as to the inappropriateness of a British naval contribution to a great European war passed by the C.I.D. in the sub-committee of 1908–9 and at the meeting of 23 August 1911, and who despite this knowledge and familiarity continued to 'harp', as the Kaiser put it,[42] on the balance of power, did not trouble to undeceive the largest group of his colleagues and a high proportion of his advisers and representatives. Why Loreburn, and other ministerial colleagues, should not have been undeceived will be clear when the real objectives of British foreign policy, and the attitude of Loreburn in particular to these objectives, are known and can be compared.

In 1901 the First Lord of the Admiralty, Lord Selborne, had pointed out that within the last five years three new Navies had sprung into existence – those of the United States, Germany and Japan. Stressing that if the U.S.A. were to build such a Navy as she could well afford, 'even the Two-Power Standard would be beyond our strength', he had suggested that the Standard be henceforth understood as a margin of strength over the Navies of France and Russia. These Powers were selected as the two against which to regulate the British Standard on the grounds that 'a naval war with France, or with France and Russia is less improbable than any other naval war which we can foresee . . .'. A *margin* of strength was necessary for two reasons: first because the Admiralty considered that simple equality of numbers could not provide the necessary 'reasonable certainty of victory'; and secondly because 'with no margin, we should be susceptible to the least hostile hint or pressure from any one of the new naval Powers at a time of war or strained relations with France and Russia'. This assessment of the naval situation, and Selborne's prediction that the result of Germany's 'definite and persistent' naval policy 'will be to place (her) in a commanding position if ever we find ourselves at war with France and Russia', were made even *before* he established, by having enquiries made of Lascelles, that the German Navy *was* being built directly against Great Britain.[43] But though all Selborne's memoranda for the Cabinet subsequent to receiving Lascelles' information contained a substantial quotation from the statement attached to the German Navy Bill of 1900, it would be rash to conclude that the prospect of a German Fleet became the sole, or even the main, determinant of British foreign policy. So far as Selborne was concerned, the prospect of a German Fleet merely strengthened his conviction that the recommended margin be adhered to.[44] So far as naval considerations were involved in the making of the Agreement with France they were considerations to do with 'the growth of the navies of the world generally' and with Britain's inability to maintain command of the sea even against all the European navies, rather than considerations to do with the development of the German Navy in particular.[45] A German Fleet to be stationed in the North Sea did alarm, disturb and annoy the British. But it did not cause them, immediately upon their perception of the potential threat, to alter their policy with a view to depriving Germany of an opportunity to intervene against them in a war between Britain and France and Russia. This contingency was taken care of by the margin of strength over and above the Two-Power Standard.

Even before the threat of the German Fleet was perceived by the Admiralty, the Cabinet had authorised Lord Lansdowne to close, if he possibly could, with the French.[46] There were good reasons, quite apart from the position of European affairs at the time, and quite apart from the existence of the infant German Navy which in 1903 consisted of a mere 12 battleships compared with a British total of 34, as to why a settlement with France was desirable. One was simply that it was ridiculous, as Arnold-Foster noted, to be on bad terms, if this could be avoided, with 'a great Nation, our points of contact and difficulty throughout the world being what they are'.[47] The most powerful reason, however, was that France was the ally of Russia and might, if on good terms with Britain, be disposed to help bring about the primary goal of British foreign policy since the late 1890s: an agreement with Russia. Throughout the nine months of the negotiation of the Anglo-French Agreement, it was Russia that was regarded as constituting the main threat to Britain's interests. In January 1904 Balfour was still insisting that 'we must see Russia as a) the ally of France b) the invader of India c) the dominating influence in Persia d) the possible disturber of European peace'.[48] The incentive offered by Delcassé for the British to enter into more cordial relations with the French was that, if some arrangement of the kind could be effected, he would exercise a restraining influence upon Russia, if not in fact intimate to her that, under certain conditions, she could not rely upon French support if she picked a quarrel with Britain. Upon this incentive Lord George Hamilton commented, in a letter to Curzon: 'I do not see how we shall be able to effect any arrangement which will be so far reaching in its effect, but that is the tendency of the negotiations, and the expectation, though possibly too sanguine, of those who are behind the scenes.'[49] It was certainly the expectation of Lord Lansdowne himself who, elaborating in September 1903 for the benefit of the Cabinet upon the ample recompense there would be for any sacrifice of moderate dimensions to the French, went on immediately: 'A good understanding with France would not improbably be the precursor of a better understanding with Russia.'[50] As Balfour made clear in the House of Commons on 1 March 1904, the Anglo-French Agreement certainly took place against a background of a changing world balance of naval power, as had the Anglo-Japanese Alliance, and cannot be dis-associated from this. It had, however, little if anything to do with the balance of power in Europe.

That it was made for purely selfish reasons, and had less to do with the balance of power in Europe than has sometimes been supposed, is all the more clear when it is realised that the Conservative Government respon-sible for it did not discern, at the time when it was made, any threat to the balance of power in Europe, and did not equate the new German naval programmes with a bid on Germany's part to secure the hegemony of Europe. Indeed Selborne was reiterating in February 1904 what he had first stated in October 1902, namely that

The more the composition of the German fleet is examined the clearer it becomes that it is designed for a possible conflict with the British fleet. It cannot be designed for the purpose of playing a leading part in a future war between Germany and France and Russia. The issue of such a war can only be decided by armies and on land, and the great naval expenditure on which Germany has embarked involves a deliberate diminution of the military strength which Germany might otherwise have attained in relation to France and Russia.[51]

Just over a month before the conclusion of the Anglo-French Agreement Sir Edward Grey had appreciated the prospect that good relations with France would open of reducing the Two-Power Standard, and had expressed the hope that, if the friendly relations with France lasted into a less troubled period, 'no opportunity would be lost of turning that friendly spirit to practical advantage by some mutual agreement with regard to stopping the increase in the Fleets'.[52] The Anglo-French Agree-ment, which he inherited when he became Foreign Secretary, was welcome from the point of view of the elimination of a naval rival. In maintaining the Agreement, he stressed this aspect to a much greater extent than his predecessor had done. Twice in 1911, at the Committee of Imperial Defence in May and in conversation with C. P. Scott in July, he said that if Britain was isolated she would be compelled, in order to keep command of the sea, to build against five or even six Powers.[53] Twice in 1912, on both occasions at the C.I.D., he spoke of how 'the growth of the navies of the world generally' had affected British foreign policy. For

if you take the total of the great European navies as they are, or will soon be, you would not be able to hold the command of the sea against them all. This has made the task of foreign policy more difficult in this respect, that it is essential that our foreign policy should be such as to make it quite certain that there are, at any rate, some nations in Europe with whom it becomes inconceivable that we should find ourselves at war.[54]

In March 1914 the House of Commons was told to expect 'that the Government of the day will preserve relations, and will continue to preserve relations, with the other Powers of Europe which will make it perfectly clear that we are not drifting into the position of having a possible combination of Powers which is greater than our own naval strength'.[55] Grey was, no doubt, encouraged to pursue this line by the advice of the Liberal First Lord of the Admiralty, Lord Tweedmouth, who told Campbell-Bannerman in November 1906 that 'good diplomacy must be trusted to secure that all the greater naval Powers should not at once be ranged against us, for we could not of course be prepared to meet such a combination'.[56]

The point here, however, is that Grey was activated by the same essentially selfish reasons as had inspired Lord Lansdowne. In Haldane's recollection, Grey had consistently maintained that Britain must stick to the entente because the real reason for it was that it was the only way of retaining command of the sea.[57] Certainly the more friends, and the more naval 'allies', Britain had, the better the position she would be in *vis-à-vis* Germany. Certainly, as a result of sticking to the entente, the navies of France and Russia were 'neutralised', and Germany deprived of any chance to increase her naval power by making naval alliances. None of this had anything to do with the balance of power in Europe. Germany did not require naval allies in order to make a bid for the hegemony of *Europe*. If Germany did acquire a naval ally, it would increase her chances of success only in a war against *Great Britain*.

In Grey's time as Foreign Secretary, certain individuals at the Foreign Office commented upon the development of German naval power in such a way as to convert what was intended as a lever for colonies at Britain's expense into an instrument designed to secure the hegemony of Europe by deterring Britain from intervening in the affairs of the continent. In paying Britain this large, and largely undeserved, compliment, they also converted the British Navy into something it had never been – a device intended to deter any one Power from bidding to dominate Europe. As recently as 1 March 1904 Balfour had stressed the fact that 'our Navy is substantially and essentially a defensive force'.[58] Before him, Lord Salisbury had pointed out to Queen Victoria that 'in all places at a distance from the sea, our diplomatists can only exhort, they cannot threaten'; in 1887 he had confided to Sir E. Malet, his Ambassador to Berlin: 'it is puzzling to me why Bismarck ever thinks us worth conciliating. None of the battles he may have to fight will be fought within striking distance of the sea – and it is only on the sea that we can be of any use at all.'[59]

The temptation to which some of his advisers yielded was one to which Grey also yielded, on occasion – as when he countered arguments that there would have been no German Navy had it not been for the ententes with the point that Britain's Agreements with France and Russia followed the German decision to build a battle fleet.[60] Nevertheless, this was not a case of *post hoc propter hoc*, and the bulk of his comments indicates that he knew it was not. For him as much as if not more than for Lansdowne, given that the Liberal Party was more inclined to economies on principle than were the Conservatives, the elimination of naval rivals was required by 'the growth of the navies of the world generally' and not just by that of Germany. In the minds of both of them, the elimination of naval rivals and the positive response to the dispositions of France and then Russia to come to friendly terms with Great Britain, one result of which was that Germany was deprived of situations of which she could take advantage, and another result of which was the prospect of a reduction in British naval building from the scale it would otherwise have had to reach, served British interests. They were not moves designed to serve the principle of the European balance of power.

Lansdowne did not have time to add an agreement with Russia to his Agreement with France, though towards the end of 1905 he was looking forward to a resumption of the negotiations.[61] It fell to Grey to take advantage of the 'stepping-stone' provided by the previous Government. Like Lansdowne, Grey regarded an Anglo-Russian agreement as the primary goal of British foreign policy. He had consistently advocated such an agreement since before the turn of the century; he had been apprehensive lest both the original Anglo-Japanese Alliance and its successor interfere with the achievement of what was for him the overriding objective.[62] He had made no secret, in the speeches he delivered before and during the general election which returned the Liberals to power, of the importance he attached to it and of the place that it would be accorded in any foreign policy for which he might be made responsible. The sentiment he expressed in a speech on 20 October 1905, for instance, concerning the necessity of supporting France at the forthcoming Conference at Algeciras, on the grounds that one did not make new friends by failing existing ones, was clearly a reference to this intention. The sentiment surfaced again at a crucial point during the Algeciras Conference. Envisaging a breakdown of the proceedings and a Franco-German war, Grey wrote that it would be very difficult for Britain to keep out of it: 'There would ... be a general feeling ... that we had behaved meanly and left France in the lurch ... Russia would not think it worth while to make a friendly arrangement with us about Asia.'[63] This sentiment also lay behind the authorisation of conversations between the British and French General Staffs in January 1906. Just as Lansdowne, in May 1905, had affirmed his readiness to join with France in resisting any pressure that the Germans might put upon her to grant them a port on the Moroccan coast, and in terms that left on the French Ambassador the ineradicable impression that an offer of an offensive and defensive alliance had been made, so Grey could not desert the French in his first days in office. It was a matter of keeping the 'stepping-stone' in being.[64]

It may seem that the involvement of Britain in a Franco-German war was a high price to pay for a chance to make an agreement with Russia, given the state she was in at this time, following her defeat by Japan and the outbreak of revolution. It may seem that, given the destruction of the Russian Navy, and the extension in 1905 of the Anglo-Japanese Alliance to cover India, the British had less reason for seeking an agreement with Russia in order to safeguard the approaches to India than they had had for many years past. It may seem, therefore, that the decision to seek an agreement with Russia can only be accounted for in terms of the balance of power in Europe. This impression would, in my opinion, be false; like the Agreement with France, that with Russia was made not for the sake of the balance of power in Europe but for the sake of Britain's own Imperial interests.

A number of things have to be borne in mind. It was presumed that Russia would re-establish herself as a naval Power. The renewed and extended Anglo-Japanese Alliance, itself partly inspired by assumptions concerning Russia's recovery, was not considered sufficient in itself to avert the consequences of this.[65] The Liberal Government was quickly made aware of the reluctance of the General Staff and of the Government of India to see Japanese troops operating on the North-West Frontier, for fear the Indians would cease to tolerate British rule if it was revealed to depend upon her oriental ally. Haldane was anxious to make economies in the Army, starting with India. Despite her internal difficulties, Russia was still capable of maintaining an Army of 250,000 men 3000 miles from Russia proper; Lord Minto, the new Viceroy, reported in alarm the arrival of Russian troop boats on the Oxus.[66] In recent years the Russians had so extended their system of railways as to bring them within striking distance of Kandahar and Kabul. There was no indication that this process would not be resumed.

Even in the first half of 1906 the British could not relax over Central Asia. It was to be expected that Russia would recover her full strength before long. The problem facing Grey and Morley in particular was how to make permanent the situation relatively more favourable to Britain[67] that had been created by the outcome of the Russo-Japanese war and its aftermath. An agreement with Russia was their solution to the problem. They were encouraged to adhere to this solution by the Report of a sub-committee of the C.I.D. set up in January 1907 to consider the Military

Requirements of the Empire as affected by the defence of India. This was chaired by Morley and included Grey, Asquith and Haldane. In May 1907 it reported tellingly in favour of 'the school who look to diplomacy rather than to arms, and hold that the foundation of our rule in India would be more securely strengthened by peace with Russia than by any success in war with Russia'. 'In default of an understanding with Russia', the process of 'insidious advance and slow absorption' on Russia's part would have to be reckoned with. Among the points made were these: that a rumour of a Russian seizure of Herat would cause a great stir amongst 'the Natives of India'; that the permanent occupation of Kabul would make it necessary for Britain 'to keep up a British force in India far exceeding the number of our present European garrison, and perhaps exceeding our capacity'; that to retain a great force of Native soldiers far from their homes for year after year, waiting on Russia's processes, would be asking more of the Indians than they had shown they were prepared to provide. Morley wrote to the Viceroy in September 1907, saying that the vital point of the Report was the conclusion that the dispatch of 100,000 men to India in the first year of a war was a military necessity: 'That is the fundamental argument for the Convention for we have not got the men to spare and that's the plain truth of it.'[68]

They received further encouragement at the end of May 1907 when the Japanese made it clear that they were as reluctant to serve in India as the Indian authorities were to see them there, and that they would confine themselves to creating a diversion on the Manchurian frontier; and from a study by the War Office of the military resources of the Russian Empire, completed in mid-1907, which stated that the number of men the Russians could pour into Central Asia was 'practically unlimited'; at the turn of 1906, moreover, the General Staff and C.I.D. had maintained that Britain was too weak to contemplate the active military coercion even of the Sultan of Turkey.[69]

In an extensive minute dealing with some objections to his Russian policy from the Military Attaché in Persia Grey made explicit what his real priorities were:

The policy of the agreement is to begin an understanding with Russia, which may gradually lead to good relations in European Questions also and remove from her policy designs upon the Indian frontier either as an end in themselves or as a means of bringing pressure to bear upon us to overcome our opposition to her elsewhere. *If this policy succeeds India will be relieved from apprehension and strain.* If it fails we shall at any rate have secured temporarily that Russia does not get a hold of the parts of Persia, which are dangerous to us and all we shall have lost will have been the chance of preventing Russia from strengthening her hold on northern Persia: a chance which I do not believe exists except in theory . . .

Hardinge added that the dangers foreshadowed by Colonel Douglas of an advance towards India through Persia 'already exist'. An agreement with Russia was 'the only hope of staving them off effectually'. To oppose the Russian advance by adopting forward policies such as pushing British influence, telegraphs and railways into Seistan and southern Persia, lending money to the Persian Government so as to bring it more and more under British control, and making every diplomatic effort at Tehran to oppose Russian influence in northern Persia, Grey argued, might actually make matters worse: 'To drop the Agreement and to adopt the forward policy would entail a certain and as I think it an intolerable increase of the military responsibilities of India and the Empire, and would provoke Russia to make it her object more than ever to worry us in Asia . . .'[70]

The removal of dangers that already existed; the relief of India from apprehension and strain; the avoidance by England of the commitment of becoming a continental state in Central Asia with a common frontier with the Russian Empire, and of the constant drain on her resources which the forward policies which she would otherwise have had to pursue merely in order to stand still in that region would have constituted: these were the reasons for the making and the keeping of the Agreement with Russia. It was India that Grey had it in mind to defend on the Sambre in February 1906, and by any subsequent gesture in the way of providing moral support for the French. The Anglo-Russian Agreement was devised in the interests of England's Imperial position, not for the sake of the balance of power in Europe. Had the policy of an agreement with Russia not been justifiable on grounds quite separate from its necessity for the equilibrium in Europe, it is certain that Morley, who regarded the balance of power in the same way that Loreburn did, and who wrote in March 1908 that 'in entering into negotiations with the Russian government . . . His Majesty's Government were actuated not only by considerations affecting the Empire as a whole, but also, very largely, by considerations relating to India alone', would not have given the policy the backing and support which Grey recognised as being quite invaluable to its success.[71]

It is quite true that Grey did say, in February 1906, that 'an entente between Russia, France and ourselves would be absolutely secure. If it is necessary to check Germany it could then be done.'[72] It is also true that, on at least one occasion when the negotiations were faltering, Grey appealed to the Russians to 'bear in mind that larger issues than even those directly involved in these Agreements are indirectly at stake'.[73] If he was thinking of Europe, it was only in an incidental way. So were some of his advisers when they welcomed the start of a contest between Russia and Austria in the Balkans on the grounds that 'we shall not now be bothered by Russia in Asia'.[74] Hardinge said at the turn of 1907 that, in the Near East, Russia 'will constantly find herself in conflict with Germany and not in opposition to us'.[75] The latter point – that Russia should not be in opposition to Britain – was the main one. A re-orientation of Russian policy towards the Balkans, and the possibility of her colliding with Germany through the pressure she would put on Austria, were welcomed at the Foreign Office less because Germany was considered a menace to Europe or to Britain than because Russia was considered a menace to the British position in the world.

As it was more to the future than to the present that the makers of the Anglo-Russian Conventions were looking, the passage of time only increased the importance to them of maintaining their achievement. Hardinge revealed in 1910, to Paul Cambon, the French Ambassador in London, of all people, that he regarded the Russian railway systems in Central Asia as 'a sword of Damocles hanging over Britain's head'.[76] So far as he was concerned, 'our whole future in Asia is bound up with the necessity of maintaining the best and most friendly relations with Russia'.[77] Nicolson shared this outlook. He wrote in April 1912:

it would be far more disadvantageous to have an unfriendly France and Russia than an unfriendly Germany. The latter . . . can give us plenty of annoyance, but it cannot really threaten any of our more important interests, while Russia especially could cause us extreme embarrassment, and, indeed, danger, in the Mid-East and on our Indian frontier, and it would be most unfortunate were we to revert to the state of things which existed before 1904 and 1907.[78]

As, with time, it became clear that Russia's recovery was indeed taking place, the consequences for Britain of not being on friendly terms with her were increasingly stressed. Nicolson wrote in April 1913 that Russia 'can, were she unfriendly, cause us very great annoyance and embarrassment in Central Asia, and we shall be unable to meet her on anything like equal terms'.[79] In May he received a letter from Hardinge, then Viceroy, expressing the devout hope 'that Russia may be pre-occupied for some years to come in the Near East with the interests of the Slav races, so that those who favour a forward policy in Asia may receive no encouragement'.[80] Rightly convinced that Grey was 'thoroughly in accordance' with his own and Hardinge's view that relations with Russia must remain on the best possible footing, Nicolson wrote again in April 1914:

The maintenance of our understanding with Russia is of the very greatest importance to us both in Europe and as regards India and our position generally in the Mid and Far East. Hardinge is continually impressing on me the urgent necessity of doing nothing which could in any way tend to alienate Russia from us . . . She could hit us where we were powerless.[81]

A few days later Buchanan wrote to him from St Petersburg: 'Russia is rapidly becoming so powerful that we must retain her friendship at almost any cost.'[82]

It was the fear of such consequences, I suggest, that accounts for Grey's categoric assertion to the German Ambassador in May 1910: 'we cannot sacrifice the friendship of Russia or of France.'[83] It was this that explains his constant anxiety to avoid any 'new departures' in foreign policy. As he told Churchill on one occasion, the risks involved were greater than the advantages.[84] Hence his concern to avoid making with Germany any agreements into which France and Russia could not also be admitted.[85] As he told the Cabinet in July 1910, the difficulty of making any political arrangement with Germany was that 'France and Russia would regard any such agreement with suspicion and all the blessings of the entente with France and Russia would go, and we might be again on the verge of war with one or other of these Powers.' He was supported in this instance by Morley, who urged from the Indian point of view that nothing be done to worsen 'our present happy relations with Russia'.[86] No more than his Ambassador to Berlin did the Foreign Secretary, who continued to believe as others had done before him that Russia was both inaccessible and invulnerable to Britain, wish to see 'all the work of the last decade brought to nought, and all our old anxieties, which we set at rest by our Ententes, brought to life again'.[87]

It was these 'old anxieties', and not the more prominently advertised fears for the balance of power *per se*, that were throughout his tenure of the Foreign Office uppermost in Grey's mind. At the height of the Agadir crisis, when the prospect of British involvement in a Franco-German war was in sight again as it had been in 1906, Grey stressed that the break-up of the Triple Entente would mean that 'we should be faced again with all the old troubles about the frontier of India'.[88] Early in 1912 he assured Hardinge that he was staking everything on pulling the Russian Agreement through all difficulties, for 'if it were to go everything would be worse'.[89] When on 3 August 1914 he told the House of Commons that the country would suffer but little more if it went into the war than if it stayed out it was of these consequences, basically, that he was thinking. Indeed in the fortnight before the declaration of war he had been forcibly reminded of, and even blackmailed with, precisely these consequences by his Staff at the Foreign Office, by certain of his Ambassadors and by the French in the person of Paul Cambon. Crowe, who on 31 July was to appeal to 'the theory of the balance of power', minuted on 25 July: 'Should the war come, and England stand aside, one of two things must happen: (a) Either Germany and Austria win, crush France, and humiliate Russia . . . What will be the position of a friendless England? (b) Or France and Russia win. What would then be their attitude towards England? What about India and the

Mediterranean?'[90] Buchanan telegraphed from St Petersburg on 2 August 1914:

I venture to submit that if we do not respond to the Tsar's appeal for our support, we shall at the end of the war, whatever be its issue, find ourselves without a friend in Europe, while our Indian Empire will no longer be secure from attack by Russia. If we defer intervention til France is in danger of being crushed, the sacrifices we shall then be called on to make will be much greater.[91]

As recorded by Grey on 1 August the French Ambassador, helping the sword of Damocles on its downward path, 'urged very strongly the obligation of British interests. If we did not help France, the entente would disappear; and, whether victory came to Germany or to France and Russia, our situation at the end of the war would be very uncomfortable.'[92]

From 1904, associating with France and then Russia looked like supporting the weaker of the two major European groupings. It resembled, in this respect, classical balance of power politics. When the Foreign Secretary and his officials spoke and wrote of 'the work of the last decade', however, they did not have Europe primarily in mind. Nicolson might write in July 1911 of 'our policy since 1904 of preserving the equilibrium and consequently the peace in Europe'.[93] Mallet might write in 1912 that 'by the policy so happily inaugurated by Balfour's Government the outbreak of war has been twice averted in the last eight years'.[94] Essentially, this was a screen erected to conceal Britain's Imperial vulnerability. Not only did those most concerned with, and most responsible for, British foreign policy know that she could make hardly any material contribution towards a balance of power in Europe; they knew that their alignment with France and Russia rather than with the Triple Alliance was for the purpose of enabling Britain more easily than otherwise to retain command of the sea and, above all, to secure the position of the British Empire in Central and East-Central Asia.

It was considered, by the British, that if there were a balance of power in Europe then this would be to their advantage. When Europe balanced itself the beneficiary tended to be the British Empire. In the eyes of those who put the roof on the house begun by Lord Lansdowne it was for Russia to provide the balance in Europe, not Great Britain. There was little point in the French looking to England's '80,000 men with good guns'. The French had to look to themselves, and to the Russians. So far as Grey was concerned, not the British but the Russian Army ought to be regarded as the 'great counterpoise to Germany on land'.[95] As Asquith put it after Grey had reported to him yet another encounter with Clemenceau at which the latter had invoked the memory of Waterloo rather than of Trafalgar, the Frenchman was ignorant if he imagines we are going to keep here a standing army of ½–¾ million men, ready to meet the Germans in Belgium if and when they are minded to adopt that route for the invasion of France. As you point out, he completely ignores the existence – from a military point of view – of his Russian ally.[96]

Grey told Nicolson and Bertie in February and March 1906 that it was Russia who would change the situation in Europe, on which the positions of France and Germany in Morocco depended, to the advantage of France; that it was Russia who would assure the peace of Europe and the 'civility' of Germany to France and to Britain.[97] It was appreciated, at this time, that, in order to fulfil this role, Russia needed time in which to recuperate and recover. This recovery took place very slowly. Even at the conclusion of the Anglo-Russian negotiations Grey was fully aware that it had not yet been effected.[98] Russia was still not ready to play her appointed part in either 1908 or 1909: in May and October 1909 Hardinge wrote: 'there still remains much to be done and it will require at least two or three years before the Russian army is prepared for war'.[99] Despite being aware of this, the British continued to invoke the power of Russia. The C.I.D. sub-committee on the Military Needs of the Empire that was appointed in October 1908 and reported in August 1909 was encouraged by the Foreign Office to presume that if Germany provoked hostilities with France, the latter 'would be able to count on the armed support of her ally Russia'.[100] On 9 August 1911, at a meeting between Grey, Haldane, Sir Henry Wilson and Eyre Crowe, the question of Russian support was raised yet again. The D.M.O., in his own words, 'shattered rather rudely' the theory advanced by the Foreign Secretary 'that Russia was a governing factor'. Grey was told that 'Russian interference would scarcely relieve the pressure from Paris'. In a paper drafted on 11 August Wilson went on to say: 'It is true that France might have the active assistance of Russia. In point of fact however, this assistance is more imaginary than real.' In the version of this paper printed for consideration at the C.I.D. on 23 August this was watered down only to: 'In point of fact, however, in the early stages of the war this assistance would not be likely to relieve the hostile pressure along the lines of collision to any material extent.'[101] The point had certainly been well made – on 23 August Wilson said the Russians were so frightened of the Germans that he did not think they would allow a single man to leave the country, and the meeting could have been forgiven had it taken away the impression that, of the two Armies, the Belgian was the more valuable.[102] These views seemed, however, to make no difference to Sir Edward Grey, who minuted in February 1912 on a letter from the French Military Attaché in Berlin to his colleague in London: 'This takes no account of the Russian Army.' If it was on the Foreign Secretary's instructions that Nicolson made this point to the French Ambassador, there would appear to be little difference between irresponsibility and downright stupidity. At any rate, the Permanent Under Secretary found the situation unchanged. He was told that the Russians were 'in a transition state. They said they would not be ready for taking a *serious* part in a campaign for about 16–18 months from now.'[103] Only in the spring of 1913 was it clear beyond all doubt that the recovery of Russia was complete.[104] Until then, she was always eighteen months to two years from being in any condition to determine the outcome of the struggle on land which Grey admitted on 23 August 1911 would be the decisive struggle, and which, throughout, he had ostensibly relied upon her to determine.

For most of the period of the ententes there was no balance of power in Europe. The British knew this. So anxious were they that Europe should at least appear to be in balance that they piled dissimulation upon dissimulation. They did their utmost to make it appear that there was 'a fair equilibrium' in Europe, and that Russia, and themselves, were providing part of it. Merely by dint of saying so, simply by force of repetition, they went a long way towards convincing themselves that the image was the reality. Theirs was a triumph of mind over *matériel*, a gamble that their treble-bluff would not be called.

The Agreement with Russia was an act of faith on the part of Great Britain. Hardinge made this clear when he said that the only hope of staving off effectually the dangers to India which already existed lay in the conclusion of an agreement 'which it is hoped the Russian Government will loyally observe'.[105]

In making this act of faith the British made two assumptions. These were that the Russian advance towards India would stop, and that Russia would undertake to hold Germany in check in Europe. Both these assumptions turned out to be false. The sentiments expressed by Grey even before becoming Foreign Secretary, in a speech on 20 October 1905, and reiterated immediately upon taking office, about the desirability of the re-establishment of Russian influence in the councils of Europe, were not shared by the Russians. Count Lamsdorff was reported by Hardinge on 6 January 1906 as interpreting English manifestations of sympathy towards Russia as 'a recognition of the necessity of a strong Russia as a counterpoise in the European system', but he was not so easily to be persuaded away from Central Asia.[106] In April 1908 the British and the French were chagrined to discover that the Russians intended to resume railway construction in the Far East.[107] At Reval in June 1908 Hardinge flattered A. Isvolsky with the prospect of Russia's being 'the arbiter of peace' in Europe.[108] There was no response. On the other hand, in July and October 1908 the British had to make serious protests against the extent to which the Russians were taking advantage of the deteriorating situation

in Persia where a constitutional struggle was raging.[109] In exaggerating
their concern with Europe and in stressing the importance of Russia's playing an active part *there* for fear that she might be active in areas of more
vital concern to them, the British succeeded all too well. This backfired
upon them in the shape of Sazonov's reflections of October 1910:

Considerations . . . prompt me to say that the London Cabinet looks upon the
Anglo-Russian Convention of 1907 as being important for the Asiatic interests of
England; but that this Convention possesses a still greater importance for England
from the viewpoint of the policy which is being pursued by England in Europe . . .
  These considerations are of great moment for us, as we may rest assured that the
English, engaged in the pursuit of political aims of vital importance in Europe,
may, in case of necessity, be prepared to sacrifice certain interests in Asia in order
to keep a Convention alive which is of such importance to them. This is a circum-
stance which we can, of course, exploit for ourselves, as, for instance, in Persian
affairs.[110]

It was far more dangerous that Sazonov should misunderstand British
priorities than that Loreburn and Scott should do so.
  The situation in Persia continued to deteriorate. Though Grey maintained in January 1912 that 'since the Anglo-Russian agreement was made
. . . the Russians have scrupulously abstained from doing anything prejudicial to the security of our Indian frontier', he was at that very time
engaged in suppressing material which would have revealed just how
unscrupulous the Russians had been, and the degree of strain their
activities in Persia were placing upon Anglo-Russian relations.[111] Nor was
the deterioration of the British position confined to Persia. During 1912
the Russians were penetrating Mongolia, Tibet and Chinese Turkestan.
Hardinge, now Viceroy of India, was alarmed to discover that they were
consolidating a position only 150 miles from Srinagar and 300 miles from
Simla.[112] Tyrrell's gloomy prediction of May 1907 that Russian assurances were only reliable so long as she was in a condition of impotency so
far as offensive policies were concerned,[113] was being amply fulfilled.
Reviewing the position reached in March 1914 Grey wrote on the 18th:

. . . as regards Persia, we wish to have practically the whole of the neutral sphere,
and have nothing to concede there to Russia; as regards Afghanistan, we cannot
concede anything to Russia, because we cannot get the Ameer's consent; as regards
Tibet, the change that we wish to have, and to which Russia's consent is necessary,
is very slight, but we have nothing to give in return.

As he summarised it: 'all along the line we want something, and we have
nothing to give'. Three days later, on receipt of another disturbing
despatch from Townley in Tehran, Grey wrote to Lord Crewe at the India
Office that matters had been brought 'to the point when we cannot post-

pone a reconsideration of the Persian Question'. He proposed that the first step should consist of a discussion between Crewe, himself, Nicolson, Crowe (who was now in charge of this department at the Foreign Office) and an official from the India Office selected by Crewe.[114] The Russians had already hinted that railway systems in Persia might be linked in such a way as to provide a through-route to India, something which would hardly have increased English or Indian peace of mind and which Grey could not see himself getting through the C.I.D. or past the criticism of the Government of India. In May 1914, at the same time that they suggested an Anglo-Russian defensive alliance, the Russians demanded the stationing of a Russian official in the most sensitive place of all so far as the defence of India was concerned, Herat. Simultaneously with this Grey wrote to Crewe that 'it looks as if the expected but dreaded break down in Persia were coming'. It was becoming increasingly clear, as the Russians delayed for a whole month a reply to a memorandum from Grey highly critical of their proceedings, and then provided one that was unhelpful in the extreme, that Russian concessions to Britain over Tibet and Persia would only be granted in return for British concessions to them in terms of support in Europe, if then.[115]

By the time war broke out in Europe in 1914 the problem of Central Asia was, then, as great as it had ever been. Russia was no longer in the state which had caused her to grant the British Empire a reprieve. She was using her strength to resume the Great Game in Asia. Her policy once more contained designs upon the frontiers of India either as ends in themselves or as means of bringing pressure to bear upon Britain to support her elsewhere. The defences of the British Empire in Central Asia, however, were in the same state. The precautions advocated by Kitchener and the Government of India in 1905–6, and accepted in May 1907 by the Committee of Imperial Defence as being necessary in the absence of a diplomatic solution, had not been taken. Faith had not been rewarded. From one point of view, seven years had been gained. From another, they had been lost.

5

The Fiction of the Free Hand

With the balance of power, the principle of the free hand dominated statements purporting to describe the aims and essentials of British foreign policy in the late nineteenth and early twentieth centuries. The two principles were brought together well in one report sent from the Paris Embassy on 1 May 1913 by the First Secretary there, whose interlocutors had declared that 'England was today the arbiter of Europe. She could do what she liked.'[1]

At the turn of the century Sir William Harcourt had invoked Canning to the effect that England should be 'the friend of all states, but the instrument of none'. Shortly afterwards, two future Prime Ministers had made similar declarations. Asquith was unable to imagine anything 'which can in the least compensate us for the loss of the freedom to act, or not to act, according as our own interests and conscience dictate'. Campbell-Bannerman referred to a 'freedom of individual action' that was 'of immense importance to this country'.[2] Campbell-Bannerman's and Asquith's Foreign Secretary was Sir Edward Grey. At a meeting of the Committee of Imperial Defence which included the Prime Ministers of the Dominions, on 26 May 1911, Grey said: 'We are not committed by entanglements which tie our hands. Our hands are free.'[3] In the House of Commons, on 3 August 1914, he maintained: 'as regards our freedom to decide in a crisis what our line should be, whether we should intervene or whether we should abstain, the Government remained perfectly free, and, *a fortiori*, the House of Commons remains perfectly free'.[4] Grey's Permanent Under Secretary, Sir Arthur Nicolson, minuted in April 1912: 'We have a very simple policy, not to tie our hands in any way with anyone, to remain the sole judges of our action.' His Ambassador to Paris, Sir Francis Bertie, was reported as being convinced that his government intended to retain, right up to the last minute, 'la pleine liberté de sa décision finale'.[5]

The free hand, in the face of French, Russian and German assaults upon it and efforts to deprive Britain of it, would appear to have borne a charmed life. It was deemed not to be affected by the conversations between British and French military and naval Staffs which began on a 'solely provisional and non-committal' basis in January 1906. As Grey described it, the position was 'that the Government was quite free, but that the military people knew what to do if the word was given'. His argument was that Britain's freedom of action was actually increased by such consultations: without them she would have less choice, in that she would have been unable to furnish effective aid to France even had she desired to.[6] In the autumn of 1911, when these talks came to the attention of the Cabinet as a whole, Grey maintained 'that at no stage of our intercourse with France since January 1906 had we either by diplomatic or military engagements compromised our freedom of decision or action in the event of a war between France and Germany'. The Cabinet took advantage of the opportunity to pass a formal resolution that 'no communications should take place between the General Staff here and the Staffs of other countries which can, directly or indirectly, commit this country to military or naval intervention'. In the following year the position was further reinforced by the Cabinet's decision that it should be 'plainly intimated' to the French, who wished to resume naval talks, 'that such communications were not to be taken as prejudicing the freedom of decision of either Government as to whether they should or should not cooperate in the event of war', and by the embodiment of this point in the letter sent by Grey to the French Ambassador on 22 November 1912.[7] In the spring of 1914, when the Russians expressed a desire for closer and more formal relations between the Triple Entente Powers the Cabinet had no hesitation in agreeing that the Grey–Cambon exchange of letters be communicated to the Russian Government, and approved Grey's language to the French that the Russians would see from them 'that both the French and British Governments were left entirely free to decide whether, in case of war, they would support one another or not'. At the Foreign Office, one senior official had been quick to contend that consultations with France related 'solely to measures which the naval authorities *would* take *if and when* their governments decided on joint warlike operations. It commits neither side and establishes no casus foederis, and saves improvising plans at critical moments when any delay may involve the gravest consequences', and to recommend Anglo-Russian naval talks on the same basis.[8]

The response of the Foreign Office to the German requests for some form of neutrality, which was that 'the hands of England would be tied so long as the engagement was in force',[9] completed the circle of the argument. If the Germans, between 1909 and 1912, were asking for something that would tie British hands, for something that went further than anything done with France, who had not been given any assurance that the

British would take no hostile action against *her*, then those hands must, in all respects, be free.

   This position appeared to be still further bolstered by the postulates that no British Government could go to war without the support of public opinion and that public opinion would be determined by the immediate circumstances in which war broke out; and also that the public would not take the side of the aggressor.[10] During the Agadir crisis of 1911, for example, Grey stressed that 'it is essential that before war comes (if it does come) it should be clear that Germany has meant war and has forced it'; 'A repetition of 1870, when France was manoeuvred into making war against Germany, would be a fatal mistake as regards public opinion here, on which everything as regards our attitude depends.' It was from this point of view that Grey kept alive the possibility of a conference: for if Germany rejected a conference, or at first agreed to one and then broke it up, she would at least emerge as 'the person who prefers war'.[11] According to Grey, the language which the French Ambassador later told Nicolson he had been using to Paris in respect of the possible attitude of England in the event of a break between France and Germany stated the position quite accurately. Cambon had said

that it would be exceedingly difficult for any British Government to take any action which was not supported by British public opinion: that in the event of Germany attacking France or wilfully breaking off the negotiations British public opinion would side with France and would enable the British Government to support France. British public opinion . . . had an instinctive sympathy with the party attacked and an instinctive mistrust and dislike of an aggressive and bullying Power . . .

Grey read the whole of this out to the Cabinet on 15 November 1911, in his own defence.[12]

This chapter will attempt to show that, despite the above claims, the free hand was a fiction; that it was the product partly of the reiteration of a particular vocabulary, which kept alive artificially a long tradition of wishful thinking which had been embodied in the speeches on foreign affairs of British politicians; partly of the appeal of the idea itself. It was all too easy for Nicolson, warning that a North Sea Convention might hamper Britain in the future, to give and to receive the impression that Britain's liberty of action was everywhere, and absolutely, 'untrammelled'.[13] This was the stuff that dreams were made on, and the wish was father to the thought. Grey might maintain that the British were bound in one respect only – to afford to France diplomatic support on issues arising from the Agreement of 1904; he might assure the House of Commons that the secret articles of that Agreement which were made public in November 1911 were not of first-rate importance and had not committed the House to serious obligations, that there were no other secret engagements, that 'for ourselves we have not made a single secret Article of any kind since we came to office'.[14] This was all strictly correct. He might attempt to reassure the Colonial Secretary that it was 'precisely because Russia knows that an Entente is not an Alliance and that an Entente does not entail any obligation on us, that she is so sensitive and anxious to know how she stands as regards our support of her . . . '.[15] Like the effort in 1906 of Nicolson's predecessor Hardinge to account for French nervousness and suspicion by 'the fact that we are not bound hand and foot' to them,[16] this was not without plausibility. Terminological inexactitude, however, was a poor substitute for the truth.

How inelastic Britain's position really was, how little freedom of action she really possessed, and how academic the semantic constructions employed to conceal this, was revealed in a practice which made nonsense of the theory.

In November 1912, C. Kinlocke-Cooke M.P. asked 'was Article IX [of the Anglo-French Agreement], stating that the French and British Governments agreed to afford to one another their diplomatic support in order to obtain the execution of the clauses . . . regarded by either Government to mean and to include military and naval support under any and what circumstances?'. For the Government, Mr Acland replied: 'An agreement to afford diplomatic support does not impose on any Power an obligation either to give or to withhold military and naval support.'[17] The distinction between diplomatic and military support had been raised at the very beginning of Grey's period of office. On 10 January 1906 the French Ambassador had asked whether, in the event of German aggression against France, Britain would be prepared to render France armed assistance. Grey's Private Secretary, Mallet, believing that there was 'only one possible answer and that is that if the aggression arises out of the entente with us and if we are given an equal voice with France in the negotiations which result in the attack, we will take our share of the fighting', urged Bertie in Paris to write in favour of the pursuit of 'a logical course'. Bertie obliged with a confidential despatch to Grey on 13 January 1906, in which he wrote:

It is true that the second article of the Anglo-French Declaration respecting Egypt and Morocco only says that H.M. Govt. will not obstruct the action taken by France for the purposes of the Declaration, and that the 9th Article only binds Great Britain to afford to France diplomatic support in order to obtain the execution of the clauses of the Declaration; but if diplomatic support failed to remove the opposition made by another Power without political interests in Morocco to France acting within the conditions of the Declaration, it is felt that the natural sequence would be that France should receive from her partner in the Declaration more than the diplomatic support that had proved insufficient for the purposes of the agreement . . .

On this occasion Grey countered the French wish for a formal engagement by threatening them with the loss of their own liberty of action. The British would have to be consulted about French policy in Morocco, hitherto 'absolutely free', and if necessary would have to press upon them 'concessions or alterations of their policy which might seem to us desirable to avoid a war'.[18]

The problem had merely been side-stepped. It had not been resolved, and it did not go away. It was raised in an acute form by the Agadir crisis. Behind Grey's admission, in July 1911, that the 'general and underlying ground of our policy' was 'to give to France such support as would prevent her from falling under the virtual control of Germany and estrangement from us',[19] lurked the unanswered questions of 'how much support?' and 'what kind of support?'. When Grey informed them that his Cabinet wanted to know whether at a conference France would in all circumstances exclude any solution that would give a foothold in Morocco to Germany, which the British were reluctant to treat as an unconditional casus belli, the French were appalled:

Le gouvernement anglais, par l'accord de 1904, a reconnu à la France et à l'Espagne, seules, des sphères d'influence politique au Maroc et a, par conséquent, dénié aux autres Puissances toute prétension politique sur ce pays. Laisser aujourd'hui le Gouvernement allemand créer un établissement d'Etat sur un point quelconque du territoire marocain serait contraire à l'accord de 1904 . . . Le Gouvernement français ne pourrait donc admettre que la Conférence éventuelle puisse être appelée à envisager la concession à un titre quelconque au Gouvernement allemand d'une portion, si petite soit-elle, du territoire marocain.

J. Caillaux, the French Premier, threatened that if France was to be deserted by England and left to face Germany alone it would be a serious blow to the entente and the consequences might be very grave. At least one member of the Foreign Office was taken aback by this display of logic: 'It is not pleasant', minuted Crowe, 'to be reminded by the French Government of our treaty obligations.'[20] With the French holding this view as to the scope and interpretation of the 1904 Agreement, and the British anxious not to occupy diplomatically ground that they were not prepared to defend by measures going beyond diplomacy, it was just as well that the Germans turned out not to be amenable to a conference. Grey was fortunate that the matter did not come to a head. What he stressed with the French was that an agreement by which Germany gave France a free hand in Morocco would still leave France bound by the Act of Algeciras. If on the other hand France could strike, at the expense of the French Congo, such a bargain with the Germans as to secure their agreement to a French protectorate over Morocco, this could be ratified at a conference of the signatories of the Act of Algeciras called for the purpose.[21] Towards the end of these negotiations, when it was clear that they would be successful, Grey no longer bothered to conceal his personal view. In May, in an unsuccessful effort to deter German action, he had told the German Ambassador that 'whilst in other questions the British Government possessed perfect freedom and could act according to their own discretion, they were bound by the Agreement with France to support her in the Morocco question'. In November he told C. P. Scott: 'As to the Morocco difficulty we were bound to give France our diplomatic support in her resistance to the dismemberment of Morocco, and diplomatic support implied, if it was to be of any value, the possibility of military support.'[22] Lansdowne, moreover, took the same line in the House of Lords a few weeks later. He thought it 'not unfair to say that in a case of this kind, an undertaking to give diplomatic support may tend to bring about an obligation to give support of another kind'. He then went on to maintain the great principle, of double-talk at least, by saying that 'each side, of course, retains its liberty of action'.[23]

Other personal views and stances of Grey's also betray the real situation. In March 1911, for instance, he was clearly none too happy at a suggestion made in Cabinet that the French Ambassador should be told that his Minister for Foreign Affairs, S. Pichon, had gone 'too far' in a recent speech in which he had by inference intimated the existence of a military understanding.[24] In April 1911 he let Bertie know that he had purposely worded his answer to a parliament question from F. W. Jowett 'so as not to convey that the engagement of 1904 might not under certain circumstances be construed to have larger consequences than its strict letter'.[25] At the Cabinet on 1 November 1911 he said that he could 'not conduct negotiations with France if he was not to be able to assume our landing forces to help France, if Germany invaded her'.[26] On the draft of the second of the resolutions passed by the Cabinet on 15 November, to the effect that communications between General Staffs relating to concerted action by land or sea should not be entered into without the previous approval of the Cabinet, he minuted: 'I think the last paragraph is a little tight.'[27] During the discussions in the summer of 1912 that preceded the exchange of letters with Cambon, Harcourt's request that words be inserted to express the view that the resumption of naval talks should not lead to the expectation of help one to another was held by Grey to be 'tantamount to telling the French that we might contemplate a war with France'. He objected, according to one colleague, J. A. Pease, that the words concerning the unprejudiced freedom of decision of either Government would give rise 'to suspicion as to why they were inserted at all'.[28] It is difficult to understand such attitudes as these on the part of the Foreign Secretary unless, as Charles Trevelyan later wrote, the entente was in his mind an alliance, 'no less real . . . because it was not written'.[29]

Grey, whose emphasis was on keeping British hands free to continue existing relations with France and Russia,[30] and for use, however empty they might be, against Germany, went through the motions of being detached. When asked by the Russians in November 1908 what England would do supposing a crisis arose in the Balkans and Germany took the part of Austria he maintained that it was impossible to come to a decision beforehand: 'so much depended upon how the quarrel arose, and who was the aggressor'. More privately, he admitted that if the eventuality did occur, 'it would be very difficult for England to keep out of it'.[31] The disinclination to discuss the eventuality did not spring from any doubts as to what the outcome of the discussion would be. It was due, on the contrary, to there being no such doubts. It was increased, on that particular occasion, by the fact that the Russian enquiry came at the end of a week spent considering the question of British intervention in a Franco-German war over an incident at Casablanca, of all places. There was equally no doubt as to what the answer would have been in that case. On the previous occasion on which it had looked as if Germany was trying to fasten a quarrel upon France in connection with Morocco the Central Powers had been told that it was 'impossible' for England to abandon France, and that she would stick to France in all emergencies, even in the case of war. Hardinge wrote in October 1906: 'Only a few months have elapsed since there was a serious risk of war between France and Germany and had war broken out it would have been very difficult, in fact almost impossible, to have prevented this country from being forced by the strength of circumstances to take part in it.' Shortly after this, when issuing an instruction that no British services personnel or diplomatists should discuss with Germans 'what assistance we may offer or may have offered to France at any time past or future', Grey did not dispute or take up with Hardinge the remark the latter had made on Spicer's surmise that Admiral von Tirpitz must know perfectly well that the report that England was ready to land 200,000 men to support France in the spring of 1906 was quite untrue: 'It was only an exaggeration of numbers, consequently not "quite untrue".'[32] In November 1908 Grey maintained that 'the world would say that France was being attacked because she had made friends with us, and for us to fold our hands and look on would not be a very respectable part'.[33] Esher's information was that Asquith, Grey and Haldane had all been prepared to intervene by sending a force to the continent.[34] And Hardinge explained to

Sir F. Villiers in Lisbon that no ship could be spared for the ceremonials attending the coronation of the King of Portugal because it had been decided to order the Channel Fleet, which had been cruising off the coast of Ireland, round into the Channel, 'so as to be prepared for all eventualities'.[35] He pointed out, in the spring of 1909, that the Russians 'must realise that, in the event of a general conflagration in which they are associated as allies of France, it is not likely that we shall not actively participate'.[36] The first Balkan War and the possibility of British involvement brought to a head the concern of the Directorate of Military Operations over the provision of shipping for the transportation of the Expeditionary Force. On this occasion, for the British record, the French Ambassador was told that so far as joining forces with Russia was concerned, much would depend on how war broke out as to whether public opinion would be aroused and that, if things did become serious, public opinion would first require an attempt to secure that Germany, France and England kept out of trouble; Cambon's own record shows that he was also told that the German Ambassador had been given what the latter took as 'a hint that cannot be misunderstood': that 'despite the fact that there were no secret agreements with France, it was for England of vital necessity to prevent that country from being crushed by Germany; England . . . would have no alternative but to come to the aid of France should Germany, as is expected . . . prove victorious over the French'.[37]

In January 1906 the Permanent Under Secretary Sir Thomas Sanderson wrote: 'It would really be preposterous that we should have a European war on the question of the organisation of the Police in Moorish ports.'[38] In August 1912 the Ambassador to Vienna echoed this attitude: 'Under present circumstances it is certainly in our interest and in that of France to give Russia every possible support, but it seems to me scarcely to be to our advantage to risk the dangers of war for the sake of who shall or shall not remain finally in possession of the Sandjak of Novibazar.'[39] To Grey, in February 1913, it seemed 'unreasonable and intolerable that the greater part of Europe should be involved in war for a dispute about one or two towns on the Albanian frontier'.[40] However preposterous, unreasonable and intolerable, the contemplation of such consequences was the absurdity to which the British were reduced. Asquith admitted to C. P. Scott in July 1911 that German fortification of Agadir, in itself, was not something worth Britain's while to go to war over. But as Nicolson had pointed out: 'the moment may arrive when we shall have to deal with the situation on far broader grounds and from a higher standpoint than are afforded by the wording of existing agreements or by the relative values of ports or dis-

tricts on the western coast of Africa'.[41] The question of Serbian access to
the Adriatic excited little interest, in itself, in London; the ownership of
Scutari was 'strictly speaking a matter of perfect indifference' there. But, as
Grey realised, should Scutari be the spark of a European conflagration, 'we
and other Powers should have to consider, not the merits of the question
of Scutari, but what our own interests required us to do in a European
crisis'.[42]

What lay behind this apparently distorted scale of values were the
requirements of British interests. British interests were protected by and
embodied in her friendly relations with primarily Russia and secondarily
France. If these relations ceased to be friendly Britain would not only have
to face further assaults on her Imperial position which she was ill-equipped
to withstand; she would also have to endure a state of isolation which she
was not prepared to support. A few days before Grey, in January 1914,
assured Harcourt that Russia's anxiety to know how she stood in respect
of British support over the issue of the German command at Constantinople was due to her knowledge that an entente was not an alliance and
did not entail obligations, he had admitted to his Ambassador in Berlin the
necessity of supporting Russia. He did not think it worth 'all the fuss
Sazonov makes about it; but as long as he does make a fuss it will be
important and very embarrassing to us: for we can't turn our back upon
Russia'.[43] Similarly over Scutari: as Nicolson put it: 'It is so essential to us
to maintain our understanding with Russia that we could not possibly run
the risk of seriously impairing it were we to adopt an attitude which she
might consider not very friendly'; as Bertie put it: 'Should Russia be
dragged into a war with Austria and Germany and should we stand aloof
the Entente will die a natural death and no power on earth will bring it to
life again.'[44] Russia might be alienated by failure to support her over questions in which she was directly interested; she might also be alienated
indirectly, by failure to support France over questions in which France was
directly interested, which would also involve the alienation of France.
Mallet's reaction to the German proposals of 1909 for British neutrality
was that 'if we fall into the trap the entente with *Russia* would at once fall
to the ground . . . '.[45] In April 1912 Nicolson drew attention to the likelihood of a British engagement to Germany causing French confidence in
Britain to wane 'even to the extent of seriously impairing our relations –
and such a result would at once react on our relations with Russia. The
consequences are not pleasant to contemplate'.[46] Grey admitted that the
closeness of Anglo-French relations enabled Germany to put pressure on
England through France, 'but unless we had the entente we should be
isolated and might have everyone against us which would be a still greater
weakness'.[47] His determination not to run 'the risk of returning to our old

position of isolation in Europe' ensured his support of France and her ally.[48]

So long as it was considered, in the words of both of Grey's Permanent Under Secretaries, both of them, and this not at all incidentally, former Ambassadors to St Petersburg, 'far more disadvantageous to have an unfriendly France and unfriendly Russia than an unfriendly Germany',[49] then so long were the British in a dilemma which was resolved by the mere stating of it. On one occasion, explaining his desire to see a working understanding between Russia and Austria on the grounds that a war between them would be 'very inconvenient', Grey continued: 'I do not think that we could take part in it, and intervene on the Russian side in a Balkan war; and yet our abstention would prove a danger to the maintenance of the present grouping of the European Powers.'[50] A fuller version was provided by Goschen:

We know that Austria won't concede anything more than she has said she will. We also know . . . that if Russia moves against Austria Germany will join the latter. Then of course France must also chip in, and we should . . . be confronted with a perfect beast of a problem.

To my mind it means a catastrophe whichever way we solved it. Because it would be a catastrophe in itself to be dragged into a terrible war for a question originally paltry in itself and one in which we have no interest whatever.

But, where should we be if we were to stand aloof? I shudder to think of it. What friends should we have left? And what figure should we cut? and moreover we should see all the work of the last decade brought to nought, and all our old anxieties, which we set at rest by our Ententes, brought to life again. It is really rather awful to think of.[51]

This was, moreover, a position that Britain had occupied from the start of Grey's time as Foreign Secretary, if not from the time of the signing of the Anglo-French Agreement. Grey had stated both the problem and his own resolution of it in a memorandum of 20 February 1906. His starting point was that if the Algeciras Conference broke down and there was war between France and Germany, 'it will be very difficult for us to keep out of it'. On the one hand there were the manifestations of Anglo-French affection leading to certain expectations on the part of the French. There would also be

a general feeling in every country that we had behaved meanly and left France in the lurch. The United States would despise us, Russia would not think it worth while to make a friendly arrangement with us about Asia, Japan would prepare to re-insure herself elsewhere, we should be left without a friend and without the power of making a friend and Germany would take some pleasure . . . in exploiting the whole situation to our disadvantage . . .

On the other hand, 'the prospect of a European War and of our being involved in it is horrible'. The question of whether Britain could keep out of a war between France and Germany had nevertheless to be faced. Grey's conclusion was: 'The more I review the situation the more it appears to me that we cannot, without losing our good name and our friends and wrecking our policy and position in the world.'[52]

France had to be supported originally, otherwise all hope of an agreement with Russia would disappear. Once an agreement with Russia had been obtained, however, and the main aim of British policy secured, her commitment in no way decreased. The necessity of supporting France remained; that of supporting Russia was added. The immediate consequences of failure to support either would have been isolation. The ultimate consequences did not bear thinking about. Crises only accentuated a chronic condition, by highlighting, and bringing closer, these consequences. It would not be '*just* pour les beaux yeux de Serbie' that England might be plunged into a European war, as Paget should have realised.[53] It would be because 'the whole policy of the Entente' demanded it. This explains why, at dinner on the night of 29 July 1914, Nicolson should speak to Balfour 'as if it were a matter of course that we should join in at once with France and Russia'.[54]

In January 1906 Grey had endeavoured to persuade both the French and German Ambassadors, as he had been informed that Lansdowne had endeavoured to do in the previous year, that in the event of a Franco-German war public feeling in England would be such that it would be impossible for England to remain neutral. This may very well have been the case, in 1905, in 1906, and in 1911. 'Policy', however, was as much, if not more, involved. For both foreign and domestic consumption, Grey maintained that 'It was not a question of the policy of the Government; what made a nation most likely to take part in war was not policy or interest, but sentiment . . .'.[55] In reality, so closely were British interests, in Grey's view of them, bound up with the making and maintenance of the ententes, that *policy* required her to go to war, irrespective of the prevailing public sentiment. Interests were interests. They did not suddenly cease to be interests. The introduction here of a public opinion which would support only defensive wars, when it was notoriously difficult to identify the provocative party, and when the possibility of manipulating, or giving a lead to, public opinion, had long been acknowledged,[56] was as spurious as the distinction between diplomatic and military support. Grey's concern to deprecate an aggressive and chauvinistic spirit in France, which was first brought to his attention in February 1912,[57] sprang from his conviction that France and Russia could not be left in the lurch, and from his anticipation of the difficulties he would have to face in persuading his colleagues, and that the Government might then have in persuading the country, that this was so. As it was, in his treatment of this aspect Grey left a loophole for public opinion that may not have been fully appreciated at the time. Cambon's statement of the position, read out by Grey to the Cabinet on 15 November 1911, included the sentence:

If France were to place herself in the wrong, and were to attack Germany or wilfully break off the negotiations, British public opinion, *in any case at the outset*, would not be on the side of France, and the British Government would not be able to assist France at the commencement, *whatever they might do later*.[58]

Grey would, no doubt, on *any* occasion requiring in his view British intervention in a continental war, have experienced difficulties with some of his cabinet colleagues. As a Foreign Secretary who by February 1906 had 'made it an object to maintain the entente with France', who in September 1906 made it clear that if the entente was broken up he must go, he would, no doubt, have had to threaten, as he did in August 1914, to break up the Liberal Cabinet.[59] The odds, however, were substantially the same as on that occasion. He would never have had the support of Loreburn or Morley.[60] But in 1908, when he contemplated a German ultimatum to France and a cabinet decision to support France,[61] as in 1906, he would have had that of John Burns, who resigned in 1914. He would also have had the support of McKenna, which was missing in 1911, if not that of Lloyd George and of Churchill, which was forthcoming in 1911.[62] In 1906, 1908, and 1911 he would have had the advantage of the connection of the dispute with the Anglo-French Agreement, in addition to the issue of Belgian neutrality.[63] There is no reason to doubt that the outcome would have been different, on any of these occasions, from what it was in 1914.

Where interests dictated, there was no freedom. Britain was not committed by obligations, published, secret or moral, but by what her interests were thought to be. So long as the reasons why the ententes were made continued to apply, Britain was committed to France and Russia. The British were being flattered, and were flattering themselves, when they were assured, and allowed themselves to repeat, and in some cases even to believe, that they were in this respect different from the continental Powers; when they heard, for instance, that it was accepted in Paris that 'La France marchera s'il y a un cas d'alliance; l'Angleterre marchera si c'est dans l'intérêt de sa politique générale',[64] and when they pretended there was a distinction here that meant something and could be sustained in practice. Both the French and the Russians were sure of the course Britain would follow if war broke out. Pichon said at the beginning of 1909 that it was not conceivable that England would not be on the same side as France in the prevailing political conditions.[65] Bertie recorded in 1914 that all French ministries had 'the conviction that in the event of war between France and Germany, England would be bound in her own interest to support France lest she be crushed'.[66] They simply wished, in their efforts to secure 'quelque chose de plus palpable', to be more sure, and to keep the British up to the mark. In their view, an alliance was the logical step. Sazonov believed 'une nécessité inexorable' would drive the British to take an active part in a war against Germany. As part of this 'inexorable necessity', he himself was ready to threaten that English neutrality would be equivalent to her suicide; this he did on 24 July 1914. His Ambassador in London, Benckendorff, added that it was because this inexorable necessity was recognised by the British that the latter saw no need to conclude an alliance: 'On sait que de toutes façons, si les choses vont au pire, il faudra marcher.'[67]

The Entente with France and Russia *was* England's 'politique générale'. She might counsel concessions upon them, and advise restraint, but there were limits to which she could do so which were easily reached. During the Agadir crisis, one official wrote that he did not like 'the prospect of the French realising it is they who have to keep the ogre quiet, for this may cause a rift in our entente'; Bertie came to London to tell the politicians that 'if we do not abstain from counselling concessions we shall render France suspicious and may throw her into the arms of Germany'.[68] In September 1911 Grey wrote to Goschen: 'I daren't press the French more about the Congo. If I do so we may eventually get the odium in France for an unpopular concession and the whole entente may go.'[69] In early 1914 Cambon's point, that French public opinion would be shocked into raising the cry of 'Perfide Albion' if the Anglo-German Agreement of 1898 came to its notice, was enough to stop in its tracks Grey's proposed revision of these arrangements for the future of the Portuguese colonies.[70]

Fundamentally, if her friends marched, Britain had to march also. She could try to dissuade unfriendly Powers from war only by pointing out that any war would in all probability quickly become a general one, and by threatening them, in terms not always obscure, with her own participation in it and against them. But if on any occasion before 1914 any of the continental Great Powers had chosen not to negotiate, not to back down, but to press matters to extremes, Sir Edward Grey would have had to admit, as his advisers did, that the initiative lay with the Powers most immediately concerned;[71] that when it came to matters which these Powers considered vital, Britain had no power to influence them, no influence even over the policies of her friends such as her relations with them were supposed, and certainly desired, to provide; that Britain was no longer master of her fate.

Rosebery's 'mournful and supreme conviction' of August 1904 that the Agreement with France was 'much more likely to lead to complication than to peace' proved all too accurate a forecast, and in more senses than his frst biographer was prepared to admit.[72] Participation in a great European war was the price Britain paid for 'the policy of the Entente'. This price could have been paid at any time. It was paid not over Casablanca, or Scutari, but over Sarajevo. It was paid in the form of casualty returns.

On 3 December 1912 Sir Arthur Nicolson drew the attention of Goschen to a phrase used recently by Count Lichnowsky to Grey. The German Ambassador had said that Britain belonged to no special group and was in a neutral position. Nicolson wished that this remark 'had been taken up a little more sharply than it was, as I cannot help feeling it was thrown out as a feeler, and as it was passed over as of no importance I am afraid Lichnowsky may have reported back that it was practically acquiesced in'. Nicolson's fears were premature. On the very day on which he wrote, the day following the speech to the Reichstag in which the German Chancellor had declared that if in the course of securing her vital interests Austria were attacked Germany would 'step firmly on to her side and would fight' to preserve her own position in Europe, Haldane had called on Lichnowsky and told him:

Under no circumstances could England tolerate the overthrow of the French . . . England could not afford after a French defeat to face a homogeneous Continental group under the leadership of a single Power, nor did she intend to do so. Should Germany therefore be drawn into the quarrel by Austria and thus come to blows with France, currents would arise in England which no Government could withstand . . .

Grey himself saw Lichnowsky on 4 December. The latter still tried to hold to the distinction that Germany had an alliance, and was therefore more closely tied than was Britain. He was told that the words used by the Chancellor 'did not apply only to the question of an Alliance, but to what the interests of a country might require'. Grey then repeated that if Austria, Russia, Germany and France were involved in war, 'no one could tell what further developments might follow'. Lichnowsky's report of his conversation with Haldane reached the Kaiser only on 8 December. The Kaiser took Haldane's words as 'a moral declaration of war', and immediately summoned a conference of his chief military and naval advisers.[73] Haldane's *démarche* gave impetus to a process which was already in train, as indicated by the speeches of Bethmann-Hollweg on 2 December and of Kiderlen on 28 November, within German governing circles. It precipitated the German decisions not to shirk what was now regarded as 'the final struggle between Slav and Teuton', actively to contemplate an 'energetic' Austrian treatment of the Serbian problem, despite the now even more distinct likelihood that this would result in a war difficult to localise; and the associated decisions to prepare new Army and Navy Bills, to seek allies wherever they could be found, and to prepare the German nation psychologically for a war against Russia, to accustom it beforehand to the idea that Germany's national interests would be involved if a war were to break out over an Austro-Serbian conflict.[74] Bethmann, who had not been present at the meeting on 8 December, and who maintained that Haldane's disclosure 'was not all that serious', that it 'merely reflected what we have long known', nevertheless for the first time gave the impression that he had accustomed himself to the idea of such a war, and did not dispute the necessity for a degree of psychological preparation.[75]

The British 'clarification of the situation' had one other result. In the conference on 8 December the Kaiser declared: 'The possibility mentioned by the Chief of the Admiralty Staff in his last audience of a war with Russia alone cannot now, *after Haldane's statement*, be taken into account.' On 1 April 1913, the 'great plan of operations for the east', which had hitherto been revised annually, was discontinued. Only the Schlieffen Plan remained. The impossibility of respecting the neutrality of Belgium was thus rendered absolute.[76]

224158

6

〰〰〰〰〰〰〰〰〰〰〰〰〰〰〰〰〰〰〰〰〰〰〰〰〰〰〰〰〰〰〰〰〰〰〰〰

The Invention of Germany

The picture of Imperial Germany drawn from certain comments made by most of the permanent officials at the British Foreign Office and by many representatives abroad in the decade before 1914 has survived, in effect, to this day. It was not a flattering one. According to Sir Charles Hardinge, Permanent Under Secretary from 1906 to 1910, it was 'generally recognised that Germany is the one disturbing factor owing to her ambitious schemes for a "Weltpolitik" and for a naval as well as a military supremacy in Europe'; in November 1909 he described her as 'the only aggressive Power in Europe'.[1] What she wanted was 'a free hand for the Continent'. This she would use 'to consolidate her supremacy in Europe'.[2] Sir Arthur Nicolson, who succeeded Hardinge, similarly maintained that 'the ultimate aims of Germany surely are, without doubt, to obtain the preponderance on the continent of Europe, and when she is strong enough, [to] enter on a contest with us for maritime supremacy'.[3] Sir William Tyrrell, who acted from 1907 to 1915 as Private Secretary to Sir Edward Grey, the Foreign Secretary, declared at the height of the Agadir crisis of 1911: 'What she wants is the hegemony of Europe.'[4] One of the Assistant Under Secretaries, Crowe, made it clear that by 'hegemony' was understood no less than the elimination of the independence of the other Powers – the removal of their capacity to pursue foreign policies independent of the dictates of Berlin.[5] Good relations with Germany, in his view, were to be had 'by any Power with which she is afraid to go to war, and by no other'.[6] Sir Cecil Spring-Rice had written from Tehran in 1910 that Germany was 'little short of a common enemy'.[7]

The essential accuracy of this picture has to a considerable extent been confirmed by the impression received of the conduct of Germany in July and August 1914. Nevertheless, it is the purpose of this chapter to suggest that the picture merits re-examination. For it does contain, as it stands, a number of questionable features. It is not entirely without internal contradictions. It does not take account of all the evidence available. Nor is it

100

consistent with major aspects of the international situation at the time, which it has been all too easy to assume that it reflects.

Looked at objectively, some of the claims made about Germany were so remarkable as to be quite hysterical. Consider, for instance, Crowe's assertion of March 1913: 'The French are convinced that when the German Government talks of a Franco-German understanding, they mean an understanding directed against England. We on our part know that underlying Germany's plan of an Anglo-German understanding, is the idea of making common cause against France.'[8] This bears a family resemblance to the impression left upon the Lord Chancellor, Loreburn, by Grey's own defence of his policies; for it seemed to Loreburn that 'Grey ... is firmly convinced that if France is not supported against Germany she would join with her and the rest of Europe in an attack upon us'.[9] Similarly, just as Goschen, then Ambassador in Vienna, had in 1907 been afraid of the consequences of emphasising Germany's comparative isolation, maintaining that 'Wilhelm II will feel that we are driving him into a corner and that he may get sick of it', so Grey in 1909 implied that Germany, if she were thoroughly isolated, might actually run amok: one of the extreme things that would produce conflict, he told the House of Commons, 'is an attempt by us to isolate Germany'.[10] Perhaps the most striking position of all, however, was that adopted by Hardinge in May 1911. Writing to Goschen, by then in Berlin, from the vantage-point of the Viceroyalty of India, he said of the Germans: 'What they want is to get some arrangement with us by which our hands are tied for a few years, and then to have a go at France, Italy, Russia, and perhaps Austria.'[11] Without hindsight, these predictions would cross the threshold of the absurd.

An examination of the context in which they were made renders them in many respects no less ridiculous. In mid-1905 Crowe, who was then a relatively junior official, commenced the writing of a memorandum on the Present State of British Relations with France and Germany.[12] This memorandum, which emerged from the Foreign Office printers on 1 January 1907, has been elevated by many historians to the status of a State Paper. It was in fact no such thing. It has also gained a reputation for being 'anti-German', as correctly identifying, several years ahead of the event of the Great War, the eventual, even inevitable, antagonist. In view of the fact that Lascelles, the then Ambassador in Berlin and a man whom Crowe regarded as far too pro-German, did not regard the Crowe memorandum as being 'anti-German', this description can hardly be allowed to stand.[13] The Crowe memorandum is in fact a most curious, confused and self-contradictory piece of work. Despite dealing in the first pages with the German moves which culminated in the resignation of

Delcassé, the French Foreign Minister, in June 1905, Crowe remained, albeit with a discernible effort, non-committal in argument if not in tone. He put forward two alternative hypotheses:

Either Germany is definitely aiming at a general political hegemony and maritime ascendancy, threatening the independence of her neighbours and ultimately the existence of England; or Germany, free from any such clear-cut ambition, and thinking for the present merely of using her legitimate position and influence as one of the leading Powers in the council of nations, is seeking to promote her foreign commerce, spread the benefits of German culture, extend the scope of her national energies, and create fresh German interests all over the world wherever and whenever a peaceful opportunity offers, leaving it to an uncertain future to decide whether the occurrence of great changes in the world may not some day assign to Germany a larger share of direct political action over regimes not now a part of her dominions, without that violation of the established rights of other countries which would be involved in any such action under existing political conditions.

Crowe was himself unable to decide between his two hypotheses. He solved this problem by contending that there was no actual necessity to make a definite choice:

For it is clear that the second scheme (of semi-independent evolution, not entirely unaided by statecraft) may at any stage merge into the first, or conscious-design scheme. Moreover, if ever the evolution scheme should come to be realised, the position thereby accruing to Germany would obviously constitute as formidable a menace to the rest of the world as would be presented by any deliberate conquest of a similar position by 'malice aforethought'.[14]

Yet Crowe had already effectively acquitted the Germans under both charges. Under the first charge, that Germany was consciously aiming at the establishment of hegemony first in Europe and eventually in the world, he pointed out an 'obvious flaw' in the argument:

If the German design were so far-reaching and deeply thought-out . . . then it ought to be clear to the meanest German understanding that its success must depend very materially on England's remaining blind to it, and being kept in good humour until the moment arrived for striking the blow fatal to her power. It would be not merely worth Germany's while, it would be her imperative duty, pending the development of her forces, to win and retain England's friendship by every means in her power. No candid critic could say that this elementary strategical rule had been even remotely followed hitherto by the German Government.

He supplemented this with a paragraph on a recent article by Dr Hans Delbrück, who had concluded that unless Germany wished to expose herself to the same overwhelming combinations which had ruined earlier French dreams of a universal ascendancy, she must renounce all such thoughts. Crowe's own conclusion was that Delbrück's article was itself evidence 'that the design attributed by other nations to Germany has been, and perhaps is still being, cherished in some indeterminate way by influential classes, including, perhaps, the Government itself, but that responsible statesmen must be well aware of the practical impossibility of carrying it out'.[15]

The second charge, that 'Germany does not really know what she is driving at', that there was in reality no great German design, but merely 'vague, confused and impractical statesmanship, not fully realising its own drift', was described by Crowe as a hypothesis so unflattering to the German Government that that very fact might be urged against its validity. It was valid only if a German statesman could be found who was unwise enough as not to recognise the extent to which the world would be set at defiance by the simultaneous combination of the edifice of Pan-Germanism, a German maritime supremacy, an assault on the Monroe doctrine, the creation of a German India in Asia Minor and a German conquest of Constantinople and the countries between Germany's existing frontiers and the Bosphorus.[16]

At the time when Crowe was putting the finishing touches to his memorandum Hardinge was discovered to hold the views that Germany was sincerely anxious to be on friendly terms with England, and that an agreement might be made with her on the basis of her acceptance of the entente with France.[17] By Hardinge's own admission of 1912, it was not until 1907, when he accompanied the King and talked to the Kaiser and Bulow at Wilhelmshohe, that he realised that it was impossible to come to any terms whatsoever with Germany, whose 'real aim and intention' was then revealed as 'to have a go at us on the first opportunity . . .'.[18] In 1908, writing to Lascelles, he still made no mention of *European* designs on Germany's part: 'When one comes to think that, as the Germans admit, their navy is being built at very great sacrifices in order to impose their will, it is quite conclusive to us that it is only upon us that they wish that their will should be imposed, for their fleet [*sic*] is already strong enough to impose it on other Powers.'[19] At the same time Cartwright complained from Munich only that Germany was doing her very utmost 'to disturb the status quo *at sea*, not in the direction of the maintenance of peace, but in that of the continuance of a permanent threat of war'. It was not until late 1909 that he wrote of the danger which might come 'to us *and to others* from an all-powerful Germany'.[20] It took Germany's intervention between Austria and Russia following the former's annexation of Bosnia and Hercegovina to dispel from Nicolson's mind any doubt that 'the ultimate aims of Germany' were 'to obtain the preponderance on the continent of Europe'.[21] Spring-Rice had spent much of the year 1904 advocating a *rapprochement* with Germany, later his 'common enemy'.[22]

Crowe's memorandum of 1 January 1907 had attempted, according to its author, to deal with 'all the ascertained facts' of German foreign policy. This it did not do. On the one hand, there was no consideration of what might be called the Egyptian lever, and only one mention of Egypt; whilst another official, in a memorandum on Anglo-German relations 1892–1904 dated 5 January 1905, had pointed out that the attitude of Germany towards this most vital concern of Britain's had been 'on the whole, correct'.[23] On the other hand, Crowe made no play with the preambles or texts of the German Navy Laws of 1898 and 1900. Facts, moreover, were capable of being ascertained quite differently. They were by no means the exclusive preserve of certain Foreign Office officials. Spencer Wilkinson, for instance, chief leader-writer on the *Morning Post* on international affairs and naval matters, who was amongst other things Crowe's brother-in-law, thought that Germany had been perfectly entitled to challenge Britain's 'gift' of Morocco to France in 1904 which had produced the crisis of 1905–6. Writing in 1909, he went on to say: 'I am aware of no (great and manifest) wrong actually attempted (by Germany).' This included German support of Austria-Hungary over the annexation of Bosnia-Hercegovina in 1908: 'he would be a rash man who, on now looking back, would assert that in either case a British Government would have been justified in armed opposition to Germany's policy'. Clearly some of Spencer Wilkinson's brother-in-law's colleagues were rash men. It also included Germany's attempt to remove British maritime supremacy. Wilkinson denied that Germany's policy was such that Russia, France and Italy were each and all of them desirous to oppose it, and to assert a will and policy of their own distinct from that of the German Government.[24]

Above all, all the hostile claims about and portrayals of Germany, at whatever point they were made, ignored the salient facts of the years in question. These were that there was no balance of power on the European continent, that the military power of Germany and Austria far outweighed that of all the other Powers and that the main characteristic of German policy was in these circumstances its *restraint*. At the turn of the century the Kaiser had said: 'Lord Salisbury is obsessed with the balance of power in Europe; there is no balance of power except me and my thirty Army Corps.'[25] He may not have been right about Lord Salisbury; he was certainly right about his Army Corps. He went on to point out the simple fact of geography for which, again, the received picture of Germany made no allowance: 'We simply *are* Central Europe, and it is quite natural that other and smaller nations should tend towards us and should be drawn into our sphere of action owing to the law of gravity.'[26] Despite the Franco-German crises over Morocco of 1905, 1908, and 1911, and despite the Russo-German crisis of 1909, Germany did nothing to justify the attribution to her of extreme aims. She took no steps to convert her undoubted ascendancy into unwanted supremacy, to *exercise* her admitted superiority. Throughout a period when it was widely recognised that France in particular and Europe in general was at her mercy,[27] the really striking things – which became salient facts of the formulation of British foreign policy in their own right – are that Germany was given no credit for foregoing opportunities to implement the aims imputed to her, and that her failure to capitalise on circumstances favourable to such aims produced no reconsideration or re-assessment of her objectives. The revelation of features that inhibited progress towards them was not allowed to inhibit the propagation of the German purpose. The information received in August 1911 from the leader of the German Socialist Party, August Bebel, to the effect that the German economy could only withstand a sixteen-day war, apparently made no difference to those who received it.[28] German proposals for British neutrality in a continental war, which occupied the years 1909 to 1912, were taken literally, as giving away what the German game was. That the Germans might be playing another game, less obvious than the one they made no effort to conceal, was a possibility that was not explored. There was a rare acknowledgement of forebearance on Germany's part by the Military Attaché in Belgium in March 1906. To those more strategically placed than N. W. Barnardiston what the Germans had made no attempts to realise remained her 'ultimate' aims and ambitions.[29]

The Germans denied that they had any intention of going to war with Britain, with France, or with anyone. There was no reason why such denials should have been taken at face value. But was there any reason for going so far beyond scepticism as the Foreign Office went? Surely 'the German menace' rested on more secure foundations than what Crowe called 'the vague and undefined schemes of Teutonic expansion ("die Ausbreitung des deutschen Volkstums")' or than the 'Imperial apothegms' to which the Kaiser was inclined?[30] Surely it was more than the product of the reverse of an argument that the British applied to themselves as regards conscription: was Germany's possession of both an Army and a Navy enough to identify her as an aggressive power? The Germans themselves could not be certain that they would not be attacked by Britain, despite British assurances. Even Crowe believed Germany had a perfect right to build as large a Fleet as she considered necessary or desirable for the defence of her national interests.[31] Surely it was based on something more substantial than an idea of which Grey was rather fond – that nations wanted to go to war roughly every forty years?[32]

It would, of course, be one thing to say that the Foreign Office simply, and genuinely, mistook German policy. That would not be outside the bounds of possibility. The occupants of high office and of high official positions have, after all, no monopoly of wisdom. They are statesmen only by virtue of the fact that they occupy certain positions, and not necessarily by any other criterion. They are not infallible, though few of them admit this so charmingly as did Lord Halifax, who, when asked by an American historian during the Second World War if he didn't regret the Munich agreement, replied: 'Oh well, if you don't make one mistake, you make another.'[33]

It would be quite another thing to maintain that elements of the British Foreign Office, and the Foreign Secretary, *deliberately* mistook the aims and objectives of Germany, and credited her with intentions they did not believe her to possess. Yet towards this conclusion much more than the lack of correspondence between the presentation of Germany as a threat to Europe and the extent to which her behaviour justified it inexorably points.

The fact of British naval superiority over Germany and the confidence of the British in their ability to maintain it did not cause their reaction to the German naval challenge to be any less strident. In October 1906 Hardinge admitted that there was no immediate naval threat to Britain from Germany. He pointed out that the Admiralty was proposing a concentration of its forces for defensive purposes 'against an attack which is not likely to be made for some years to come'.[34] Admiral Sir A. K. Wilson went even further. Commenting in May 1907 on current Admiralty War Plans he remarked, of the case of a purely Anglo-German conflict, that 'it was difficult to see how such a war could arise', and that 'neither country would have much opportunity of doing the other any vital injury'.[35] Grey himself noted in November 1907 that the Germans were 'a long way behind' in dreadnoughts: 'We shall have 7 Dreadnoughts afloat, before they have one, without our laying down any more. In 1910 they will have 4 to our 7, but between now and then there is plenty of time to lay down new ones if they do so.'[36] In February 1908 the Foreign Office received the Annual Report on the German Navy for 1907, drawn up by Captain Dumas, the Naval Attaché. One of the facts to which he drew attention was that the German naval authorities 'at present greatly dread the power and aims of England'. This was not lost on Crowe, whose summary pointed out 'the important fact that for the next 3 or 4 years Germany will be practically unable to begin a war with England owing to the backward state of the necessary preparations'.[37] In November 1908 Grey wrote in euphoric terms: 'We were the only Power against whom Germany could invent even a fiction about attack without being completely ridiculous, and of course we had not the least intention of attacking her. She could invent such a fiction about us only because we were the one Power that was out of her reach.'[38] The fact was that the Foreign Office knew that the German Navy posed no insurmountable threat to British superiority at sea; that the risk of invasion, as distinct from raids, was minute; that the Germany were more afraid of attack by Britain and of a British strike against the German Navy than vice versa.[39] And yet, in the middle of this period of security rendered even more secure by the fact that the Germans continued to supply the steel of which British dreadnoughts were being built, Grey was not beyond or above identifying himself with the inculcated views of the man in the street, to whom it seemed, he said, that 'with 21 of the most aggressive vessels in the world concentrated at Wilhelmshaven and looking straight at our shores, there was a risk of invasion should there be any unfortunate turn in the relations between this country and Germany'. He complained to the German Ambassador that 'it might also be noticed that lectures were given in Berlin, publicly, the subject of which was how to invade England'.[40] In April 1908, a few weeks after noting that the risk of invasion was 'too great for the Germans to run it in cold blood', and always would be so long as Britain had 'sufficient superiority of Navy', Grey raised with the visiting and ingenuous Canadian, Mackenzie King, the spectre of a German attempt to conquer England: 'We must not allow (Germany) to get in the position where she could ever dominate us . . . Once she could land an army on this island she could devast [sic] England . . . that means the end of the Empire.'[41] This was, no doubt, one way of soliciting contributions from the Dominions to British sea power, sparing both the taxpayer and the social order. In the following August Grey wished to place before the Cabinet a report from Colonel Trench, the Military Attaché to the Berlin Embassy, which he avowedly regarded as alarmist; this ploy would, he said, serve 'as an antidote for those who only hear or believe in the soft side of German opinion'. Asquith was neither enthusiastic nor impressed. In his view, 'German opinion may be "mobilised", but they know quite well that, so far as we are the objective, they cannot for a long time to come get within striking distance.' Grey's idea was not pursued.[42] (Hardinge, for his part, was not unprepared to make some play with the fact that what purported to be full German plans for an invasion of Britain had, supposedly, been left on a train by, supposedly, a German Staff Officer travelling through France, and handed in to the authorities.[43] Such carelessness, of course, even if it had actually occurred, did not argue that the Germans were not serious, but Hardinge can hardly have been so unsophisticated as to equate plans with intention. All General Staffs made plans. It was their raison d'être. In August 1905 Sir George Clarke, the then Secretary of the Committee of Imperial Defence, had asked the Prime Minister for permission to put the General Staff to work on the problem of Belgian neutrality: 'It would give them useful occupation', he said.[44] Had Hardinge known of the Admiralty's plan for the fighting of a war against Germany and the United States in combination, he would hardly have inferred that the British Admiralty was eager to start such a war.)

Thus far, Germany stood guilty until proven innocent, on two counts. 'Painting the German devil on the wall' was a job at which the Foreign Office were busy in several other respects and with quite different motivation from the one referred to by Spring-Rice when he used this graphic phrase.[45]

No one reading Crowe's memorandum of 1 January 1907 would have gathered that Anglo-German rivalry was *not* the dominant feature of the decades he reviewed, and that avoiding German blackmail was *not* the first priority of the policy of entente with France and Russia pursued by Lansdowne and Grey. In this sense, the memorandum was distinctly unbalanced. Sanderson felt it necessary to emerge from retirement to point out the context in which German demands had been made and met. The fact was that German opposition 'would have been very inconvenient when we had Russia with France at her back in antagonism to us . . . '.[46] Grey, who had understudied Rosebery in the 1890s, stated several times that during the years when there was supposed to be an Anglo-German entente, Germany had taken toll of England when it suited her. There had indeed been constant friction:

It was not very comfortable, even so far as Germany was concerned; *but as regards Russia and France, the situation was very much worse.* The diplomatic atmosphere between ourselves and Russia and France in those years was such that the least incident in any part of the world, whether the Russian seizure of Port Arthur, the Russian action on the Pamirs on the Indian frontier, or French action in Siam – the least incident of that kind – at once excited the press of both countries, and there were rumours of wars more than once.[47]

In June 1909 he recounted to Goschen how 'before 1904 we had constantly been on the brink of war with either France or Russia; for instance, when I was at the Foreign Office in 1893, we had been thought to be on the brink of war with France about Siam; soon after that, there had been talk of war with Russia about Port Arthur . . . '.[48] The 'friendly understanding' with the Triple Alliance, he told C. P. Scott of the *Manchester Guardian* in November 1911, had not prevented trouble on either side: 'Germany was exacting and troublesome and we were repeatedly on the brink of war with France and Russia.'[49] To be on 'the brink of war' with two Great Powers was rather more serious than to find one other Power, which could other-

wise be disregarded, merely 'exacting and troublesome'. It was the operation against Great Britain of the Franco-Russian Alliance, of which Grey
had had personal experience, which had left an indelible impression upon
him. It was a repetition of that experience that he was determined to avoid.
A letter to Leo Maxse in November 1901 reveals what his priorities were
at that time: 'The first practical point is to establish confidence and direct
relations with Russia and to eliminate in that quarter the German broker,
who keeps England and Russia apart and levies a constant commission
upon us, while preventing us from doing any business with Russia.' Grey
went on to suggest, moreover, that German 'brokerage' or blackmail was
less thoroughgoing than Crowe, for one, was later to make out:

I expect the plea of the German Government is that, though public opinion forces
them to be rough and uncivil in the Reichstag and though they drive hard bargains
where they have direct interests, yet where we are interested, as in Egypt, they have
given us quiet backing or not molested us. There is some truth in this, but it is a
position, which was never comfortable for us and is becoming daily less comfortable and secure; the business of the British Govt. is to bring about a better one and
the first step is an understanding with Russia.[50]

German demands were certainly more endurable than poor relations,
verging on war, with France and especially Russia. Grey was being less
than fair when he remarked to Campbell-Bannerman in September 1907
that 'if the Germans succeed in detaching France from us we shall soon get
the rough side of German diplomacy again'.[51] Britain would also have got
the rough side of French and Russian diplomacy, which would have been
even rougher than that of Germany. This was why Grey supported
Lansdowne's policy, and wished to continue and to complete it. Those in
the Foreign Office whom Spring-Rice overheard early in 1902 talking 'as
if we had but one enemy in the world and that Germany', were being
totally unrealistic unless they were referring, as they probably were, to
Germany's determined efforts to keep Britain on bad terms with the
Franco-Russian Alliance. Two cabinet ministers give the lie to Spring-
Rice's informants: St John Brodrick in April 1903 was clearly contemplating Britain's being 'seriously set upon by France and Russia'; Arnold-
Foster wrote to Lansdowne in the following December: 'Our people are
weary of war. Russia is an enemy, Germany is an enemy, France is an
enemy by Treaty if not by conviction.'[52] Grey lapsed on one occasion in
1912 into saying that he had always felt that the German policy of political
blackmail was the real reason for the change of British policy since the
1890s.[53] It may, with the help of the line taken by the German press during
the Boer War, have turned the British people against Germany; it did not,
and could not, turn Germany into a greater menace to the British Empire
than Russia was, or than Russia and France were.

Nor did the German Fleet really revolutionise international politics to the extent claimed by Spring-Rice at the time and by certain historians subsequently.[54] Once Germany possessed a Fleet British Foreign Secretaries could no longer treat Germany as they wished to treat her, as Lord Kimberley had treated her in October 1894 over Delagoa Bay, as a *quantité négligéable*.[55] Grey was quite correct in saying that 'if the German fleet were once strong enough to challenge ours, we should be continually having to choose between war and diplomatic humiliation'.[56] Not only would 'our very independence depend on Germany's goodwill,' but Germany's increased potential for blackmail might lead the British to revert to the 'concessionary policy' of the last years of Lord Salisbury which so many F.O. officials so deeply deplored. It was most unlikely, however, that German naval power would ever achieve parity with, never mind superiority over, British and Imperial naval power. The necessity to choose between war and diplomatic humiliation was a problem that could clearly be solved by British naval building, as the 'We Want Eight' crisis of 1909 demonstrated. What British naval building could not ensure was that the only diplomatic situation in which German 'blackmail' could hope to prosper would not recur: the alienation from Britain of France and Russia.

Late in 1904 Lord Selborne, the First Lord of the Admiralty, explained to Balfour that the reason why the Germans could keep their Fleet concentrated at its two home ports was that 'the only object aimed at by German naval policy is to have a fleet of battleships which might intervene with decisive effect on one side or the other during a war in which England was engaged with France and Russia'. In January 1905 his colleague Austen Chamberlain gave his understanding that the strength and composition of the German Navy had been

officially justified on the ground that, though obviously insufficient to obtain victory single-handed, it would, in the event of war between our two countries, leave our fleet so weakened as to be unable to face the probable combination of other Powers against us, whilst if we were actually engaged in war with such a combination, it would enable Germany to throw a decisive weight into the scales and to impose terms of peace upon us.[57]

This was not unlike the position which some officials took. Bertie, the Ambassador in Paris, said in June 1904: 'We have nothing to fear from Germany if we remain on good terms with France. (Germany) cannot without the active support of a naval Power such as France injure us.' The following year he said that he was afraid that 'if we were engaged in war with another Power Germany with a largely increased naval force might turn the scale against us'.[58] Hardinge's opinion of 1908 was that 'the

German fleet is intended not to invade us but to put pressure on us at a critical moment, when we are involved in difficulties elsewhere'. Nicolson, in 1910, agreed: 'Of course (Germany) does not wish to go to war with us. But I would not venture to assert that, when she considers the moment favourable, she would not be prepared to go to war if we were without friends and were still recalcitrant to her demands.'[59]

In other words, there already was a premium, so far as the British were concerned, on good relations with France and Russia. All the German Fleet did was to increase this premium. Yet by December 1909 Cartwright was taking it as 'self-evident' that Britain drew closer to France and Russia 'as an insurance against the growing danger which might come to us and to others from an all-powerful Germany'! That the ententes were in response to the German Navy was an impression Grey also sometimes gave.[60] Moreover, by consistently omitting, when they quoted the German Navy Law, the words 'to protect Germany's sea trade and colonies', by concentrating instead on the words that followed – 'Germany must possess a fleet of such strength that a war with her would shake the position of even the mightiest Naval Power' – the Foreign Office converted the German Navy into a device designed to secure British neutrality in a continental war.[61]

Nor was the claim that an isolated Germany would run amok all that it appeared to be. Commencing in July 1908 and lasting into 1912 a number of suggestions emanated from the ranks of British diplomats to the effect that the evident dissatisfaction of Austria and Italy with the Triple Alliance might be taken advantage of to detach either or both of them away from it. All these suggestions were strongly resisted by Grey. He consistently opposed any interference between Germany and either of her allies. He entirely disapproved of anything that would expose Britain to the charge of attempting to isolate Germany.[62] When the idea of encouraging Austria to 'cast aside' German influence was first elaborated Grey shared the reaction of Spicer, who asked:

Would this policy not be fraught with considerable danger? The balance of power in Europe would be completely upset and Germany left without even her nominal allies. Is it not more than likely that she would consider this humiliating position intolerable and risk everything in defence of her honour, dragging Europe into what would be the most terrible war in all history?

It was quite true, Grey maintained, 'that an attempt to isolate Germany by setting Austria against her might precipitate a conflict'.[63] Again in February 1909 he seconded Spicer's opinion that if Austrian relations with France, Russia and Britain were cemented, it 'might easily bring about a very dangerous situation, for if Germany is deserted by the only ally on whom she feels able to depend, she will be quite certain to regard this as the final link in the "EinKreisung" policy of Great Britain, and may then be seriously tempted to resort to the fortunes of war to burst through the iron ring encircling her . . . '.[64]

The Germans were certainly very concerned not to appear to be isolated. Articles in the *Cologne Gazette* and *Neue Freie Presse* at the time of King Edward's meeting with the King of Italy at Gaeta in April 1907, for instance, which had suggested that it was Edward's intention to isolate and humiliate Germany, had produced a fall of six points in German securities on the Bourse, and a general feeling in Berlin that war was imminent. Grey and Hardinge were much relieved when the King's visit to Rome in 1909 did not produce the same reaction.[65] German 'nervosity' at this time, however, reflected her fear that she would be attacked, rather than any disposition on her part to make an attack. Moreover, the British had known since at least February 1907 precisely how tenuous was Italy's connection with the Triple Alliance, having been told of the Franco-Italian Agreement of 1902 under which Italy had agreed not to join in any German attack upon France.[66] Although they did not know the actual stipulations of the Triple Alliance, and did not receive until October 1911 the text of the Barrère–Prinetti exchange of 1902, the position of Italy in the Triple Alliance was so anomalous that Crowe in January 1909 thought it could be assumed 'that Italy is unlikely in the highest degree to consent to take part in any hostilities directed against either England or France'.[67] In April 1909 he found it 'somewhat remarkable that Germany and Austria should be so anxious to retain Italy in the alliance, because they can hardly be unaware of Italy's resolve not to join in any war against either France or Russia if such a war was to find her opposed also to England'.[68] Hardinge conceded later in the year that the Germans and Austrians would not count on Italy's help in a continental war: 'The Triple Alliance is useful to Germany and Austria simply because it prevents Italy joining a coalition against them.'[69] In these circumstances it is even less likely that Germany would have run amok if effectively deprived of Austria too, than it is that she would have done so if suddenly confronted with an alliance of the Entente Powers against her.

The British wished to see the Triple Alliance remain as it was for quite other reasons. It was in an unstable condition. Italy, because of her long coastline, was and would always be dependent on the goodwill of France and England. From their point of view, it was 'all to the good that Italy remain in the Triple Alliance and be a source of weakness'.[70] If she were detached, she would be 'rather a thorn in the side than any assistance to France and ourselves'.[71] The British, at least, had responsibilities enough. Moreover, were the Triple Alliance denounced, it might be expected that the Germans would make every effort to re-establish the DreiKaiserBund. This was a possibility that was particularly exercising Hardinge in March and April 1909. His fear was that Isvolsky might yield to German dictation, 'should Germany demand that Russian foreign policy should in the future come within the Austro-German orbit'.[72] The DreiKaiserBund would have, it was feared, the effect it was believed always to have had – it would free Russia from Balkan concerns and allow her to resume the Imperial struggle with Britain which the latter had admitted was one that she could not win.[73] Any alleviation of Austro-Russian difficulties would have had the same effect. It was no good Cartwright's suggesting that Britain put herself forward as the Power through whom such a *rapprochement* might be brought about, in order to end the tradition that it could only be accomplished through Berlin. It was not in the interests of Britain that there should be any such *rapprochement*.[74] Rivalry between Count A. L. von Aehrenthal and Isvolsky, as Hardinge admitted, was 'considerably to our advantage'.[75] It also helped to maintain bad relations between Germany and Russia which, again, were 'very much to our advantage'.[76] It fulfilled Hardinge's forecast of October 1907 that Russia and Germany would not find it easy to work together in the Near East.[77] The possibility that Austria was capable of pursuing a policy independent of Germany, and desired to do so, as Cartwright frequently indicated, was therefore not admissible. The Foreign Office, with the initial exception of Tyrrell, continued to treat the two as indivisible, and for 'Vienna' always to read 'Berlin'.[78] It was for these reasons that Sir R. Rodd's tentative proposal of October 1911 that England try to formulate an agreement with Italy similar to that between Italy and France really received the short shrift it did; it was for these reasons, and not simply because Austria showed all the signs of being 'a star that may dissolve', that Grey was determined to keep his distance, and not to change his course.[79]

Similarly, the Foreign Office treated the undoubted and sustained efforts of German diplomacy to split the Triple Entente into its constituent parts as a way of furthering the establishment of German hegemony in Europe. The sort of political agreement proposed by Kiderlen in April and pursued by Bethmann-Hollweg from September 1909 would, said Grey, 'serve to establish German hegemony in Europe . . . '. The duration of such an agreement, wrote Hardinge, 'would be strenuously employed by Germany to consolidate her supremacy in Europe'. Others wrote to the same effect.[80] They appeared to overlook the possibility that Germany could wish to see the ententes disappear without also wishing to pursue an aggressive policy on the continent of Europe. For one thing, in the absence of the ententes, Germany would be restored to a position from which she could take advantage of British differences with France and Russia to renew her pressure for British concessions. Germany was given none of the benefit of the doubt in this matter because what the British were really afraid of was the 'immediate isolation' that would result from any Anglo-German political agreement or from the doubts that this would cast upon the degree of their commitment to supporting France and Russia.[81]

It was all very well Nicolson's insisting, in January 1913, of German efforts that he detected to detach Britain from her friends: ' – the object is obvious: we should from every point of view be in a most parlous position, as would international peace, were such efforts to be successful'. When Tyrrell wrote, during the Agadir crisis, that the 'real inwardness' of this German move was 'to test the Anglo-French entente. It should be viewed from that point of view alone! Everything else is a side-issue on this occasion ... What she wants is the hegemony of Europe', he too was trying to have it both ways.[82] The fact was, as Nicolson admitted in February 1911, that 'we are not strong enough to stand alone'.[83] If the ententes disappeared, international peace would have been in a much less parlous position than Great Britain herself. That Europe would be obliged to look to Germany, as Grey put it,[84] was by no means so clear as that Britain would be forced to look to herself. That the isolation of England – 'the isolation of England attempted by any great Continental Power so as to dominate and dictate the policy of the Continent' – would produce German hegemony, that each European Power would 'inevitably have to submit to German dictation',[85] was first to invent motives and then to exaggerate the ease with which they could be accomplished. If the Germans had attempted to reduce the European Powers singly, as in one of Hardinge's predictions, what became of the combination of the rest, as Crowe, following Delbrück, had outlined in his memorandum of 1 January 1907, for instance? Nor would the Germans have found it as easy to create a continental coalition against England as Grey pretended they would have found it. They were credited with trying, and failing, to do this on at least one occasion.[86] The British were fully aware that the Treaty of Frankfurt and to a certain extent the person of Clemenceau, who in July 1905 had told Mallet that France would not be bribed into being embroiled with Britain even by the offer of the return of Lorraine, remained obstacles to the very best Franco-German relations.[87] In the circumstances it was rather more realistic to presume, as Hardinge did in May 1909, that Germany would merely ask France and Russia for a guarantee of their neutrality in the event of a war between Germany and England. Only the active support and participation of France and Russia, however, would increase Germany's chances of success in such a war. And

Hardinge was quite confident that, so long as Britain maintained 'an undoubted supremacy at sea', she could cope with Germany alone.[88]

Without the ententes, it was not that Europe would have been more vulnerable to Germany. It was that Britain would have been vulnerable to everyone. What was really at stake in their preservation was the fate of the British Empire at the hands, in the first place, of France and especially of Russia.

That the power of Germany frightened and overawed her neighbours in Europe was only to be expected. The British Foreign Office, however, embellished the clumsiness of German diplomacy that merely represented in many cases her nervousness and anxiety and sense of *amour propre* and legitimate grievance to such an extent that they effectively invented for her designs of a hegemonial character upon Europe. They did so because 'the German menace' served to conceal British weakness. It served to divert attention from the British Empire's vulnerability and to rivet it upon Germany. It provided the ententes, which had been made because Britain was unable any longer to maintain unaided her position in the world against the competition which she faced, with a more respectable *raison d'être* than that of merely trying desperately to hang on to what she had. In this connection, even the German Navy came to the aid of the British. For by playing to Britain's only strength, it helped to reduce, if not by any means to solve, their problem of convincing France and Russia of why they should support, or not take advantage of, a Power whose agreements with them had shown could not support itself. As Nicolson wrote from St Petersburg: 'If doubts became prevalent here that our supremacy on our own element were in serious danger, our value as friends would rapidly depreciate.'[89] Both the naval and the British card, however, were played for far more than they were worth. 'It must be remembered', claimed Hardinge, 'that the one obstacle to German hegemony in Europe has been the strength and independence of the British navy'; 'the Germans quite realise that the British fleet may . . . be a deciding factor in the situation, and they would consequently like to neutralise our position'; 'England, it is fully realised, is the one Power capable of offering . . . effectual resistance to the realisation of any such ambitious schemes.' According to Crowe, in 1909, 'so long as the British navy is strong enough to defeat the German, Germany is unlikely to contemplate the acquisition of Holland . . . '. According to another official in 1911, it was a fact that 'this country is the only one sufficiently strong to prevent the German will being imposed on all other European Powers'. This was a stance to which the officials continued to adhere, despite the recognition by some of them, in lucid intervals, that Britain's military contribution to the sort of European war that was predicted would be of infinitesimal proportions. Hardinge continued to adhere to it despite the demonstration which he witnessed at the proceedings of the C.I.D. sub-committee on the Military Needs of the Empire that British naval aid to France would be both too little and too late. Bertie, when Caillaux maintained in November 1911 that the furnishing of 156,000 British troops would not have been enough to enable France to reject German demands over Morocco, offered the French Premier the solace that the British Fleet could protect France from German attack by sea. Caillaux's retort was: 'So could mines and submarines.'[90]

The propositions that the prospect of British intervention in a continental war deterred the Germans from embarking upon one, and that Britain's refusal to commit herself to neutrality secured the peace of Europe were, as a group of Grey's opponents within the Cabinet recognised,[91] absurd. So was the proposition that Germany, because she was afraid of losing her colonies, her sea-borne commerce, and even her Navy, in the course of a struggle which nevertheless resulted in the achievement of what was supposed to be her main aim, hegemony, should forego that aim – all the more so as she could be expected to recoup many of these losses in kind at the expense of the vanquished. So was the proposition that the delay in attempting to implement German hegemony was due, as Hardinge once put it, to the fact that she was 'not strong enough to be absolutely certain of coping successfully with France on land and with England at sea'.[92] This obscured the question of whether Germany wanted to go to war with France or with England, or with both simultaneously.

The British stance made only inverted, contorted and perverted sense. The only common denominator of the nonsensical propositions was the enormous credit reflected upon Britain. It was because the British needed this credit so badly that they leapt to the conclusions they did, in the absence, or directly contrary to, the evidence, and turned the whole situation upside down, in which position it made the only sense that it could make. In order for Britain to be 'the only Power who can resist the achievement (of German hegemony)' Germany had to be aiming at this.[93] Britain, and the British Navy in particular, could not be deterrents unless there was something to deter. Therefore the Germans had to have certain designs. German denials that they ever possessed 'such ambitions and such fantastic aims';[94] German expressions of opinion that, even had they done so, they would not have regarded Britain as in any way an obstacle to their achievement, had to be treated as false. As a matter of fact, the German General Staff consistently refused to alter what they considered their major plans of operations in the case of a war of Germany against France and England to cater even for large-scale landings of British troops on the

German or Danish coasts. The furthest H. von Moltke went in this direction was to admit, in March 1907, that it would be 'unwelcome' for the Army if the English achieved unrestricted naval mastery in the North Sea soon after the start of a war, and had as a result the possibility of transporting troops in chosen directions. The view he expressed in 1911, that 'in any future war, whether it be between Germany and England or between Germany and France, the outcome will be decided on land', was by no means a state secret.[95] Because of this also, there was more to the British attitude than mere suspicion and circumspection.

The British stance was one which *necessarily* excluded a number of obvious things. It excluded any emphasis such as was placed by Sanderson in 1905 on the difficulties facing the German Government and on the very real restraints on Germany's pursuit either of Weltpolitik or of European hegemony. Sanderson wrote:

Before they went to war with France they purchased the neutrality of Russia by promising to accept a modification of the Black Sea articles of the Treaty of 1856. At the end of the war they forced upon France a frontier which de Courcel told me, and I believe with truth, that no French statesman or general could accept as a permanent and satisfactory settlement. The subject is mentioned as little as possible either in France or Germany, but it is the skeleton always present in the cupboard. Since that time German commerce has enormously increased and the German Government have been driven by popular aspirations into various Colonial acquisitions. Their naval inferiority is therefore now a serious matter not to be ignored. They are confronted with a Russo-French Alliance; the Triple Alliance is less effective than it was: Austria is weaker from internal dissensions, and is working with Russia in the Balkans, Italy from financial and other reasons has made friends with France; and we have followed suit. It is true that France shows no sign of an aggressive disposition, but she has obstinately refused to be reconciled to her loss of territory . . . [It] seems to me that quite irrespective of Colonial ambition Germany must feel it necessary to increase her navy and that unless she can feel sure that we will not at some untoward moment throw ourselves on the side of France, she must as a matter of precaution cultivate the goodwill of Russia far more than it is convenient for her to do.[96]

Bertie, who in November 1901 had pointed out that in Europe Germany found herself surrounded by other states,[97] never subsequently drew attention to this.

The British stance also necessarily excluded any admission that the Germans might be content with their European position, which their persistence in building a Navy at the expense of their Army which increased in size by only 30,000 men between 1893 and 1912 might have been taken as indicating, since it had been so taken by Lord Selborne in 1903 and 1904.[98] It necessarily excluded any recognition that the Germans might wish, as a result of the diplomatic revolution which a neutrality agreement with Britain would produce, simply to improve the prospects for German Weltpolitik.[99] It necessarily excluded all doubts, and all doubters (amongst whom was the Minister for War, Haldane, with whom Grey was on more intimate terms than with anyone else in the Cabinet) that German intentions were aggressive in nature.

The outbreak of war, of course, only confirmed those who had maintained this stance in the error of their ways. The incorrigible Hardinge, for instance, wrote to Grey in 1915:

I often think of the five years I spent with you at the F.O. and wonder if any mistake was then made in our policy, and if anything we might then have done could have possibly staved off this war. I think not. It seems as though there can be no doubt that the careful preparation for war was then in full swing, and that the ideal of German hegemony in Europe and of worldwide domination had already sunk too deep into the convictions of the governing class in Germany to make it possible that war should be averted. Everything points to this now, though to some it may have been obscure in the past.[100]

The invention of Germany, for this is what, on the part of many advisers and takers of advice, it amounted to, fulfilled important psychological needs. The more unflattering the portrayal of Germany, the more flattering that of Great Britain. The greater the menace of Germany, the better able were some people to persuade themselves that they had a role to play. The picture which many at the Foreign Office had of themselves depended on their picture of Germany. Portraying Germany as they did was the only way for them to restore their self-respect. For Britain's international position in the period of the ententes fell far short of what, in the eyes of most of them, it might have been. The ideals of Bertie, for instance, of remaining 'the country holding the balance between the Dual and Triple Alliances', and of maintaining 'our liberty to pursue a British world policy', were quite unrealised.[101] Britain was able to pursue a world policy at all only as a result of her alignment with France and Russia, which entailed the same consequences of embroilment in European affairs as had once caused Bertie to argue against an alliance with Germany. When Tyrrell in 1913 gave the impression that 'we can now snap our fingers both at the Triple Alliance and at France and Russia', he was, essentially, reverting to type. His distaste for the 'stupid and demoralising policy' of 'relying on other nations to fight our battles' momentarily got the better of his judgement. The ideal got in the way of the reality.[102] Britain's international position also fell far short of what it was fondly imagined to have been in the past. This image emerged from the woodshed clearly at the outbreak of the Great War. It was put best – or worst – in the leader written for *The Times* of 6 August 1914 by Valentine Chirol, once of the Foreign Office.

His version of events was that the British people was drawing its collective sword in 'the old cause':

that once again, in the words which King William inscribed upon his standard, they will 'maintain the liberties of Europe'. It is the cause for which Wellington fought at the Peninsula and Nelson at Trafalgar; the cause which saw its crowning triumph on the field of Waterloo. It is the cause in which Oliver's Ironsides and their French comrades beat the finest infantry of Spain, and for which Drake and Howard of Effingham routed the Armada – the cause of the weak against the strong, of the small peoples against their overweening neighbours, of law against brute force, of the Commonwealth of Europe against the domination of the sword.

It was a measure of Hardinge's desperation and determination to be playing a role of such significance that he should make the wholly untenable assertion that 'the one obstacle to German hegemony in Europe has been the strength and independence of the British Navy, a fact fully realised in Germany *at the time of the Boer War . . .* '.[103] It was a measure of Nicolson's anxiety to achieve continuity with the heroic past that he should say that, although Britain had, before 1900, been on bad terms with France and Russia and been inclined to shape her course with that of the Triple Alliance, nevertheless, 'our policy had not changed – it was the same which had existed for centuries – Great Britain had always been and was still in favour of maintaining the equilibrium in Europe'.[104] It was a measure of the extent to which this desire had got out of control that Crowe in July 1914 should maintain that Britain had to engage in the war, otherwise 'the general principle on which our whole foreign policy has hitherto been declared to rest would stand proclaimed as an empty futility . . . A balance of power cannot be maintained by a State that is incapable of fighting and consequently carried no weight.'[105] With this the wheel came full and vicious circle.

Grey and his officials used their image of the past as a model for the present. Germany was tailored to suit the role the British needed to play in order to be able to live with themselves. This process was encouraged by the relative immunity of the British Isles to direct German attack, and by the concentration of naval force in the North Sea which could be taken as portending the situation in which the last and indubitable bid for hegemony had resulted.[106] In an attack on the Foreign Office in November 1911 Noel Buxton M.P. drew attention to 'the feeling prevalent in the official world that the Kaiser is some danger to the world – that he is in fact the modern Napoleon Buonaparte'. Earlier that year Grey had told the Dominion Prime Ministers the truism that 'If Germany was to use her strength . . . to obtain the dominating Napoleonic position in Europe, then I think there would be trouble'; in August 1914 he told the Cabinet:

'German policy is that of the great European aggressor, as bad as Napoleon.'[107] By turning their minds back a hundred years, by identifying William II with Napoleon I, the Foreign Office and their chief were able to continue in the great tradition to which they felt they ought to belong. The invention of Germany was an indispensable part of the projection of Britain.

7

<oooooooooooooooooooooooooooooooooooooooooooooooooooooooooooo>

The Military Entente with France

In November 1914 the Historical Section of the Committee of Imperial Defence produced a 'Report on the Opening of the War'. In his notes towards this Report Julian Corbett maintained that 'our arrangements with the French Naval and Military Staff . . . fettered our freedom of action', with the result that 'our Army . . . became committed as an integral part of the allied line, and we had to forego all the advantages of operating independently on a line of our own and at our own selected moment, in order to break into the German scheme after it had developed'.[1]

Corbett's position is now widely shared. John Terraine has spoken of 'the binding force' of the British Government's commitment to a pre-arranged plan.[2] Paul Guinn has said that when the crisis of continental war arose in the summer of 1914, 'no resistance could avail against the long-matured General Staff preparations'; and Samuel Williamson that the continuance of the staff talks assured the primacy of the strategy of continental intervention, that 'the staff talks . . . were responsible for British presence on the western front'.[3] Nicholas d'Ombrain, in the course of demonstrating emphatically that the C.I.D. failed to operate as a centre for strategic planning, has held that as a result of this failure, 'the Government discovered in 1914 that its imagined freedom of choice had been jeopardised'.[4]

All the above writers have closely connected the sending of the British Expeditionary Force to France and the kind of strategy which resulted from this with the pre-war conversations between the British and French General Staffs and the arrangements which these bodies made. They all imply that these arrangements not only had a momentum of their own which caused them to be put into action in August 1914, but also that they constituted in some way an obligation on the British Government. A re-examination of questions associated with the military conversations will show that British plans were more flexible than has been thought, and that the real motive for dispatching the B.E.F. was of a kind not hitherto given its due weight.

The question of obligation will be addressed first. In April 1911 Sir Edward Grey provided the following justification for, and account of the origins of, the military conversations:

Early in 1906 the French said to us, 'Will you help us if there is war with Germany?' We said, 'We can't promise, our hands must be free.' The French then urged that the military authorities should be allowed to exchange views, ours to say what they could do, the French to say how they would like it done, if we did side with France. Otherwise, as the French urged, even if we decided to support France, on the outbreak of war we shouldn't be able to do it effectively. We agreed to this.[5]

Having dodged in this manner the 'great question' of whether, in the event of German aggression against France, Great Britain would be prepared to render France armed assistance,[6] the British Government continued studiously to reserve its freedom of action. Despite continued contacts between the British and French military authorities, the Government rigorously maintained, as did the sub-committee of the C.I.D. on the Military Needs of the Empire in its Report of July 1909, that the expediency of sending a military force abroad or of relying on naval means alone was a *matter of policy* which could only be determined when the occasion arose by the Government of the day, as distinct from an *obligation*.[7] The primacy of *policy* was stressed again in November 1911, when Asquith pointed out that 'all questions of policy have been and must be reserved' for the decision of the Cabinet and that it was 'quite outside the function of military or naval officers to prejudge' such questions. It was formally embodied in the cabinet resolutions of that month.[8] It was also included in Grey's letter to Cambon of 22 November 1912, which was quite as much the work of the Cabinet as of Grey himself, and in the course of the formulation of which a phrase suggested by Cambon, which would have had the effect of binding the two Governments, if they decided to cooperate in war, to carry out the plans made by the General Staffs, was rejected.[9] In March 1913, when Lord Hugh Cecil asserted in the House of Commons that there was a widespread belief that Britain was under an obligation to send a large armed force out of the country to operate in Europe, Asquith interrupted to deny categorically that this was the case. As he explained to Grey, such a challenge was one that he could not ignore.[10] Although Paul Cambon dwelt on the unfortunate effects of what Asquith had said, the Ambassador admitted that the Prime Minister's statement was true.[11] Sir Henry Wilson, who as Director of Military Operations had done more than anyone to further the cause of military planning with the French, got the impression from this incident that the Cabinet had decided *not* to help the French on land. Although he called them 'Cowards, Blackguards, and

Fools', he did not dispute that they were free to decide whether or not to aid France in this way.[12] Even the optimistic Isvolsky had had to point out from Paris the difference between the Franco-Russian Convention and the Anglo-French 'accords' – that the latter, being signed only by the General Staffs, were for that reason not 'obligatoire pour le Gouvernement'; and it indicates the little regard in which what had been done was held on the part of the French authorities, whatever 'hopes' they might have entertained, that Bertie in June 1913 was still receiving feelers and picking up hints 'that there ought to be something definite to rely on'.[13]

If there was no legal obligation, was there nonetheless a moral obligation? Esher held that 'the mere fact of the War Office plan having been worked out in detail with the French General Staff has certainly committed us to fight, whether the Cabinet likes it or not'; 'Of course there is no treaty or convention, but how we can get out of the commitments of the General Staff with honour, I cannot understand.'[14] McKenna thought so too: he told Asquith in October 1911 that 'so long as conversations were carried on between the General Staffs, the danger (of British troops being used in France) existed'.[15] Sir William Nicholson, the C.I.G.S. from 1908 to 1912, would also appear to have thought so: he wondered in December 1911 whether Henry Wilson's and Churchill's alternative proposal for the allocation of the Expeditionary Force would be acceptable to France; when first faced with this proposal he had said that he did not condemn it in the abstract, 'but we have to consider our available military forces and the secret discussions we have had with the French military authorities'.[16] Grey certainly thought the French were entitled to some return on their expectations. In September 1911 he did not deny that an expectation of support existed. Nor did he see how such an expectation could have been avoided, or how it could be prevented in the future.[17] Although he seconded Asquith in November 1911, when the Prime Minister said that the French Government recognised that there was no legal obligation, Grey, according to Hobhouse, clearly regarded the communications between experts which had already taken place 'as committing us to cooperation with France, if her action had been non-provocative and reasonable'.[18] According to Loreburn's recollection Grey had said at this time, regarding the secrecy of the military conversations: 'I always said we ought to be fair to the Cabinet.'[19] And that the Foreign Secretary had actually encouraged French expectations of support, which may account to some extent for his attack of conscience, is clear from Sir Arthur Nicolson's protest to him in August 1914 that 'you have over and over again promised M. Cambon that if Germany was the aggressor you would stand by France', and from his reply: 'Yes, but he has nothing in writing.'[20]

On the other hand Asquith, according to Hobhouse, emphasised that, despite what had transpired between the French and British experts before November 1911, 'he still felt himself quite free, under any circumstances, free to refuse cooperation'.[21] And Haldane, who had over the years been more closely associated with the staff talks than any other minister, appears to have shared Asquith's view. For in August 1914 he told Lansdowne that it was

clearly recognised that our liability to send out the Expeditionary Force was one to which we could not be expected to give effect except in circumstances which enabled us to do so without incurring too serious a risk. *If* there was an implied engagement, it was quite a different one from that implied in the arrangement under which France had undertaken to keep her Fleet in the Mediterranean on the understanding that ours was concentrated in the North Sea.[22]

Conceptions of honour, and assessments of the extent to which it was engaged, clearly varied. It was indeed something for each minister to look into his heart and determine, which is what Grey invited the members of the House of Commons to do on 3 August 1914. Those ministers who believed there *was* a moral obligation would undoubtedly have been on stronger ground if, as Esher wrote at one point, 'by naval and military conventions entered into with our friends and allies, not perhaps specifically, but by inference and assumption, we are pledged to definite acts of war upon which the plans of other nations turn'.[23] However, this was not so. Joffre, the Chief of the French General Staff, told his War Board in April 1913 that, because London 'wanted to make no engagement in writing ... we will thus act prudently in not depending upon English forces in our operational projects'.[24] The constant caveats that the *Governments* were not committed by plans for joint action worked out by the General Staffs had had their effect. Very little was made of Esher's consideration at the British War Council of 5 August 1914. As it was, those ministers who were opposed to the use of the B.E.F. on the continent, and those who were inclined to believe that the conversations which only came to their attention in the aftermath of the C.I.D. meeting of 23 August 1911 had committed Britain 'partially', were alike reassured by the cabinet resolutions of November 1911 and the letter to Cambon of November 1912, which they took as restoring the situation by cancelling any incipient moral obligations, and as safeguarding the future.[25] As for Grey, the expectations which he shared and encouraged were the product of more than simply the staff conversations. Those of which he wrote as early as February 1906 had not built up just since January 1906, when the conversations had first been authorised.[26] They dated from April 1904, if not July 1903; from the beginning of the policy of the Entente, and they grew as it lasted.

The premise upon which the plans of both the War Office and the Admiralty for giving armed support to the French were based was that without such support the French would be defeated by the Germans. General Ewart, Wilson's predecessor as Director of Military Operations, cast his reflections upon France early in 1909 in the following way:

The course of events in recent years has altered the balance of power in Europe once again and, as in the past, our foreign policy aims at redressing the inequality by supporting the weaker side. The chief weakness of our potential allies lies in a doubt as to the ability of one of them to withstand the military forces of the stronger group until the military strength of their partner can be brought to bear, or until the slow, if perhaps sure, pressure of sea power can take effect.[27]

Wilson, two years later, was more direct: 'In the case of our remaining neutral Germany will fight France single-handed. The armies of Germany and the fleets of Germany are much superior to those of France, and the results of such a war can scarcely be doubted . . . It follows that in a single-handed war France would in all human probability be defeated . . . '.[28]

Both Admiralty and War Office agreed with the maxim that the best way to win campaigns was to have decisive numbers at the decisive place at the decisive time. Their solutions to the problem of relieving pressure on the French Army were geared either to the achieving of superior numbers for the Entente against the Germans or the obverse of this – the engineering of inferior numbers for the Germans against the *French*. As Churchill put it apropos military intervention: 'The reason for sending a British army either to France or Belgium is to secure, either by addition to the French or by subtraction from the German force, a preponderance of strength on the decisive front at the decisive moment.'[29] The 'decisive point' was defined by Henry Wilson as 'the point where the German and French armies met for a decision'.[30]

Asquith opened the War Council of 5 August 1914 with these words: 'The situation was not unlike one which had constantly been considered, but with regard to which no decision had ever been reached.'[31] What he meant was that no particular one of the plans put forward for saving the French had formally been decided upon. This was strictly correct. However, by that time the strategic option originally proposed by the Admiralty was, for a number of reasons, no longer available.

On two occasions before the war the alternative schemes of the Admiralty and the General Staff for providing the French with armed support had been examined on their merits. The first of these was provided by a sub-committee of the Committee of Imperial Defence called by Asquith in October 1908 to consider circumstances in which the British

Army might be called upon to operate either alone or with other Powers.[32] At the meetings of this sub-committee the Admiralty proved most reluctant to reveal its intentions. It did emerge, however, from an outburst on the part of Sir John Fisher, the First Sea Lord, at the first meeting on 3 December 1908, that he considered that the British Army should be restricted to operations consisting of sudden descents on the German coasts, the recovery of Heligoland and the garrisoning of Antwerp. He went on to speak of 'ten miles of hard sand on the Pomeranian coast which is only ninety miles from Berlin. Were the British Army to seize and entrench that strip, a million Germans would find occupation.'[33] His preference was evidently for such coastal operations: he wrote to Esher in March 1909 that he had been studying one 'of inestimable value only involving 5,000 men and some guns, and horses about 500 – a mere fleabite! but a collection of these fleabites would make Wilhelm scratch himself with fury!'.[34] The sub-committee, however, accepted the General Staff's view that 'no relief could be given to the armies of France by any threat by the British Army to make a descent on the coast of Germany, since the latter Power has ample troops both for watching its own coasts and for an attack on France, and those detailed on the former service would not in any case be used for active operations'. It also considered that such economic pressure as would be exerted by a blockade of Germany would not be felt 'sufficiently soon to save France' if she was attacked in overwhelming force. Consequently, the General Staff plan was considered by the sub-committee to be the more valuable one, and the schemes of the Admiralty were, in McKenna's words, 'discarded'.[35]

The second occasion was in the course of the Agadir crisis of 1911. Nervous, and unsure about Germany's real intentions, the Government called a meeting, although not a full one, of the Committee of Imperial Defence, for 23 August. This was, in Major A. Grant-Duff's words, 'to settle their plans in case of the worst'. At this time the Admiralty revealed that it had failed to improve on the idea of 'fleabites': Imperial Germany was still expected to scratch herself to death. Both McKenna and Sir Arthur Wilson, Fisher's successor, spoke unconvincingly of a close blockade of the whole German North Sea coast, and of one division of the British Army embarked in transports and taking part in operations against Wilhelmshaven and Heligoland, Bremerhaven and Cuxhaven, in this way retaining 10 German divisions on the coast and away from the main theatre of war, and thereby making a material contribution to the Allied cause.[36] They were thoroughly routed by the Army, Sir William Nicholson gaining his revenge for Fisher's having in 1908 called the dispatch of British troops to the front in a continental war 'an act of suicidal idiocy' by demonstrating that the class of operations envisaged by the Admiralty was not only anachronistic and 'doomed to failure' but, in his considered opinion, 'madness'.[37]

In the aftermath of this meeting Asquith could not avoid saying that 'Sir A. Wilson's "plan" can only be described as puerile, and I have dismissed it at once as wholly impracticable. The impression left on me, after consideration of the whole discussion . . . is that, in principle, the General Staff scheme is the only alternative . . . '.[38] Under pressure from Haldane, which included a threat to resign, for a modernisation of the Admiralty which would create an institution which would in future cooperate more readily with the War Office, the Prime Minister in October moved Churchill there from the Home Office, and converted the principle into practice.[39] Sir Henry Wilson saw Churchill on 21 November 1911 and recorded afterwards: 'He will play in with us [i.e. the W.O.] all he can . . . '.[40] Churchill himself wrote to Haldane on 8 January 1912: 'Now let us at once begin the transport arrangements. They have hung fire since September.'[41] Moreover, in Churchill's time there, the Admiralty substituted an observational blockade of the German coast for a close blockade. As a result they removed themselves from a position from which they could have launched any combined operations in that area.[42]

These developments since 1908, together with the fact that the premise on which all planning was based was no less strong, and the consciousness of it more widespread – as indicated by Churchill's and Lloyd George's questions at the session of 23 August 1911 about the likelihood of a French defeat – meant that in 1914 the Government effectively had only the alternatives provided by the War Office to turn to.

In conversation with Esher on 4 October 1911, Asquith, whilst condemning the Admiralty's proposals and disclosing his own reluctance to see more than four divisions of the British Army dispatched to France, said that he still wanted 'the Belgium plan' to be 'worked out'.[43] He was referring to the scheme presented by the General Staff to the 1908–9 sub-committee. This scheme admitted of the deflection of the British Army across the French frontier to the right of the Belgian Army. It also remarked that 'If . . . before we were actually committed to French soil, it became evident that Germany intended to disregard the neutrality of Belgium and Luxembourg, the question arises whether we could not give more assistance to France and the common cause by landing our expeditionary force in northern Belgium, and by operating thence against the flank of the German advance.' Such action, it was thought, would have the advantage of directly covering Antwerp. The General Staff gave preference to a plan in which 'the British force shall be concentrated in rear of the left of the French army, primarily as a reserve', and it was this plan which the sub-committee described as a valuable one, and of which it concluded that all the necessary details should be worked out. The General Staff, however, had gone on to say that the possibility of the British force's being called upon to cover Antwerp had not been lost sight of, and that plans would also be worked out for landings in Belgium with a view to this operation.[44]

d'Ombrain, for one, has claimed that after this reference to it, the Belgian scheme was ignored. This, however, is far from being the case. For one thing, a war game was played at the Staff College in November 1910 and selected papers from this, under the heading 'Belgian Scheme', were forwarded to the Directorate of Military Operations, by request, early the following year.[45] Historians have concentrated upon the development of the 'W.F.' scheme, which d'Ombrain, probably correctly, interprets as shorthand for 'With France'. ('W.F.' was certainly not shorthand for 'Wilson-Foch': filed under this title in the Public Record Office index to D.M.O. material there is a memorandum of 30 June 1911 on the progress of the scheme for the dispatch of the Expeditionary Force *to the Continent* over the last six months in which Major Gorton says that the scheme 'first known as the W.F. scheme and afterwards as E2.11' was originated in 1905 by General Grierson at the time of the Moroccan 'imbroglio'.)[46] It has not been appreciated that there was also a 'With Belgium' scheme. This was not allocated any initials, nor was any great amount of separate planning done upon it. Both were unnecessary. For the 'Belgian' scheme was to a large extent interchangeable with the 'W.F.' scheme. It was an option available to the British Army once it had disembarked at French ports, and it was an option that was still available in August 1914. Had it been taken up, the course of the war would not have been the same.

In their plans to save the French from defeat the General Staff had, from the outset, to contend with a number of imponderables. They did not know, when they began, whether they would be involved in a war with Germany in defence of Belgian neutrality, or in a war between Germany and France. If in the latter, they did not know whether the neutrality of Belgium would be maintained or whether it would be violated by Germany, nor, if it was violated, to what extent or at what point in the war: whether the Germans would confine their operations to the area south of the river Meuse or whether they would deploy to both north and south of that obstacle; whether the Germans would invade Belgium at the start of a Franco-German war or at some later stage in the course of such a war. They did not know how the Dutch would react to a violation of their territory that a German advance north of the Meuse would involve, nor what effect a closure of the Scheldt might have upon the safety of Antwerp. They did not know what the attitude of the Belgians themselves would be to any violation of Belgium, whether confined to the country south of the Meuse or not. They had also to consider the extra-European situation.[47]

Matters were advanced somewhat by the sub-committee of 1908–9 taking the view that 'the decision of the question of whether Great Britain should intervene on behalf of France cannot . . . be left to turn on the mere point of violation of Belgian neutrality'.[48] But the General Staff remained unable to fix the 'decisive place' and the 'decisive time' with any precision. Captain Ommanney criticised Grant-Duff's memorandum of January 1907 for stopping short 'at the most interesting and vital point which is whether [British troops] should be employed in France or Belgium'.[49] In July 1908 Grant-Duff was saying that the decisive point of the struggle would be 'where the main armies of France (or the Allies) and of Germany met': 'it would be wisest to concentrate all that we can in that theatre of war in which our small force can earliest make themselves felt. That theatre is France or Belgium . . . '.[50] Henry Wilson's definition of this, in September 1911, was 'either in, or in the neighbourhood of, the Ardennes'. As a result of his own extensive fieldwork on the geography of the Franco-German frontier he had become convinced that the main German effort would be made through the 90 mile gap between Verdun and Maubeuge. He believed, and continued to believe, that Germany would not move north of the Meuse.[51]

Because of, rather than despite, these imponderables, the schemes produced by the War Office advocated and contained a degree of flexibility. They met the General Staff's self-imposed requirement of November 1908 that 'We have . . . in considering what military measures we might take, if it were necessary to give aid to either France or Belgium . . . so to frame our plans that they may be capable of instant modification during the first days of mobilisation, should the developments of the situation demand it.'[52] In this they were helped by a fact to which the General Staff drew attention in April 1907, namely 'That the same set of railway lines from Calais, Boulogne, and Havre would lead British forces disembarking at these ports equally to the French left or the Belgian right.'[53]

Although a poor opinion of the state of the Belgian Army and reservations about whether the Belgian Government would actively defend its country against invasion had helped the War Office to prefer the scheme it did in late 1908,[54] the Directorate of Military Operations in Sir Henry Wilson's time was fully alive to the value to England and France of a positive attitude on the part of the minor states of the Low Countries. In conversation with the French Military Attaché in March 1911 Wilson had considered a German violation of Belgium as certain, and revealed that he counted on the four divisions of the Belgian Army.[55] In April, in a note for the C.I.G.S., he stated: 'It would possibly, and indeed probably, change the whole course of the campaign if the Belgians could be induced to put their fortresses of Liège and Namur into a better state of defence and if they would trust more to their field army and less to their fortress of Antwerp.'[56] Wilson needed no prompting to discuss with Churchill the value to Britain and France of a Belgium actively hostile to Germany, and in reply to the latter's question at the end of August 1911, 'What should be our foreign policy, speaking of course from the military point of view?', he replied:

My opinion is that, for the single and specific case of an unwarranted attack by Germany on France or an attempt by Germany to seize or absorb Belgium, England and France should have an offensive and defensive alliance and in this Belgium would join . . . Denmark ought to be brought into it and I take it for granted that Russia is already there.

A Belgium, hostile to Germany, would mean that the line of the Meuse was secure, that the fortresses of Namur and Liège and the work at Huy were impregnable. It would mean an open and friendly country for us to operate in, it would therefore mean a constant and ever increasing menace to the German right flank and the German line of communication; and most important of all, it would mean that the superiority in German numbers could not be brought into play.[57]

Wilson sent a copy of this to his chief, Sir William Nicholson, and in another letter elaborated and defended conclusions which, he said, were the outcome of years of study. Nicholson was unreceptive. The acceptance of the proposal, he claimed, 'would involve a radical change in our scheme for supporting France in the event of that Power being attacked by Germany'. Whilst he appreciated that 'our Expeditionary Force cannot reinforce the left of the French line if it is to be used in Belgium in the manner indicated', he missed Wilson's most important point concerning numbers. This was that from the 'safe' base of northern Belgium 'a force of 8 or 10 divisions could operate on the right flank of the German advance'.[58]

Wilson was not deterred by Nicholson's response. Having on the night of 4 September put his views personally before Sir Edward Grey, and not without effect, on 9 September he impressed on the French Military Attaché, Colonel V. J. M. Huguet, the value of Belgian active support and of Anglo-Belgian operations. Huguet immediately went to see Cambon, and on his return told Wilson what the latter had until then been ignorant of – 'where the French G.S. want us to go and what their plans are'.[59] On the very next day Wilson began to write a long paper on the political and military situation of Europe which Churchill had requested a few days before. In this he maintained that the importance of a Belgium friendly to France and England 'can scarcely be overrated', dwelt at length on the difficulties which would face a German force advancing to the south of the Meuse and Sambre from sudden and surprise attacks of the 'Belgian and English' Armies, and reminded the Government that 'the larger the force detached by the Germans from the decisive point the better it would be for France and ourselves'.[60] The day after he finished this and sent it to the C.I.G.S. the Foreign Office sent Ronald Macleay, who had been selected to go over to Brussels to find out how the land lay, to him for briefing.[61] In October he was convinced that 'we ought to be able to snaffle these Belgians', and put further pressure on Sir Arthur Nicolson for overtures towards them.[62] Huguet was being more than generous, and more loyal to Wilson than the other way round, when he maintained that Wilson remained 'loyal' to joint action with France. It was Nicholson, not Wilson or French, who remained loyal. French, the Commander-in-Chief designate of the British Expeditionary Force, was in September 1911 using the phrases 'on the Belgian frontier' and 'We could put into Belgium' interchangeably.[63] It had not been coincidence but rather the result of what at the very least was ambivalence on the part of Henry Wilson, that the French had provided him when he was in Paris on 29 September with all the relevant information on the concentration areas of the French northern Armies and for the B.E.F.[64] There was, after all, a considerable difference between taking up a position in the triangle Maubeuge–Brussels–Liège (as Churchill was suggesting) or along a line Liège–Givet–Mézières, and concentrating between Arras, St Quentin and Cambrai as in the 'W.F.' scheme.[65]

Henry Wilson's answers to questions posed by Churchill and passed on to him by Nicholson at the end of October 1911 make the position even more clear, and deserve to be quoted in full:

Q.1. What, if any, would be the advantages to be gained from a friendly and allied Belgium and what modifications would it be worth while making in the present plan?

A.1. The advantage would be very great, and if estimated in divisions might amount to the withdrawal of 14 to 16 German divisions from our main theatre. *No great modifications in our present plan would be required.*

Q.2. On what day could an Anglo-Belgian Army be concentrated behind the Liège-Namur line? Could it be concentrated by the 17th day?

A.2. The answers to these questions depend on what day the British and Belgian mobilisations are ordered. If these mobilisations are ordered on the *same day* as those of France and Germany, the Anglo-Belgian Army could be concentrated on the 15th or 16th day, possibly, with good arrangements, by the 14th day.

Q.3. Should it go through Maubeuge or through Lille, or by Ostend and Ghent, or several of them? And what should be the base?

A.4. The British force would enter Belgium from France and not from the Belgian coast. The base would be in France.[66]

Wilson returned to these arguments in April 1912: if Belgium actively opposed Germany, the action of the Armies of the Triple Entente would be at a great advantage; even if Germany seized Liège the use of the Belgian railways could be denied her, and the combined British and Belgian forces would be in a position seriously to harass the German right flank and communications; 'if Belgium is co-belligerent with the British and French armies the freedom of action afforded to the combined British and Belgian forces would probably neutralise the superior German numbers'.[67] He was confident that, if the Belgians called on Britain for help directly their territory was violated, he could put 150,000 men at the decisive point in time. G. T. M. Bridges, the Military Attaché in Brussels, mishandled his approaches along these lines to General H. A. Jungbluth the Belgian Chief of Staff and General V. L. Michel the Belgian War Minister by implying that the British would come whether they were asked or not, and possibly before Belgian territory had been violated. The Foreign Office had to step in to disavow any such intentions.[68]

Wilson still did not consider the Belgian option as closed. In October 1912 he transmitted to Grey through Colonel J. E. B. Seely a minute in which he pointed out the difference to England and the French of the value of a friendly Belgium, which he put at 12 to 16 divisions.[69] And in November 1912 as a result of his insistence that the Belgian position be cleared up Sir John French once more approached the Foreign Office.[70] When at the end of that month he told General de Castelnau that on no account must the French be the first to violate Belgian neutrality, this was still more in the direction of keeping the Belgian option open and reducing Belgian disquiet concerning the entente than it was to do with agreeing with Paris on the treatment of a hostile Belgium.[71] Finally, at the War Council on 5 August 1914, Wilson revealed that a month before he had sent three officers to France: 'They had worked out an alternative scheme [to the standing 'W.F.' scheme] in cooperation with the French General Staff, according to which the British force might concentrate at Amiens, whence they could very easily be despatched in any direction, according as the situation might develop.'[72]

The appreciation that the 'W.F.' scheme was not the only one available may have encouraged Staff Officers, both before the war and at its outbreak, to express differing views as to the best strategy for the Army to adopt.[73] Why, however, in August 1914, when the Belgian scheme was admitted to be still technically feasible, when it had been claimed that it would occupy greater German numbers than six British divisions fighting on the French left[74] and that this difference of between six and 12/16 'may quite easily decide the campaign one way or another',[75] and when the imponderable of the attitude of the Belgians themselves was removed in a favourable sense, was the 'W.F.' scheme preferred?

The decision for war was a *political* decision. It was taken on the ground of the Entente. So far as the maintenance of cabinet unity was concerned there can, as Hazlehurst says, be no doubt about the significance of the Cabinet's decision of 1 August 'that we could not propose to Parliament *at this moment* to send an expeditionary military force to the continent'.[76] J. A. Pease, for example, President of the Board of Education, wrote on 3 August: ' . . . to resign at this moment only adds to the necessity of finding more warlike instruments and colleagues, who may go further than we are prepared to go and might urge our troops being sent abroad and so extend the field of our troubles'.[77] Once the ultimatum to Germany expired, however, Britain and France were both at war with Germany. Then, the sending of the B.E.F. to France was also a political decision. It followed from the first. It too was based on 'the policy of the Entente'.

The sense of the War Councils held on 5 and 6 August 1914 was that four divisions and a cavalry division should be sent to France to await events and to be ready to do as the French wished. This was the view of Sir John French, of Lord Roberts, of Sir Charles Douglas and Sir D. Haig. No decision was taken as to the line of operations, and on 6 August French and Lord Kitchener agreed with Hamilton's suggestion of the 5th that concentration should not be further forward than Amiens.[78] There may have been some military reasons for this decision: to try to join up with the Belgian Army might have involved a flank march – a risky operation; and there was the possibility, raised before and raised now by Haig, of 'defeat in detail'.[79] There was more safety in numbers.

Political considerations, however, were the overriding ones. In the 1908–9 sub-committee both the Foreign Office and the General Staff had stressed the 'moral effect' on the French of the cooperation of English soldiers – what Grant-Duff in July 1908 had called 'the undoubted moral and political effect on the French Army and the French nation of the ocular presence' of a British force in the field. Esher had presumed, correctly as it turned out, that political considerations would govern the sending of some assistance to give 'that moral support upon which stress has been laid'.[80] In August 1911 both Grey and Wilson admitted that the moral value of the B.E.F. was greater than, perhaps double, its material value.[81] And on 2 August 1914, Paul Cambon, in Grey's words, 'dwelt on the moral effect of our sending only two divisions'.[82] The War Councils, attended only by those ministers – Asquith, Grey, Haldane, Churchill – who had most identified themselves with the Entente, had been called to further to the greatest extent possible in the circumstances, the Entente policy. The B.E.F. was sent off because it existed; to France because it was thought the French needed it, because all pre-war planning had been for the sake of the French, and the premise for it that the French would otherwise be defeated; because Britain and France were now in effect allies, because it was acknowledged that naval force alone could not force a decision, and because Grey had said, for instance in April 1907, that, should Britain fight, she would do so with all her resources, naval and military.[83] When the Cabinet heard the War Council's decision it was not disposed to argue. It had, after all, only just survived the decision for war. It had no wish to repeat the process when the outcome was sure to be the same.[84]

When war came there was no obligation on the British Government springing from the military conversations themselves. Nor was the 'French' plan adopted because it was the only one that had been worked out.[85] The existence of a plan, or of plans, was no more decisive than the lack of them had been in November 1908, when Asquith, Grey and Haldane had all been ready to send a force to the continent.[86] The plans only helped, only removed the need to improvise. They did not compel.[87]

What did compel the course of action adopted was the Entente itself, which the conversations were only part of and subsidiary to. Grey himself had always insisted that such obligation as there was resided in the Entente. He had told the House of Commons on 30 March 1911: 'The extent of the obligation to which Great Britain was committed was that expressed or *implied* in the Anglo-French Convention laid before Parliament.'[88] As he told the French, this had been so worded 'as not to convey that the engagement of 1904 might not under certain circumstances be construed to have larger consequences than its strict letter'.[89] Although Grey and the Cabinet had withstood Paul Cambon's attempts of late 1912 to make the conversations binding, Grey had not challenged Cambon's remark of that summer: 'there was nothing but a moral "Entente", which might however be transformed into a formal "Entente" if the two Governments desired, when an occasion arose'.[90]

Britain's military options, then, were reduced to that taken by political considerations. Her freedom of action in August 1914 was prejudiced and curtailed only by the inflexibility of her pre-war foreign policy. If the definition of a healthy foreign policy as one in which there was a real possibility of a change of policy may be allowed to stand, then that of Great Britain had long since become unhealthy. Like all the other Great Powers, Britain had been too much committed, for too long, to a particular policy and to particular Powers. Her military planners had produced alternative schemes within this framework. No provision had been made for an alternative foreign policy.

8

∽∽∽

The Cabinet's Decision for War, 1914

On Sunday 2 August 1914, Asquith received a note from Bonar Law and Lord Lansdowne in which the Conservative leaders offered their 'unhesitating support' to the Government in any measures it might consider necessary for the object of supporting France and Russia. Of this communication Grey wrote in his memoirs: 'The message was first read and then laid aside; it could have no influence on our discussion.'[1] In an article published in 1973 Donald Lammers concluded that 'the state of our information does not justify ascribing a high or determining importance to Conservative statements and actions in connection with the British decision to go to war'. In doing so he added his name to those of Robert Blake, Roy Jenkins, Keith Robbins, Samuel Williamson and Cameron Hazlehurst, who have in his words maintained that 'the Conservative letter counted for almost nothing and the relentless march of events almost everything in the way of changing or settling ministerial minds' in the European crisis of late July and early August 1914.[2]

It is my object here to do the following things: to establish when, and on what grounds, the British decision to take part in the European war was taken; to suggest that the part played by the Tories can be measured only when taken in conjunction with other political factors; to argue that the role of party political considerations was greater than has customarily been maintained; to contend that the argument that the German invasion of Belgium was crucial is one that has been far too readily employed,[3] and that the 'march of events' (which is, in effect, what the argument amounts to) was not by any means as 'dominating' as Churchill at one point forecast that it would be.[4]

As already shown, the Asquith Cabinet contained a majority of ministers who were prepared to purchase peace through concessions to the Power they were encouraged to regard as the most likely disturber of it, Germany; who were suspicious of the connection with France and detested that with Tsarist Russia; and who wanted in no circumstances to see a British Army employed on the continent of Europe. It contained a minority who appreciated that the days of isolationism were over and who believed that the friendship of France and Russia was much more important to Britain and the British Empire than that of Germany would be. The respective numbers of this majority and this minority had been dramatically revealed in the autumn of 1911 when Loreburn, McKenna, Harcourt and Morley were so disturbed by certain developments in the course of the Agadir crisis of that summer that they pressed the Cabinet to a division on two resolutions concerning the content and conduct of foreign policy, and secured a decision in their favour by fifteen votes to five. The five were Grey, Haldane, Churchill, Lloyd George and Asquith. Although Loreburn retired in June 1912 and handed down his leading role in opposition to Edward Grey's foreign policy to the Colonial Secretary, Harcourt, there is no reason to suppose that the balance within the Cabinet altered between late 1911 and July 1914. How was it, then, that Asquith was able to take into a continental war a Cabinet that was united on the decision and depleted only by an elderly Liberal intellectual – Morley – and by the product of an electoral bargain with the Labour Party – Burns?

Enough contemporary material is now available concerning the proceedings of the Cabinet to identify Sunday 2 August as the day when the decision to intervene in the war was made. At the three previous Cabinets those ministers who wished to pursue a policy of non-intervention in the impending European war had been given some reason to think that their cause might prevail. On 29 July, after reviewing British treaty obligations to Belgium and considering the precedent afforded by the behaviour of the Gladstone Government in 1870, the Cabinet decided that 'the matter if it arises will be rather one of policy than of legal obligation'. As the documents seen were interpreted as indicating that Great Britain did have an individual obligation to help Belgium if she was attacked, this was a concession to the 'peace party'.[5] Burns recorded that 'the situation was seriously reviewed from all points of view' and concluded: 'It was decided not to decide.'[6] On 31 July, and following the Cabinet's agreement, in the words of J. A. Pease, President of the Board of Education, to the 'policy' that 'British opinion would not now enable us to support France – a violation of Belgium might alter public opinion, but we could say nothing to commit ourselves', Harcourt pencilled a note for Pease: 'It is now clear that *this* Cabinet will not join in the war.'[7] On 1 August the Cabinet decided against any immediate sending of the British Expeditionary Force to the continent, a decision which, to the surprise of Sir Henry Wilson, was not opposed by the Liberal Imperialists. Asquith, Grey and Haldane had had a private meeting before the Cabinet assembled. It was believed that

Germany might still be induced not to embark on a war with Russia, and at 11.30 a.m. Asquith wrote to the C.I.G.S. saying that army training was not to be suspended, and putting on record the fact that the Government had never promised the French the Expeditionary Force.[8] The Cabinet also forbade Churchill to proceed to the full mobilisation of the Navy, no doubt eliciting the remark that Morley remembered making to the First Lord of the Admiralty: 'We have beaten you after all.'[9] As far as John Burns was concerned, there had still been 'no decision'.[10]

By 8.00 p.m. the following day the decision had been taken. It was to his invitation to the first Cabinet of Sunday 2 August that Walter Runciman later added the legend 'the Cabinet which decided that war with Germany was inevitable'.[11] This meeting lasted from 11.00 a.m. to nearly 2.00 p.m. At it, Grey was authorised to assure the French Ambassador that if the German Fleet came into the Channel or through the North Sea to undertake hostile operations against French coasts or shipping the British Fleet would give all the protection in its power; Burns, maintaining that any such message meant war, announced his retirement.[12] At the second Cabinet, which lasted from 6.30 p.m. to 8.00 p.m., it was agreed that 'it should be made evident that a substantial violation of the neutrality of (Belgium) would place us in the situation contemplated as possible by Mr. Gladstone in 1870, when interference with Belgian independence was held to compel us to take action'; Burns, who had been asked to attend the evening meeting, remained adamant about resigning; Morley, who in the morning session had said that he would resign if Britain went to war, told Asquith as the Cabinet rose that he feared that he, too, must go.[13] Later that evening the Attorney General, Simon, who in the course of an afternoon drive to Battersea in search of Burns had told Pease that he thought he might have been slow and should have joined Burns, penned a letter of resignation; taking the same line as Burns, he wrote:

The statement which Grey made to Cambon this afternoon, and which he does not propose to reveal to Germany until the announcement is made in the House of Commons tomorrow, will, I think, be regarded as tantamount to a declaration that we take part in this quarrel with France and against Germany. I think we should not take part, and so I must resign my post.[14]

Sunday had seen the 'tussle' with the Cabinet which the previous evening Grey had determined would take place.[15] The time, he declared, had come for plain speaking. While he regarded the obligation towards Belgium as binding, nevertheless, if the German Fleet menaced the British position down the Channel and attacked the French coast in those waters, he could not stay in office unless Britain blockaded the German Navy into the Baltic. A variety of sources attest to the position Grey took at this meeting: 'I believe war will come and it is due to France they shall have our support . . . ';[16] ' . . . We have led France to rely upon us, and unless we support her in her agony, I cannot continue at the Foreign Office . . . ';[17] ' . . . We cannot take half-measures – either we must declare ourselves neutral, or in it. If we are to be neutral [I] will go . . . '.[18] Sunday also saw the arrival of the letter from Bonar Law and Lord Lansdowne either in time for the start of the Cabinet (according to Austen Chamberlain's account) or (according to Leo Maxse) 'shortly after mid-day' – in either case before Grey, as Pease recorded, became more pro-war (after one and a half hours) and threatened he could not stay if the Germans crossed into Belgium.[19] The Conservatives had thus provided Grey officially with a plank that had previously been missing from his platform: he had, according to Cambon, been pleading lack of support from the opposition as a reason for inaction.[20] There was also the unmistakable alignment of Asquith with Grey, his telling H. Samuel in the afternoon: 'I shall stand by Grey in any event.'[21]

Moreover, in the course of the day Samuel played a part which, while not entirely overlooked, has yet not been fully appreciated. He engineered two formulas – one in the morning, making British intervention dependent on a German bombardment of the northern coasts of France, a second in the afternoon, making British intervention dependent on a 'substantial violation' of Belgian neutrality – the two together having as their object to make it 'an action of Germany's and not of ours which will cause the failure'. He also secured the assent of numbers of his colleagues to these formulas by attending meetings at Lord Beauchamp's after lunch, at Lloyd George's at 6.00 p.m., and by visiting McKenna in between.[22] Sunday saw, finally, a reversion to 'obligation' in the case of Belgium, at the expense of the 'policy' of 29 July.[23]

Monday 3 August was, by comparison, an altogether quieter day. At 10.55 a.m. the Foreign Office heard that the Germans had issued an ultimatum to the Belgians; this was confirmed in the afternoon.[24] At 12.30 p.m. news was received that German troops had crossed the Belgian frontier.[25] In the Cabinet which met at 11.15 a.m. Asquith was faced with the resignations of Burns, Morley, Simon and Beauchamp. Lloyd George, whose course on Sunday had concerned Asquith more than that of anyone else, announced that the invasion of a neutral state made all the difference to him. Harcourt (who on Sunday had noted in response to Grey's urging that Britain must protect the Channel: 'I can't decline this') now seconded the Chancellor.[26] Grey addressed the House of Commons in the afternoon. The Cabinet met again at 6.00 p.m. to consider, somewhat inconclusively, what might be said to Germany in view of her ultimatum to Belgium; that evening it emerged that Simon and Beauchamp had been won over by the Prime Minister.[27]

On 4 August Lloyd George told C. P. Scott of the *Manchester Guardian* that 'up to last Sunday only two members of the Cabinet had been in favour of our intervention in the War . . . '.[28] There can be no doubt that he was referring to Winston Churchill and Edward Grey. In his memorandum of the proceedings of the morning Cabinet of 2 August, however, Runciman wrote:

Grey proposes definitely
(I) to announce to France and Germany that if the German ships enter the Channel we should regard that as a hostile act.
(II) on Belgian neutrality, we do not commit ourselves at present. We are consulting Parliament.
Crewe would not hesitate to go to war over the English Channel. Several others agreed.[29]

Who were the 'several others'? They may well have included Haldane, A. Birrell, Masterman and, though less categorically, Samuel and McKenna. Haldane believed, as Hobhouse later said that he did, that Germany wanted to destroy Britain 'in detail'.[30] Birrell, the Secretary of State for Ireland, is associated with Crewe to the extent that it was to meet these two that those who lunched at Beauchamp's that day (Morley, McKinnon Wood, Samuel, Harcourt, Simon, Lloyd George) agreed to reconvene at Lloyd George's at 6.00 p.m.[31] Masterman was familiar with the implications of the German strategic railways, which he had seen at first hand; that morning he had passed across to Lloyd George a note which read: 'If I *had* to decide now I would guarantee Belgium and the Fleet policy. If Germany accepts that, no war. But I am with McKenna and Runciman in fighting for *time*, sooner than break up the Cabinet . . . '; late that night he was strongly advocating immediate intervention.[32] Runciman later *claimed* that he had acted with Grey throughout – according to the editor of *The Times*, however, who had lunched with the 'utterly unsound' Beauchamp on 1 August, and who had visited McKenna before the Cabinet met for the first time on 2 August, Runciman was one of a group with Beauchamp and Simon that Morley believed were all pledged to go together and that he was surprised to be told had not all actually resigned with himself; McKenna and Samuel were grouped by Asquith with Crewe as members of an intermediate body, and, with Haldane, described by him as 'very sensible and loyal'.[33]

The existence of Crewe and the 'several others' is not without significance. It ended the isolation of Grey and Churchill in their opposition to peace, and revealed that there was a considerable split in the ranks of the Cabinet. What, however, accounts for the readiness of Crewe and others to go to war over the English Channel, and for the disposition of those who met at No. 11 Downing Street at 10.15 a.m. on Sunday 2 August (Lloyd George, Harcourt, Beauchamp, Simon, Runciman, Pease) and agreed that 'we were not prepared to go into war now, but that in certain events we might reconsider [the] position such as the invasion wholesale of Belgium'?[34] Were their motives connected with the 'march of events'?

The Cabinet on 31 July was told of the exchange between Bethmann-Hollweg and Grey of the previous day: of the German readiness, provided Britain remained neutral, to give assurances that she would make no territorial acquisitions at the expense of metropolitan France, that she would respect the neutrality and integrity of Holland so long as her adversaries did, and that, provided Belgium did not take sides against Germany, her integrity would be respected after the conclusion of the war; and of Grey's response, which was that for Britain to bind herself to neutrality on such terms was a proposal that 'cannot for a moment be entertained'.[35] On 1 August the Cabinet would have learned of the French and German replies to the British enquiry as to whether they were prepared to engage to respect the neutrality of Belgium so long as no other Power violated it: the French had given this assurance, whereas the German Foreign Secretary G. von Jagow had led the British Ambassador to understand that he 'rather doubted whether they could answer at all, as any reply they might give could not fail, in the event of war, to have the undesirable effect of disclosing to a certain extent part of their plan of campaign'.[36] These developments do not seem to have made on ministers anything like the impression that they made on officials at the Foreign Office, at the War Office and on opposition circles.[37] It is impossible to deny that an appreciation of the position reached by this stage was not present in the minds of ministers, impossible to deny that it may have operated at a subconscious level, that it may have been taken for granted in accounts written both at the time and later. The evidence, however, suggests that at the very least it was overridden by other considerations – that even the reports which arrived in the course of 2 August of the Germans in Luxemburg and of the Germans in France[38] (however inaccurate these were) played no more than a subsidiary role in determining the British decision for war. Even on 3 August Pease was writing: 'News not very reliable as to war operations.'

What inspired the activity and produced the decisions of 2 August was the political problem of the future of the Liberal Party. On 1 August Grey had declared that 'if an out-and-out and uncompromising policy of non-intervention at all costs' were adopted, he would resign; a 'profound impression' had been made on the Cabinet by Churchill's reading of a letter in which F. E. Smith said that having consulted some of his colleagues he had no doubt – particularly on the assumption that Germany contemplated a violation of Belgian neutrality – that 'the government can rely upon the support of the Unionist Party, in whatever manner that support can be most effectively given'.[39] On 2 August, Grey, as we have seen, returned to the attack; he was joined by Asquith – a combination the power of which Morley was later to recall;[40] the letter from Bonar Law and Lord Lansdowne, with its emphasis on supporting France and Russia, finally cut the ground away from beneath the feet of the non-interventionists: there was now no way in which the country could avoid war. The conditions that were gone into and the formulas that were produced in the course of the day represented the Cabinet's accommodation to its recognition of the implications of this coincidence of political circumstances.

The Cabinet's dilemma was summarised in Samuel's letter to his wife of 2 August: 'Had the matter come to an issue, Asquith would have stood by Grey in any event, and three others would have remained. I think all the rest of us would have resigned. The consequence would have been either a Coalition government or a Unionist Government either of which would certainly have been a war ministry.' This theme – the avoidance of these consequences – is unmistakably present throughout that day and the day following. Masterman at one point threw across to Lloyd George a note: 'For Heaven's sake let us all stand together.'[41] This was the main burden of the notes which Lloyd George received from Churchill, and of the appeal that the former made in his turn on the morning of Monday 3 August.[42] Pease on the Sunday afternoon tried to bolster the then wavering Simon with the argument that 'we should stick together as long as we could', and placed before Burns the view that 'for the majority of the Cabinet to now leave meant a ministry which was a war one and that was the last thing he wanted'.[43] Asquith considered it as in the line of his duty to remark on Monday morning that 'Coalitions have hardly ever turned out well in our history.' He also said that he could not persuade himself that 'the other party' was led by men, or contained men, capable of dealing with the national situation. As Pease reported to his wife: 'The P.M. is anxious we should see this thing through as a Party and does not want a Coalition and says he wants as many of his colleagues to stay with him as he can get so as not to go outside the Party.'[44] On 4 August, Simon told Christopher Addison M.P. 'that an important consideration with him was that . . . if a block were to leave the Government at this juncture, their action would necessitate a Coalition Government which would assuredly be the grave of Liberalism'.[45] Pease wrote on 5 August to Charles Trevelyan, who had resigned from the Board of Education the day before:

'If we all chucked as you have done, the alternative Government must be one much less anxious for a peace policy than ourselves.'[46] Trevelyan received another letter from Runciman, who linked himself with Harcourt, Lloyd George and Pease: 'That one is miserable beyond measure is natural enough but in our view that is not in itself sufficient to justify us in handing over policy and control to the Tories.'[47] War-making could not be left to the war-mongers.

The conditions on which Britain would enter the war, and the terms in which the Cabinet formulated policy on 2 August, were, in effect, those on which Edward Grey would stay, and the ministry not break up. The search which went on throughout that day was for something short of 'an out-and-out and uncompromising policy of non-intervention at all costs'. The decision rested on the grounds on which Grey wanted it to rest – on the policy of the Entente.

That it was a truism that Belgium was but, in Crewe's words, 'a highway to France' had long been appreciated.[48] That it was really France which was at stake had been acknowledged by the Cabinet in its 'decision' of 31 July. On 2 August, it was this issue which Grey, leaning heavily on Paul Cambon's appeal to the entente policy and to one of its results – the fact that the northern coasts of France were relatively unprotected – made the Cabinet face. It was the misgivings of some members of the Cabinet about responding to this appeal which led to the difficult discussion of the morning of 2 August, and to the feeling which manifested itself in the afternoon that 'Burns was right', both as to his judgement of the implications of the decisions made and the course of action that he personally proposed to take.[49] Burns himself clearly relied heavily on the Cabinet resolution of November 1911, 'that no communications should take place between the General Staff here and the Staffs of other countries which can directly or indirectly commit this country to Naval or Military intervention', but to no avail.[50] Once the conditions on which Britain would intervene were being dealt with the decision for war had effectively been taken even if, technically, it was left to the Germans. Burns recognised that the damage had been done, that there was no middle way: that if unconditional neutrality was rejected, it was 'war with both hands, naval and military'. As he told Pease: he had loyally done everything in his power to meet the situation, 'but could not declare war on Germany as Grey was doing by his message to Cambon'.[51] He went to No. 10 Downing Street on the following morning and made play with some more material from 1911 damaging to the Liberal Imperialist cause.[52] It was not only too late: it was beside the point.

Faced with desertion by Grey and Asquith, their most prestigious colleagues, and with the readiness of the opposition to pursue a war policy, the neutralists reneged on their pacifism. Considerations of unity and of the future prospects of the Liberals as the party of Government constrained all but two ministers to accept the conditions Grey made. These factors are what converted Grey's letter to Cambon of November 1912, which like the Cabinet resolutions of the previous year had been originally conceived and subsequently regarded as a safeguard for the peace party, into the 'singularly thin and deceptive document' into which it turned before Morley's very eyes.[53]

Grey's personal responsibility for the British decision for war was considerable. It was not confined to his insistence that the Cabinet come to the decision *he* wanted, to his refusal even to contemplate seeking the neutrality of France as well as of Germany in British home waters – which a section of the Cabinet pressed him to do on the grounds that 'if the Germans could be assured of food and trade supplies they might be bought off'[54] – or to his threat to resign if that decision were not immediately arrived at.

In August 1912, Churchill had pointed out to Grey and Asquith in the strongest terms that Britain's freedom of choice would be sensibly impaired if the French could say that they had denuded their Atlantic seaboard and concentrated in the Mediterranean on the faith of naval arrangements made with the British. He had wanted there to be nothing in any naval and military arrangements made between Britain and France which would have the effect of exposing either to a charge of bad faith if when war came one of them decided to stand out of it: France would possess a 'tremendous weapon to compel our intervention' if she could say 'on the advice of and by arrangement with your naval authorities we have left our Northern Coasts defenceless. We cannot possibly come back in time.'[55] In the summer of 1912 the French Naval Attaché, St Seine, had revealed, and Poincaré, and finally even Paul Cambon, had admitted, that the French decision to concentrate their naval forces in the Mediterranean was a spontaneous one, and had not been arrived at in consequence of conversations between the British and French experts.[56] The dangers to which Churchill had drawn attention were carefully avoided at that time by the rejection of words suggested by Cambon which would have bound the two Governments to carry out plans made by the General Staffs, and by a reiteration of the principle that consultations between military and naval experts did not restrict the freedom of either Government to decide at a future time whether or not to assist the other by armed force.[57] Despite this, however, in August 1914 precisely what Churchill had forecast in 1912 would happen if the pitfalls he pointed out were not avoided *did* happen. The French did make the claim Churchill had been at pains not to furnish them with the means to make, and the result was as decisive as he had predicted that it would be.

On the afternoon of 1 August, Paul Cambon had what Nicolson, in providing Hardinge later with 'the secret history of what passed on the two to three days prior to August 3rd', dubbed 'a happy inspiration'.[58] According to Nicolson, Cambon 'pointed out that it was at our request that France had moved her fleets to the Mediterranean, on the understanding that we undertook the protection of her Northern and Western coasts'; according to his own report Cambon told Grey that 'nous étions exposés . . . à des démonstrations des escadres allemandes sur nos côtes d'autant plus dangereuses que, d'accord avec l'Angleterre, nous avions concentré le gros de nos forces navales dans la Méditerranée'.[59] What Cambon 'pointed out' was simply not the case. Yet his contention was not challenged or queried either by Nicolson, who urged Grey to 'remind the Cabinet of the above fact', or by Grey. Instead it was used by the Foreign Secretary, at the beginning of the first Cabinet on 2 August, as the first of the devices he employed to lever his colleagues into a decision for war, a determination to which a letter delivered by hand on the Saturday to his Private Secretary from the editor of the right-wing *Morning Post* may well have contributed. For not only did Gwynne, wanting 'a lead, a strong manly lead', remind Grey 'that he tolds the *honour* of England in his hands, that 80% are behind him and that he has enormous personal power if he likes to use it with which he could force his views on the Cabinet and the country'; he also told Tyrrell: 'We have been led by the F.O. under your chief's guidance to be prepared for this [Anglo-French naval and military cooperation]. We have worked hard to prepare public opinion for it and now when we get to the jump, as it were, we are refusing it.'[60] Even more remarkably, in the House of Commons on 3 August he read most of the letter of 22 November 1912 to Cambon, including the sentence which flatly contradicted the Ambassador's recent assertions: 'The disposition, for instance, of the French and British fleets respectively at the present moment is not based upon an engagement to cooperate in war.'[61] On that occasion he adopted, in effect, the line taken by Poincaré in 1912 that the independent decision of the French Government would not have been taken had the French been able to suppose that in the event of Germany making a descent on the Channel and Atlantic ports of France England would not come to the assistance of France; the House was told: 'The French fleet is in the Mediterranean, and has for some years been concentrated there because of the feeling of confidence and friendship which has existed between the two countries.' Grey also managed, somewhat incoherently, to combine this appeal to sentiment with the argument that, if the French withdrew from the Mediterranean in order to defend their northern and western coasts, as was only to be expected failing a positive commitment from Britain, the latter, because she had not kept there a Fleet equal to dealing alone with a combination of other Fleets, might find her interests, in the shape of vital trade routes, exposed 'to the most appalling risk', perhaps by the departure of Italy from her attitude of neutrality.[62] Thus, so the House was led to believe – for there is no record of the discussion, at any of the Cabinet meetings, of this particular British interest – Britain had to give in 1914 the quid pro quo she had avoided in 1912.

With his speech to the House of Commons of 3 August, Grey gave a lead to public opinion which in informed circles it had always been appreciated that he would be able to do. His speech complemented, in regard to the country, his seizure of the initiative in the Cabinet, and his forcing of the issue there at a time when he was in all probability aware that Liberal opinion in the country and in Parliament was, if anything, hardening against intervention in such a way as to indicate that if the decision was left any later the Government might have 'a difficult passage' in rallying a united Party to meet the threat of war.[63] It was most probably in the cause of Party unity, at a time when the Cabinet had already taken a decision for war, and not as the result of any oversight, that Grey concealed, by omitting to read to the House the last sentence of his letter to Cambon, the fact that planning between the French and British General Staffs had taken place.

Although aided and abetted by Asquith, who exploited the initial breach in the Liberal Government with his stress on coalitions and the blackmail and bribery of his colleagues, and who would have been a party to what one observer thought he detected – an attempt to get the Speaker of the House of Commons to forestall any discussion or debate following Grey's speech on 3 August;[64] and by Churchill, who probably passed on the information gathered by F. A. Whyte, whom he encouraged to 'rub in' to Liberal M.P.s the necessity for the German General Staff to invade Belgium; there is no doubt that Grey was, as Hobhouse put it, 'the author of our rupture with Germany'.[65] Grey was later to say that, at the outbreak of war, one of his strongest feelings was that he himself had no power to decide policy, and was only 'the mouthpiece of England'. At the time, he admitted his responsibility when he said 'how unhappy it made him to be the cause of such dissent and trouble among such friends'.[66]

Once the decision for war had been taken what remained to be determined were the grounds on which it should be *advertised*. Samuel had thrown out the balance of power and substituted British interests and treaty obligations.[67] The process of making the decision respectable continued on Monday when, according to Pease's account: 'We discussed what Edward

Grey should say (to Cambon) – urging him to allude to British Interests in addition to moral obligation to support France conditionally at sea.'[68]

It is at this stage that the 'march of events' may have played a part, may have reduced the number of resignations from the Cabinet from four to two. The Solicitor General, Buckmaster, told Addison 'that, before the receipt of the German Chancellor's proposal in Paper 85, Simon, Harcourt, Pease, Burns and Morley as well as himself, had intended to resign if we became involved; but that, after its receipt, they decided to stick to the ship, with the exception of Morley and Burns . . . '.[69] Hazlehurst says that 'Further news of German bellicosity shook the determination of Simon and Beauchamp and undermined the residual reservations of the other waverers'.[70] Lammers uses with approval Simon's own testimony to C. P. Scott that it was the Belgian issue which counted for most in the retraction of his resignation.[71] Buckmaster's tale is plainly nonsense: it fits with none of the facts. Like the claims of Simon, Harcourt and Lloyd George, it has about it the air of being an argument of convenience, helpful in rescuing them from the 'hole' into which the determination to resign of Burns and Morley had placed them.[72] Morley, who 'kept the faith', as he put it, when all about were losing it, appreciated that 'the precipitate and peremptory blaze about Belgium was due less to indignation at the violation of a Treaty than to natural perception of the plea that it would furnish for intervention . . . '.[73] Trevelyan, who met Harcourt in the lobby of the House of Commons after Grey's speech on 3 August, recorded: 'I had a good talk with (him). But he is of the opportunist type in the long run.'[74] Harcourt was not the only one. It is likely that the behaviour of ministers at this stage was as much a product of political factors as the decision for war had itself been – likely that Simon and Beauchamp retracted because no one followed them, that Lloyd George, who delayed his move till the last minute, did not resign because he had no one to lead. In the case of Simon it would be as well to remember that there was such a thing as 'office' for its own sake, in addition to what Morley called 'the natural "cohesion of office" '.[75]

Given that we are dealing, after all, with professional politicians, it is a priori more likely that the 'march of events' served as an excuse to put actions both taken and not taken in the best possible light than as a genuine explanation for conduct. Grey had written to Runciman in October 1911: 'You are almost the only man in the Cabinet who has a real perhaps even a preferable alternative to office and this gives you an independence of opinion which is rare and that I should miss terribly'; Pease, who on 3 August 1914 renewed his attempt of the day before to get his wife to agree that not to resign was the really courageous course, was confronted almost immediately by her taking up a phrase in the first of these two letters: 'What do you mean by "sticking to the ship" – did you intend resigning? You could not do it now in a moment of difficulty and no business prospects to look forward to.'[76]

The breach in the British policy of non-intervention was made by the possibility, which was raised by Grey's and the Liberal Imperialists' adherence to the entente policy, of what Samuel called 'a political crisis'.[77] It was at least as much the object of Samuel and of others who fought for time to avoid this as to put Germany in the wrong; the attitude of the Conservatives was an essential part of this political equation. The argument from silence which Lammers thinks suggestive is in fact no argument at all.[78] John Burns remembered the Conservative contribution.[79] So did Runciman.[80] So did Masterman.[81] But one would not expect publicity to be given to this factor. Morley's silence on this matter is of less significance than that of others – it was of more consequence to those who stayed or returned. They were understandably reluctant to reveal the real explanation for their actions. The argument employed both at the time and by historians that the 'march of events' was 'dominating' is too simple. It may have helped to *confirm* a decision already made on political grounds,[82] but it did not *determine* that decision. Nor did it remove the residual suspicions of some contemporaries. Loreburn wrote to C. P. Scott on 25 September 1914:

I hold silence about the beginning of [the war] and avoid all that class of subject because we are now in a fight which taxes all our resources and energy and we ought all to encourage those who are fighting. And whatever may be said about it, no one can deny that Germany has behaved extremely ill and that if she persisted in attacking Belgium there was a just cause for us to defend Belgium. It can do no good and may do harm to discuss the origin now.[83]

Notes

The following abbreviations are used in the notes.
Unpublished sources
Add. MSS   British Library
I.O.L. MSS   India Office Library

Published sources
B.D.   G. P. Gooch and H. W. V. Temperley (eds.), *British Documents on the Origins of the War, 1898–1914* (London, 1926–38)
D.D.F.   *Documents diplomatiques français 1871–1914*, Ministère des Affaires Étrangères, Commission de publication des documents relatifs aux origines de la guerre de 1914 (Paris, 1929–62)
G.P.   J. Lepsius, A. Mendelssohn-Bartholdy, and F. Thimme (eds.), *Die Grosse Politik der Europäischen Kabinette 1871–1914* (Berlin, 1922–7)
Hansard   Hansard's *Parliamentary Debates*

Learned journals
B.I.H.R.   *Bulletin of the Institute of Historical Research*
E.H.R.   *English Historical Review*
E.S.R.   *European Studies Review*
H.J.   *Historical Journal*
J.B.S.   *Journal of British Studies*
J.C.H.   *Journal of Contemporary History*
J.M.H.   *Journal of Modern History*

1. The Poverty of the Entente Policy

1 W. L. Langer, *The Diplomacy of Imperialism* (New York, 1951 edn), p. 78.
2 G. W. Monger, *The End of Isolation* (London, 1963), p. 110.
3 Langer, *Diplomacy*, p. 506; Hansard, 4th Series, lviii, cols. 1347, 1418, 10 June 1898.
4 Monger, *End of Isolation*, pp. 19, 36–7.
5 Memo by Salisbury, 29 May 1901, *B.D.*, ii, no. 86. Salisbury was so little

impressed by the capability of the French that he said that all they could do, if they went to war, would be 'to confiscate a couple of P. & O. steamers'. Salisbury to Selborne, 18 June 1901, Selborne MSS 26.

6 Memo by Bertie, 9 Nov. 1901, *B.D.*, ii, no. 91.

7 Memo by Lansdowne, 11 Nov. 1901, *ibid.*, no. 92; see Arnold-Foster Diary, 20 Nov. 1903, Add. MSS 50335.

8 Monger, *End of Isolation*, p. 17; Langer, *Diplomacy*, pp. 721–2.

9 Langer, *Diplomacy*, p. 506; Hansard, 4th Series, cii, col. 1175, 13 Feb. 1902; Haldane to Rosebery, 14 Aug. 1916, Rosebery MSS box 24.

10 G. E. Buckle (ed.), *Letters of Queen Victoria*, 3rd Series (London, 1930), i, p. 195.

11 Minute by Salisbury, 27 Mar. 1897, Sanderson MSS F.O. 800/2.

12 Monger, *End of Isolation*, p. 5.

13 *Ibid.*, pp. 12, 110.

14 I. Nish, *The Anglo-Japanese Alliance* (London, 1966), pp. 175–6; C.I.D., 111th meeting, 26 May 1911, CAB 2/2/2.

15 Cromer to Balfour, 15 Oct. 1903, Cromer MSS F.O. 633/6.

16 Memo by Clarke, 16 July 1906, CAB 38/12/40; Sanderson to Spring-Rice, 6 Aug. 1907, Spring-Rice MSS F.O. 800/241.

17 *B.D.*, v, p. 550; A. C. Murray, *Master and Brother* (London, 1945), pp. 116–17.

18 Lloyd George to Asquith, 2 Feb. 1909, Asquith MSS vol. 21.

19 Grey to Asquith, 5 Feb. 1909, *ibid.*

20 C.I.D. Report on the Military Defence of India, 30 Dec. 1902, CAB 38/1/14. Hamilton wrote in February 1903 that these studies had impressed the Cabinet, and especially Brodrick, Selborne, Lansdowne and Ritchie, with 'a fuller sense of Britain's liability in the event of war with Russia and the magnitude of the military assistance which India would undoubtedly require'. Monger, *End of Isolation*, p. 111.

21 A. J. Marder, *From the Dreadnought to Scapa Flow*, i (Oxford, 1961), pp. 179, 182–5, 283.

22 Admiralty memo, 15 Feb. 1906, ADM 116/866B. In November 1906 Tweedmouth added that 'alliances and good understandings however close and excellent for the time have never been found everlasting and ample preparation must be made to meet emergencies as they arise'. Campbell-Bannerman MSS Add. MSS 41231.

23 Hansard, 5th Series, lix, col. 2189, 18 Mar. 1914.

24 C. P. Scott MSS, 25 July 1911, Add. MSS 50901; Hardinge to Bryce, 4 June 1909, Bryce MSS USA vol. 29.

25 *B.D.*, vi, no. 332.

26 Report of C.I.D. sub-committee on the Military Requirements of the Empire: India, p. 5, May 1907, CAB 38/13/20.

27 *B.D.*, iii, p. 418.

28 Cartwright to Grey, 12 Jan. 1907, F.O. 371/257/2390.

29 Minute by Spicer, 23 Mar. 1908, *ibid.* /458/9933; Dumas to Lascelles, 30 July 1908, ADM 116/940B.

30 Goschen to Hardinge, 8, 28 May 1909, Hardinge MSS vol. 15.
31 Minute by Hardinge, 28 Oct. 1907, F.O. 371/262/35519; Hansard, 4th Series, cxcvi, cols. 560, 1768–9, 12, 23 Nov. 1908; Hardings to Bryce, 15 Jan. 1909, Bryce MSS USA 28; to Goschen, 1 Feb., to Villiers, 17 Feb. 1910, Hardinge MSS vol. 21.
32 Hansard, 4th Series, cxxx, col. 1405, 1 Mar. 1904.
33 B.D., vii, nos. 402, 405.
34 Bertie to Nicolson, 6 Aug. 1911, Carnock MSS F.O. 800/349; B.D., vii, no. 461; CAB 371/107/79.
35 Bertie to Crowe, 21 July 1911, Bertie MSS F.O. 800/171; Bertie to Grey, 12 Jan. 1912, Grey MSS F.O. 800/53.
36 When in his letter to his naval colleague in London the French Military Attaché in Berlin pointed out that there was a want of foresight in the British concern to secure an agreement on naval armaments with Germany, that Britain would gain nothing 'for it will be the French and Italian fleets which will augment the German fleet', and that the Anglo-German negotiations would facilitate military preparations, Grey mistook the criticism as one of the British failure to adopt conscription. Feb. 1912, Carnock MSS F.O. 800/353.
37 Memo by Hicks-Beach, Oct. 1901, CAB 37/58/109.
38 Memo by Ritchie, 21 Feb. 1903, CAB 37/64/15.
39 Minutes by Grey, 13 Jan., 16 Apr. 1908, F.O. 371/457/1185, /13143.
40 Minutes by Hardinge, 23 Mar. 1908, ibid. /458/9933; 10 Nov. 1909, B.D., vi, pp. 310, 121; no. 182.
41 Memo by Dumas, 12 Feb. 1908, and minutes by Crowe, B.D., vi, pp. 121, 132.
42 Grey to Bryce, 12 Dec. 1909, Bryce MSS USA 29.
43 Crowe to Villiers, 21 Feb. 1907: 'it is difficult to believe that anyone responsible can be serious about (these proposals)': Villiers MSS F.O. 800/23. Crowe was selected to attend the Conference.
44 G.P., xxiv, no. 8226, 13 Aug. 1908.
45 The Times, 7 June 1909.
46 B.D., vi, no. 182. In fact the German efforts to secure a British neutrality agreement were heavily influenced by right-wing political opposition, on financial grounds, to the German Navy. The German Government hoped the financial strain might be relieved, and this opposition decline, if the British could be persuaded that large naval increases on their part were unnecessary. V. R. Berghahn, 'Naval Armaments and Social Crisis: Germany before 1914', in G. Best and A. Wheatcroft (eds.), War, Economy and the Military Mind (London, 1976), pp. 74–7.
47 K. Robbins, Sir Edward Grey – a Biography (London, 1971), pp. 248–9.
48 Sandars to Balfour, 25 May 1912, Balfour MSS Add. MSS 49768; G. M. Trevelyan, Grey of Fallodon (London, 1937), pp. 176–7.
49 B.D., vi, no. 591.
50 B.D., xi, no. 86.
51 J. Morley, Memorandum on Resignation (London, 1928), pp. 5–6.

52 A. J. P. Taylor, *The Struggle for Mastery in Europe 1848–1918* (Oxford, 1954), p. xxxiv.
53 J. Gooch, 'Sir George Clarke's Career at the Committee of Imperial Defence 1904–1907', *H.J.*, xviii, no. 3 (1975), p. 566. See also Chirol to Steed, 19 July 1907, Chirol MSS.
54 Milner MSS box 194; O. Sitwell, *Great Morning* (London, 1948), p. 125; Glenesk-Bathurst MSS.
55 A. J. A. Morris, 'Charles Trevelyan and Two Views of "Revolution" ', in Morris (ed.), *Edwardian Radicalism* (London, 1974), pp. 143–7.
56 M. V. Brett and Viscount Reginald Esher, *Journals and Letters of Reginald, Viscount Esher*, 4 vols. (London, 1934–8), iii, p. 61, 4 Oct. 1911; War Council minutes, 5, 6 Aug. 1914, CAB 42/1/2, /3; CAB 16/28A.
57 M. de Cecco, *Money and Empire* (Oxford, 1974), pp. 62–75.
58 Memo by Balfour, 21 Dec. 1903, Balfour MSS Add. MSS 49728, my italics; memo by Robertson, Mar. 1906, Grey MSS F.O. 800/102; Grey at 111th meeting of C.I.D., 26 May 1911, p. 11, CAB 2/2/2.
59 *B.D.*, ii, no. 322; Grey to Spring-Rice, 16 Apr. 1906, Spring-Rice MSS F.O. 800/241; Nicolson to Findlay, 18 Oct. 1910, Carnock MSS F.O. 800/344.
60 In the letter referred to in n. 36 above, for instance, the Frenchman also said that if the French refused to be constrained by Germany 'we shall find ourselves embroiled in a war in which England will be but of very little assistance to us'. On 13 September 1911 the French Military Attaché in London dined with Lord Kitchener and Sir J. French, amongst others. French maintained that 'we could put 85,000 men into the field and that's all'; what is more, these men would be put 'into Belgium'. Gwynne to Lady Bathurst, 14, 17 Sept. 1911, Glenesk-Bathurst MSS. See also F. Fischer, *War of Illusions* (New York, 1975), pp. 166–9, 390; G. Ritter, *The Schlieffen Plan* (New York, 1958), pp. 69–71.

2. The Politics of Liberal Foreign Policy I

1 *The Times*, 1 June 1905.
2 *Ibid.*, 7 Nov. 1905.
3 *Ibid.*, 17 Nov., 22 Dec. 1905, 8, 9, Jan. 1906.
4 Mallet to Hardinge, 4 Apr. 1905, Hardinge MSS vol. 7.
5 Lord Crewe, *Lord Rosebery*, 2 vols. (London, 1931), ii, pp. 594–5.
6 Chirol to Hardinge, 24 July 1905, Hardinge MSS vol. 7. In 1904 he had remarked on 'a large number of people who still support the Government merely because they believe a Radical Government would be a public danger in the present situation of "Weltpolitik" '. *Idem* to *idem*, 2 Nov. 1904, *ibid.*; see also Chirol to Lascelles, 18 Apr. 1905, Lascelles MSS F.O. 800/11.
7 Knollys to Haldane, 16 Sept. 1905, Haldane MSS 5906.
8 Morley to Spencer, 2 Oct., to Ripon, 7 Oct. 1905, cited by T. Boyle, 'The Formation of Campbell-Bannerman's Government in December 1905: a Memorandum by J. A. Spender', *B.I.H.R.*, xlv (1972), p. 288.

9 Minute by Mallet on Spring-Rice to Lansdowne, 2 Dec. 1905, Lansdowne MSS F.O. 800/141.
10 Hardinge to Lansdowne, 24 Oct. 1905, *B.D.*, iv. no. 202. In a series of letters to Spender in August and September Spring-Rice had attempted to improve the line taken by the *Westminster Gazette* towards continuity, and to convince its editor that Lansdowne's policies 'were in their inception liberal policies, and in strict conformity with liberal principles'. Spring-Rice to Spender 11, 14 Aug., 17, 26 Sept. 1905, Spender MSS Add. MSS 46391.
11 Hardinge to Maxse, 8 Dec. 1905, Maxse MSS.
12 Bertie to Grey, 12 Dec. 1905, Bertie MSS F.O. 800/164, Mallet to Nicolson, 23 Dec. 1905, Carnock MSS F.O. 800/336. See M. Asquith, *Autobiography* (London, 1962 edn), p. 243; S. Gwynn (ed.), *The Letters and Friendships of Sir Cecil Spring-Rice*, 2 vols. (London, 1929), ii, p. 18; Tyrrell to Nicolson, 25 Dec. 1905, Carnock MSS F.O. 800/336.
13 *The Times*, 21 Oct., 7 Nov. 1905.
14 Lansdowne to the King, 22 Nov. 1905, Hardinge MSS vol. 7.
15 Harcourt to Campbell-Bannerman, 30 Nov. 1905, Campbell-Bannerman MSS Add. MSS 52518.
16 Lansdowne to Grey, 9 Dec. 1905, Grey MSS F.O. 800/108.
17 Lansdowne to Hardinge, 12 Dec. 1905, Hardinge MSS vol. 9.
18 Haldane to Knollys, 12, 13 Sept. 1905, Asquith MSS vol. 10; *idem* to *idem*, 19 Sept. 1905, Haldane MSS 5906.
19 *The Times*, 14, 21 Oct. 1905.
20 J. A. Spender, *Life, Journalism and Politics*, 2 vols. (London, 1927), i, pp. 191–2.
21 J. A. Spender and C. Asquith, *Life of H. H. Asquith Lord Oxford and Asquith*, 2 vols. (London, 1932), i, p. 172; Haldane to his sister, 21 Nov. 1905, Haldane MSS 6011.
22 Morley to C.-B., 25 Nov. 1905, Add. MSS 41223; Harcourt to C.-B., 30 Nov. 1905, *ibid.* 52518; Verney to Nicolson, 4 Dec. 1905, Carnock MSS F.O. 800/336.
23 Harcourt to C.-B., 30 Nov. 1905, Add. MSS 52518.
24 Gladstone to C.-B., 27 Nov. 1905, *ibid.* 41217; Morley to C.-B., 28 Nov. 1905, *ibid.* 52518.
25 Gladstone to C.-B., 30 Nov. 1905, *ibid.* 52518 (tel.); 41238 (letter).
26 Morley to C.-B., 27 Nov. 1905, *ibid.* 41223; J. A. Spender, *The Life of the Right Hon. Sir Henry Campbell-Bannerman*, 2 vols. (London, 1923), ii, pp. 193–5.
27 Harcourt to C.-B., 30 Nov. 1905, Add. MSS 52518.
28 Grey to C.-B., 4, 7 Dec. 1905, *ibid.* 41218; memo by Gladstone, 5 Dec. 1905, Gladstone MSS Add. MSS 45992; Grey to Asquith, 25 Nov. 1905, Asquith MSS vol. 10; Morley to C.-B., 25 Nov. 1905, Add. MSS 41223; Spender and Asquith, *Life of Asquith*, i, pp. 174–5; Asquith, *Autobiography* (London, 1962 edn), p. 243.
29 Morley to C.-B., 1 Dec. 1905, Add. MSS 52518; Harcourt to Sinclair, 7 Dec. 1905, *ibid.* 41220; Spender, *Life of Campbell-Bannerman*, ii, p. 195; H. H. Asquith, *Memories and Reflections*, 2 vols. (London, 1928), i, p. 195; Morley

to C.-B., 7 Dec. 1905, Add. MSS 52518; Harcourt to Sinclair, 6 Dec. 1905, *ibid.*; Spender to Fitzmaurice, 12 Dec. 1905, *ibid.* 41214; Spender, *Life, Journalism and Politics*, i, p. 132; Asquith to C.-B., 7 Dec. 1905, Add. MSS 41210.

30 Gladstone to C.-B., 7 Dec. 1905, Add. MSS 41217; to Morley, 28 Dec. 1905, *ibid.* 52518.

31 Holstein, for one, regarded the change of Government in England as 'an unexpected stroke of luck for us which we should make use of'; in January he wrote: 'The fall of the embittered and anti-German Tory Government . . . makes the possibility of an Anglo-German rapprochement more easy.' Holstein to Brandt, 23 Dec. 1905, to Bulow, Jan. 1906, in N. Rich and M. H. Fisher, *The Holstein Papers*, 4 vols. (Cambridge, 1963), iv, pp. 377, 381; Tyrrell to Nicolson, 25 Dec. 1905, Carnock MSS F.O. 800/336.

32 C.-B. to Ripon, 13 Dec. 1905, Add. MSS 41225; Grey to C.-B., 13 Dec. 1905, *ibid.* 52514.

33 Mallet to Bertie, 10 Oct. 1905, Bertie MSS F.O. 800/184; *idem* to *idem*, 11 Jan. 1906, *ibid.* /164.

34 Bertie to Knollys, 31 Jan. 1906, *ibid.* /174.

35 Brett and Esher, *Journals and Letters of Reginald, Viscount Esher*, ii, p. 161, 20 Apr. 1906.

36 Hardinge to Lascelles, 16 May 1906, Lascelles MSS F.O. 800/13.

37 Chirol to Steed, 10 Sept. 1909, Chirol MSS. *Idem* to *idem*, 23 Sept. 1909: 'if the Lloyd George–Churchill section comes out on top, I see many indications that one of the first results will be a rapprochement with, or rather a surrender to, Germany': *ibid.*; also Chirol to Nicolson, 15 Nov. 1909, Carnock MSS F.O. 800/342.

38 Tyrrell to Bertie, 22 Oct. 1909, Bertie MSS F.O. 800/186. In 1912 Bertie was to describe Harcourt as being 'from ambition, overweening self-confidence *and* ignorance . . . a dangerous "politician" in foreign affairs': to Mallet, 12 May 1912, *ibid.* /171.

39 J. Wilson, *CB: A Life of Sir Henry Campbell-Bannerman* (London, 1973), p. 532.

40 Morley, *Memorandum on Resignation*, p. 7.

41 Pease Diary, 24 Oct. 1911, Gainford MSS.

42 W. S. Churchill, *The World Crisis 1911–18*, 2 vols. (London, 1923), i, p. 46.

43 Runciman to Harcourt, 24 Aug. 1911, Runciman MSS.

44 T. Wilson (ed.), *The Political Diaries of C. P. Scott 1911–28* (London, 1970), pp. 42, 53: 20 July, 6–8 Sept. 1911.

45 Hardinge to Nicolson, 18 Mar. 1907, Carnock MSS F.O. 800/339; Crowe to Villiers, 21 Feb. 1907, Villiers MSS F.O. 800/23.

46 Monger, *End of Isolation*, pp. 285–6; Morley to C.-B., 15 Jan. 1907, Add. MSS 41223; Grey to C.-B., 31 Aug. 1907, Grey MSS F.O. 800/100, to Ripon, 8 Sept. 1907, Add. MSS 43640; D. A. Hamer, *John Morley* (Oxford, 1968), p. 346.

47 H. Nicolson, *Lord Carnock* (London, 1930), p. 308; O'Beirne to Nicolson, May 1909, Carnock MSS F.O. 800/342; Nicolson to Grey, 7 May 1909, and

minute by Hardinge, F.O. 371/730/17375; Hardinge to Lowther, 18 May 1909, Hardinge MSS vol. 17.

48 Buchanan to Nicolson, 25 July 1912, Carnock MSS F.O. 800/358.

49 Harcourt to Grey, 8, 14 Jan. 1914, Grey MSS F.O. 800/91.

50 See for example minute by Crowe, 2 Mar. 1908: 'There was never the slightest chance of our coming to an understanding with Germany as regards a limitation of armaments'. F.O. 371/458/7103.

51 Bryce to Fitzmaurice, 28 Nov. 1907, Bryce MSS E31; Fitzmaurice to Ripon, 10 Oct. 1908, Ripon MSS Add. MSS 43543; Spender, *Life, Journalism and Politics*, i, pp. 213–14; Loreburn to C.-B., 10 May 1906, C.-B. MSS Add. MSS 41222; Hamer, *John Morley*, pp. 322–32, 341, 345–6; Morley to Grey, 22 June 1909, Grey MSS F.O. 800/98; Morley to Minto, 6 Feb. 1908, 21 May 1909, I.O.L. MSS Eur.D 573/3, /4.

52 Chirol transmitted the Radical views of C. P. Trevelyan to Hardinge on 24 July 1905, Hardinge MSS vol. 7; and of Churchill to Nicolson on 19 Jan. 1909, Carnock MSS F.O. 800/342.

53 Nicolson to Hardinge, 2 Mar. 1911, Hardinge MSS vol. 92.

54 *Ibid.*; note by Runciman, 25 Jan. 1911, Runciman MSS box 5.

55 Memo by Crowe, 20 May 1911, *B.D.*, vi, pp. 635–6.

56 See K. M. Wilson, 'The Agadir Crisis, the Mansion House Speech, and the Double-Edgedness of Agreements', *H.J.*, xv, no. 3 (1972), pp. 518–19; T. Boyle, 'New Light on Lloyd George's Mansion House Speech', *H.J.*, xxiii (1980), pp. 431–3; R. J. Scally, *The Origins of the Lloyd George Coalition* (Princeton, N.J., 1975), pp. 224–7.

57 Morley to Burns, 14 June 1916, Burns MSS Add. MSS 46283; to Asquith, 27 July 1911, Asquith MSS vol. 13; to Carrington at the Board of Agriculture Morley wrote: 'The Chancellor of the Exchequer went rather far about Germany don't you think.' Carrington Diary, 24 July 1911, Bodleian MSS Film 1107; Loreburn to Grey, 27 July 1911, Grey MSS F.O. 800/99.

58 H. Wilson Diary, 15 Aug. 1911; Harcourt to Runciman, 26 Aug. 1911, Runciman MSS; Marder, *From the Dreadnought to Scapa Flow*, i, pp. 392–3. Asquith wrote to Haldane on 9 Sept. 1911: 'Morley has evidently been told of the meeting of the sub-committee: I wonder by whom? He is quite the most impossible colleague that ever entered a Cabinet.' Haldane MSS 5909.

59 Notes by McKenna of conversation with Asquith, 20 Oct. 1911, McKenna MSS 4/2; C. P. Scott Diary, 23–4 Oct. 1914, Add. MSS 50901; Pease Diary, 24 Oct., 1, 15 Nov. 1911; Asquith to the King, 2, 16 Nov. 1911, CAB 41/33/28, Asquith MSS vol. 6.

60 Haldane MSS 6011, 16 Nov. 1911.

61 C. P. Scott Diary, 7, 22, Jan. 1912, 23–4 Oct. 1914, Add. MSS 50901; Loreburn to Harcourt, 17 Feb., 6 June 1912, Harcourt MSS. Loreburn himself wrote to Haldane in July 1912 of 'our wide differences of opinion . . . My difference with you has always been this – you have been an Imperialist au fond and always; in my opinion, it is quite impossible to reconcile Imperialism with the liberal creed which we professed; and on the face of which we received the support of the country'. Haldane MSS 5909.

62 Hardinge to Sanderson, 10 July 1912, Hardinge MSS vol. 92.

63 H. Wilson Diary, 11 Jan. 1912; minutes by Crowe 2, 24 Apr. 1912, *B.D.*, x (ii), no. 285, F.O. 371/1373/17161.

64 Notes by Harcourt, 14, 16 Mar. 1912, Harcourt MSS; Pease Diary, 14, 16, 29 Mar., 10 Apr. 1912.

65 Pease Diary, 16 July 1912; *B.D.*, x (ii), nos. 400, 414–15.

66 *The Daily Telegraph*, 26 Oct. 1912.

67 Nicolson to Bertie, 23 May 1912, Carnock MSS F.O. 800/356; to Grey, 25 Sept. 1912, *ibid.* /363; to Hardinge, 3 June 1912, Hardinge MSS vol. 92; memo by Bertie, 23 June 1913, Bertie MSS F.O. 800/166.

68 *The Times*, 22 June 1906.

69 Balcarres Diary, 27 July 1911, Balcarres MSS; Hansard, 5th Series, xxviii, col. 1829, 27 July 1911; *ibid.*, xxxii, col. 67, 27 Nov. 1911; *ibid.* (Lords), x, col. 389, 28 Nov. 1911.

70 Memo by Balcarres of talk with Elibank, 22 Nov. 1911, Bonar Law MSS 24/3/70; Gwynne to Law, 20, 22 Nov. 1911, *ibid.* 24/3/63, /73. See also Sandars to Balfour, 17 Sept. 1911, Add. MSS 49767.

71 Memo by Elibank for Grey of conversations with Stolypin and Isvolsky, 19, 23 Jan. 1909, Elibank MSS 8801.

72 Stamfordham to Nicolson, 4 Oct. 1912, Carnock MSS F.O. 800/359.

73 A. Chamberlain, *Politics from Inside* (London, 1936), pp. 471–3, 8 Mar. 1912.

74 Grey to Nicolson, 1 Oct. 1912, Carnock MSS F.O. 800/358.

75 Chirol to Hardinge, 1 May 1913, Hardinge MSS vol. 93.

76 Bertie to Tyrrell, 20 Aug. 1908, Bertie MSS F.O. 800/170.

77 Hardinge to Cartwright, 11 Jan. 1910, Hardinge MSS vol. 21; to Goschen, 11 Jan. 1910, *ibid.*

78 Hardinge to Nicolson, 1 Feb. 1910, *ibid.*

79 Hardinge to Nicolson, 12 Oct. 1909, Carnock MSS F.O. 800/342. Some deceit was also involved: as Hardinge wrote to Nicolson on 28 Oct. 1908: 'Grey has constantly, during the past year, had to appear in the House of Commons as the advocate of the Russian Government. We have had to suppress the truth and resort to subterfuge at times to meet hostile public opinion.' Hardinge MSS vol. 13.

80 T. P. Conwell-Evans, *Foreign Policy from a Back-Bench 1904–18* (Oxford, 1932), pp. 58–9.

81 Margot Asquith to Elibank, 14 Jan. 1912, Elibank MSS 8803; memo by Elibank for Asquith, 25 Feb. 1912, *ibid.* 8802; Asquith to Elibank, 22 Apr. 1912, *ibid.* 8803; Maxse to Chamberlain, 29 Feb., 1 Mar. 1912, A. Chamberlain MSS AC4/1/768, /769; Chamberlain, *Politics from Inside*, pp. 438–9, 5 Mar. 1912.

82 C. P. Scott Diary, 23–4 Oct. 1914, Add. MSS 50901; Balfour to Sandars, 21 Sept. 1911, Sandars MSS c. 764. See K. M. Wilson, 'The Opposition and the Crisis in the Liberal Cabinet over Foreign Policy in November 1911', *International History Review*, iii (1981), pp. 403–4.

83 Memo by Balcarres, 20 May 1912, Bonar Law MSS 38D/5; Nicolson to Grey, 22 May 1912, Grey MSS F.O. 800/94.

84 J. Wilson, *Campbell-Bannerman*, pp. 527, 531; Grey to Ripon, 27 July 1906,

Ripon MSS Add. MSS 43640; Trevelyan, *Grey of Fallodon*, p. 122; Ripon to Grey, 8 Oct. 1908, Ripon MSS Add. MSS 43640.

85 Hardinge to the King, 24 Aug. 1908, Hardinge MSS vol. 14; Grey to Asquith, 22 Aug., Asquith to Grey, 24 Aug. 1908, Grey MSS F.O. 800/100; Tyrrell to Marsh, 22 Dec., Grey to Churchill, 24 Dec. 1908, *ibid.* /89; Grey to Churchill, 22 Apr. 1909, *ibid.*

86 Pease Diary, 20 July 1910, 21 June, 21 Nov. 1912; Asquith to the King, 9 Mar. 1911, CAB 41/33/5, 3 Feb. 1912, and Crewe to the King, 17 May 1912, Asquith MSS vol. 6; note by Harcourt, 29 Feb. 1912, Harcourt MSS.

87 T. Wilson, *The Political Diaries of C. P. Scott*, p. 57.

88 Asquith to Grey, 5 Sept., Grey to Asquith, 8 Sept. 1911, Grey MSS F.O. 800/100.

89 Asquith to Crewe, 7 Oct. 1911, Crewe MSS C/40. Grey told McKenna blandly on 11 October that he was in the dark as to what was really in Asquith's mind. He certainly knew what was in Haldane's mind, and approved of his pressing Asquith for a transfer to the Admiralty. Grey to McKenna, 11 Oct. 1911, McKenna MSS 4/4; Haldane to Grey, 2 Oct., Grey to Haldane, 5 Oct. 1911, Haldane MSS 5909.

90 E. David (ed.), *Inside Asquith's Cabinet* (London, 1977), p. 108. It must not be taken from Asquith's action that he wanted the B.E.F. to go to *France*. On 4 October he had told Esher that he inclined to an occupation of Belgium on political and military grounds; on 20 October he told McKenna that he was opposed to the scheme of using British troops in France and that there was no danger of this so long as he was Prime Minister: journal, 4 Oct. 1911, Esher MSS; Marder, *From the Dreadnought to Scapa Flow*, pp. 250–1.

91 Haldane to his sister, 16 Nov. 1911, Haldane MSS 6011.

92 Memo by Bertie, 25 July 1912, Bertie MSS F.O. 800/165; Goschen to Hardinge, 15 July 1911, Hardinge MSS vol. 92; Spender, *Life, Journalism and Politics*, i, p. 156.

93 Asquith to the King, 4 July 1911, CAB 41/33/20; Pease Diary, 4 July 1911; *B.D.*, vii, nos. 405, 433–4; 461; *D.D.F.*, 2nd Series, xiv, nos. 124, 129.

94 C. P. Scott Diary Add. MSS 50901, f. 203.

95 Hardinge to Nicolson, 13 Oct. 1908, Carnock MSS F.O. 800/341.

96 Grey to Sanderson, 12 Sept. 1908, Grey MSS F.O. 800/111.

97 Loreburn to Grey, 23 Mar., Asquith to the King, 20 July 1910, *ibid.* /99, Asquith MSS vol. 5; Pease Diary, 20, 29 July 1910.

98 Minute by Grey on Goschen to Grey, 9 May 1911, *B.D.*, vi, p. 623; Nicolson to Goschen, 14 Feb. 1911, Carnock MSS F.O. 800/347; Grey to Bertie, 22 Apr. 1909, Grey MSS F.O. 800/51.

99 Pease Diary, 8 Mar. 1911, 29 Mar. 1912.

100 Grey to Goschen, 4 July 1912, *B.D.*, vi, no. 593; Nicolson to Hardinge, 21 Nov. 1912, Hardinge to Nicolson, 19 Dec. 1912, Carnock MSS F.O. 800/360, /361; Grey to Harcourt, 7 Mar. 1913, Harcourt MSS.

101 Grey to Maxse, 21 June 1904, Maxse MSS.

102 Trevelyan, *Grey of Fallodon*, p. 84, 13 Aug. 1905; Grey to Spender, 19 Oct. 1905, Spender MSS Add. MSS 46389.

103 *The Times*, 21 Oct. 1905.

104 *B.D.*, iii, no. 299.

105 Grey to Haldane, 3 Sept. 1906, Haldane MSS 5907.

106 Pease Diary, 1 Nov. 1911; note by Harcourt of conversation with Grey and Haldane, 14 Mar. 1912, Harcourt MSS; Grey to Harcourt, 10 Jan. 1914, Grey MSS F.O. 800/91.

107 Memo by Bertie, 25 July 1912, Bertie MSS F.O. 800/165.

108 Monger, *End of Isolation*, p. 331; Grey to Lascelles, 18 Sept. 1907, Lascelles MSS F.O. 800/13.

109 C. P. Scott Diary, 1 Dec. 1911, Add. MSS 50901.

110 A. M. Gollin, *The Observer and G. L. Garvin 1908–14* (Oxford, 1960), p. 79; W. S. Blunt, *My Diaries*, 2 vols. (London, 1919–20), ii, p. 446, 22 July 1914.

111 Pease Diary, 29 Mar., 10 Apr. 1912.

112 Memo by Bertie, 25 July 1912, Bertie MSS F.O. 800/165.

3. The Politics of Liberal Foreign Policy II

1 Minute by Crowe, 2 Feb. 1911, F.O. 371/1117/3884.

2 Nicolson to Mallet, 2 Mar. 1914, Carnock MSS F.O. 800/372.

3 Mallet to Spring-Rice, 29 Feb., 30 Mar., 29 Oct. 1904, Spring-Rice MSS 1/49.

4 Mallet to Short, 6 May 1905, Balfour MSS Add. MSS 49747, to Sandars 17, 18 May 1905, *ibid.*, to Spring-Rice, 16 May 1905, Spring-Rice MSS 1/49.

5 Mallet to Spring-Rice, 2 May 1906, Spring-Rice MSS 1/49.

6 Lister to Lansdowne, 30 June, 7 July 1905, Lansdowne MSS F.O. 800/127.

7 Mallet to Bertie, 11 Jan. 1906, Bertie MSS F.O. 800/164; Bertie to Grey, 13 Jan. 1906, *B.D.*, iii, no. 213.

8 Bertie to Nicolson, 14 May 1911, Carnock MSS F.O. 800/348; memo by Bertie, 25 July 1912, Bertie MSS F.O. 800/165; *B.D.*, x (ii), no. 388. In April 1909, Mallet had warned Grey that if in the event of an Anglo-German war the Mediterranean was abandoned to the French Fleet, 'it would be rash to assume that, *without an alliance* the French would come to our assistance . . . '. Mallet to Grey, 11 Apr. 1909, Grey MSS F.O. 800/93.

9 Nicolson to Grey, 24 Mar. 1909, Carnock MSS F.O. 800/337.

10 Hardinge to Nicolson, 30 Mar. 1909, *ibid.* /342; Nicolson to Hardinge, 3 Apr. 1909, to Grey, 8 Apr. 1909, *ibid.* /337; Nicolson to Hardinge, 21 Apr. 1909, Hardinge MSS vol. 16.

11 Nicolson to Hardinge, 2 June 1909, Carnock MSS F.O. 800/337.

12 H. Wilson Diary, 1 May 1912.

13 Minute by Crowe, 2 May 1912, F.O. 371/1365/18120.

14 Memo by Crowe, 8 May 1912, *B.D.*, x (ii), no. 386. This is the revised text approved by Grey. The idea that such a paper be prepared by the F.O. emerged from a meeting between Wilson, Troubridge, Hankey and Crowe on 29 April. H. Wilson Diary, 29 Apr. 1912; *B.D.* x (ii), no. 381.

15 Wilson Diary 4, 8, 17 May 1912; *B.D.*, x (ii), no. 385.

16 Nicolson to Goschen, 11 Mar. 1913, Carnock MSS F.O. 800/364, to O'Beirne, 17 Nov. 1913, *ibid.* /371, to Buchanan, 10 Feb., 10 Mar. 1914, *ibid.* /372, /373.

17 Nicolson to de Bunsen, 27 Apr. 1914, *ibid.* /373.

18 Buchanan to Nicolson, 5 Feb. 1914, *ibid.* /372; to Grey, 18 Feb. 1914, Grey MSS F.O. 800/74; to Grey, 31 Mar. 1914, F.O. 371/2092/15087.

19 F.O. 371/2092/10333; Sazonov to Benckendorff, 19 Feb. 1913, R. Marchand (ed.), *Un Livre noire*, 2 vols. (Paris, 1922–3), ii, p. 307.

20 Benckendorff to Sazonov, 25 Feb. 1914, Marchand, *Livre noir*, ii, p. 308; memo by Hardinge, 4 May 1909, *B.D.*, v, App. III.

21 *B.D.*, iii, no. 213; Bertie to Mallet, 15 Apr. 1907, Bertie MSS F.O. 800/164, to Nicolson, 14 May 1911, Carnock MSS F.O. 800/348; memos by Bertie, 25 July 1911, 23 June 1913, Bertie MSS F.O. 800/160, /166; *B.D.*, x (ii), no. 388.

22 Nicolson to Townley, 7 Apr. 1914, Carnock MSS F.O. 800/373; Buchanan to Nicolson, 16 Apr. 1914, *B.D.*, x (ii), no. 538.

23 Nicolson to Spring-Rice, 14 Aug. 1907, Spring-Rice MSS F.O. 800/241.

24 Memo by Balfour, 12 June 1912, Balfour MSS Add. MSS 49731.

25 Hardinge to Villiers, 1 Apr. 1909: 'I have always felt about the French that it would not be difficult for Germany to stampede them.' Hardinge MSS vol. 17.

26 Nicolson to Grey, 8 Apr. 1909, Carnock MSS F.O. 800/337; Hardinge to Spring-Rice, 4 June 1909: 'a German-Russian rapprochement is a possibility which must not be lost sight of'. Hardinge MSS vol. 17; F.O. 371/2091/6329.

27 Grey to Lascelles, 18 Sept. 1907, Lascelles MSS F.O. 800/13; minute by Grey, Oct. 1907, *B.D.*, iv, no. 544; Grey in the House of Commons, 29 Mar. 1909, Hansard, 5th Series, iii, col. 58, and 27 Nov. 1911, *ibid.*, xxxii, col. 60.

28 Nicolson to Bertie, 6 May 1912, *B.D.*, x (ii), no. 384, to Buchanan, 7, 21 Apr. 1914, Carnock MSS F.O. 800/373.

29 *B.D.*, iii, no. 216.

30 C. H. D. Howard, *Britain and the Casus Belli 1822–1902* (London, 1974), pp. 20–1.

31 *Ibid.*, p. 17.

32 Hardinge MSS vol. 17.

33 Howard, *Britan and the Casus Belli*, pp. 127–9; G. E. Buckle (ed.), *Letters of Queen Victoria*, 3rd Series (London, 1930), i, pp. 268–9; Salisbury to Sanderson, 15 Jan. 1902, Lascelles MSS F.O. 800/10, to Currie, 18 Aug. 1892, Lady Gwendolen Cecil, *Life of Salisbury* (London, 1932), iv, pp. 404–5.

34 See Rich and Fisher, *The Holstein Papers*, iv, p. 83; *B.D.*, ii, no. 86.

35 Nicolson to Bertie, 17 May 1911, Bertie MSS F.O. 800/180; *idem* to *idem*, 23 Apr. 1912, *ibid.* /165; *B.D.*, iii, p. 401.

36 Hardinge to Nicolson, 12 Apr. 1909, Carnock MSS F.O. 800/342, my italics, to the King, 28 Apr. 1909, Hardinge MSS vol. 18, to Goschen 27 Apr. 1909, *ibid.* vol. 17, to Nicolson, 12 May 1909, Carnock MSS F.O. 800/342. In an undated letter of May 1909, O'Beirne wrote to Nicolson: 'the best that can be

hoped for is to keep things going as they are, until we have a change of Government'. Carnock MSS F.O. 800/342. See also Nicolson, *Lord Carnock*, pp. 307–8.

37 See above n. 24. There was room also in The Constitution According to Austen Chamberlain: *Politics from Inside*, p. 425, 24 Feb. 1912; A. Chamberlain, *Down the Years* (London, 1935), pp. 66–7.

38 Memo by Balfour, 12 Dec. 1901, Balfour MSS Add. MSS 49727.

39 Lord Goschen in *The Times*, 27 Feb. 1896.

40 Nicolson to Mallet, 2 Mar. 1914, Carnock MSS F.O. 800/372, to de Bunsen, 27 Apr. 1914, *ibid.* /373, to Buchanan, 10 Feb. 1914, *ibid.* /372, to Mallet, 27 Apr. 1914, *ibid.* /373.

41 Grey to Maxse, 12 Oct. 1902, Maxse MSS.

42 Edward Hamilton Diary, 13 Feb. 1902, Add. MSS 48679.

43 Percy to Balfour, 13, 18 Jan. 1905, Balfour MSS Add. MSS 49747; Sandars to Balfour, 17 Jan. 1905, *ibid.* 49763.

44 Nicolson to Spring-Rice, 21 June 1907, Spring-Rice MSS F.O. 800/241.

45 B.D., ii, no. 94.

46 Howard, *Britain and the Casus Belli*, pp. 123–4; G.P., viii, p. 83.

47 Lansdowne to Hardinge, 4 Sept. 1905, Hardinge MSS vol. 7. Hardinge nevertheless omitted this passage when reading the despatch to Lamsdorff: Hardinge to Lansdowne, 13 Sept. 1905, *ibid.* vol. 6.

48 B.D., iii, no. 439.

49 Nicolson to Hardinge, 3 Apr., 2 June 1909, Carnock MSS F.O. 800/337; Hardinge to Nicolson, 25 May 1909, Hardinge MSS vol. 17.

50 Nicolson to Bertie, 23 Apr. 1912, Bertie MSS F.O. 800/165, to O'Beirne, 31 May 1912, Carnock MSS F.O. 800/355.

51 Grey to Nicolson, 16 Oct. 1912, Bertie MSS F.O. 800/165.

52 Memo by Bertie, 27 Sept. 1913, *ibid.* /179; minute by Grey on de Bunsen to Nicolson, 5 Apr. 1913, Carnock MSS F.O. 800/365; Grey to Nicolson, 4 Oct. 1913, *ibid.* /370. In March 1907, in regard to a French proposal for a tripartite arrangement between France, Spain and Britain, Hardinge had pointed out the necessity of absolute secrecy: 'Otherwise it would be seriously resented by Germany who would regard it as aimed at her; it would appear as a tightening of the net spread around German political activity; and might act as a sufficient provocation to Germany to drive her into hostile action of some kind.' Before the French proposal was made Grey had been prepared to offer Spain 'an undertaking to help her to protect her islands and Moroccan coast against aggression in return for guarantees to us on her part, which would increase the security of Gibraltar'. Memo by Hardinge, 25 Mar. 1907, *B.D.*, vii, no. 19; Grey to Campbell-Bannerman, 11 Jan. 1907, Campbell-Bannerman MSS Add. MSS 52514; minutes on de Bunsen to Grey, 7 Jan. 1907, *B.D.*, vii, no. 9.

53 Goschen to Nicolson, 24 Apr. 1914, Carnock MSS F.O. 800/374; on 23 May he added that a naval understanding with Russia would be made a pretext by some groups for an increase in the German naval programme (*ibid.*).

54 Mallet to Sandars, 20 Apr. 1905, Balfour MSS 49747.
55 Bertie to Mallet, 15 Apr. 1907, Bertie MSS F.O. 800/164.
56 Memo by Bertie, 23 June 1913, *ibid.* /166.
57 Memo by Bertie, 25 June 1914, *ibid.* /171.
58 Bertie to Grey, 30 July 1914, *ibid.* /166; minute by Crowe, 31 July 1914, *B.D.*, xi, no. 318.
59 Minute by Hardinge, 5 Sept. 1906, F.O. 371/79/30158.
60 O'Conor to Grey, 31 Mar. 1906, *B.D.*, iii, p. 87.
61 Goschen to Lascelles, 16 June 1907, Lascelles MSS F.O. 800/13.
62 Bertie to Lansdowne, 31 July 1905, Lansdowne MSS F.O. 800/127. The intermediary was Betzold, a French financier and intimate of Rouvier. See also Chirol to Steed, 2 June 1905, Chirol MSS.
63 Bertie to Grey, 20 Jan. 1913, Grey MSS F.O. 800/54.
64 Russell to Goschen, 3 Mar. 1911, forwarded to Grey, *B.D.*, vi, no. 442.
65 Bethmann-Hollweg to Lichnowsky, 16 June 1914, *G.P.*, xxxix, no. 15883: 'Had the rumours (of an Anglo-Russian naval convention) proved true, even though only in the form that the English and Russian navies had come to an agreement to cooperate by fighting together against Germany in the event of a future war – an agreement similar to that made by England with France at the time of the Morocco crisis – Russian and French chauvinism would not only thereby have been greatly stimulated, but public opinion (in Germany) would have become subject to a not unjustifiable disquiet that would have found its expression in a "navy scare" and led to the renewed envenoming of our slowly improving relations with England. In the midst of the nervous tension in the grip of which Europe has found itself during the last few years, the result might have proved incalculable.'
66 Fischer, *War of Illusions*, pp. 139, 224.
67 Bertie to Grey, 17 Apr. 1907, Grey MSS F.O. 800/50.
68 Mallet to Sandars, 20 Apr. 1905, Balfour MSS Add. MSS 49747; Spring-Rice to Chirol, 13 Apr. 1905, Spring-Rice MSS 1/20; note by Chaumié, 6 June 1906, *D.D.F.*, 2nd Series, vi, Annex 1; Huguet to Etienne, 18 Nov. 1905, *ibid.*, viii, no. 137.
69 French Military Attaché (Berlin) to French Military Attaché (London), 9 Feb. 1912, Carnock MSS F.O. 800/353. The French Military Attaché in London had been present at a meeting in September 1911 at which H. A. Gwynne had been told by Sir J. French that Britain could not meet the French wish for 120,000 men on the Belgian frontier. Gwynne concluded 'That is why the French have to give "compensation" and they know it'. Gwynne to Lady Bathurst, 14, 17 Sept. 1911, Glenesk-Bathurst MSS.
70 Memo by Bertie, 16 Feb. 1912, Bertie MSS F.O. 800/171.
71 Memo by Bertie, 25 July 1912, *ibid.* /165; Grahame to Tyrrell, 5 Dec. 1912, Grey MSS F.O. 800/53; memo by Bertie, 23 June 1913, Bertie MSS F.O. 800/166.
72 Memo by Balfour, 12 June 1912, see n. 24.
73 Memos by Bertie, 25 June, 4 July 1914, Bertie MSS F.O. 800/171, /177. In

July 1912 Grey was at pains to convince the House of Commons that separate groups of Powers did not mean opposing diplomatic camps: Hansard, 5th Series, xl, cols. 1994–5. Sir G. Buchanan, *My Mission to Russia*, 2 vols. (London, 1923), i, pp. 192–6; Buchanan to Nicolson, 4 Apr. 1914, Carnock MSS F.O. 800/373.

74 Hansard, 4th Series, cxxxv, col. 523, 1 June 1904.

75 Grey to Bertie, 29 Dec. 1907, Carnock MSS F.O. 800/340.

76 Minutes by Crowe, 28 May 1906, 10 May 1909, *B.D.*, iii, no. 416, *B.D.*, vi, no. 179. See also Cartwright to Grey, 8 Jan. 1908, F.O. 371/457/1308. Bertie to Nicolson, 16 Mar. 1911, Carnock MSS F.O. 800/347; Grey to Bertie, 7 Feb. 1912, *B.D.*, vi, no. 498.

77 Minute by Grey on Goschen to Grey, 21 Aug. 1909, *B.D.*, vi, no. 187; Grey to Bertie, 30 Aug. 1909, Grey MSS F.O. 800/51.

78 Grey to Goschen, 26 Oct. 1910, Grey MSS F.O. 800/62; minute by Grey on Goschen to Grey, 21 Oct. 1910, *ibid.*; Buchanan to Nicolson, 12 Jan. 1911, Carnock MSS F.O. 800/347.

79 Haldane to Asquith, 1 Sept. 1922, Asquith MSS vol. 34; Grey at the 111th meeting of C.I.D., 26 May 1911, CAB 2/2/2.

80 Nicolson to Hardinge, 10 Sept. 1906, Carnock MSS F.O. 800/337.

81 W. Kent, *John Burns* (London, 1950), p. 238; Burns Diary, 6 Aug. 1914, Add. MSS 46308.

82 Morley to Burns, 14 June 1916, Burns Diary Add. MSS 46283; C. P. Scott Diary, 27 Nov. 1914, 22 Jan. 1912, 1 Dec. 1911, *ibid.* 50901; Loreburn to Runciman, 2 Apr. 1912, Runciman MSS.

83 See Harcourt's copy of Churchill memo, 15 June 1912, 'The Naval Situation in the Mediterranean', Harcourt MSS 590.

84 Chamberlain, *Politics from Inside*, p. 485, 4 May 1912; Pease Diary, 21 June 1912; Morley to McKenna, 3 July 1912, in S. McKenna, *Reginald McKenna* (London, 1948), p. 147: 'My own mind is quite made up. No alliance, with or without a mask.'

85 Grey to Nicolson, 2 Apr. 1909, Carnock MSS F.O. 800/342.

86 Trevelyan, *Grey of Fallodon*, p. 122; *B.D.*, vi, no. 10.

87 Pease Diary, 21 June 1912.

88 MacDonald to Hardinge, 31 Aug. 1905, Hardinge MSS vol. 7; Tyrrell to Spring-Rice, 25 May, 21 June 1907, Spring-Rice MSS F.O. 800/241; de Bunsen to Nicolson, 1 June 1912, Carnock MSS F.O. 800/357.

89 Memos by McKenna, 24 June, 3 July 1912, CAB 37/111/79, /86.

90 Note by Lansdowne for the Cabinet, 16 Dec. 1901, Nish, *The Anglo-Japanese Alliance*, p. 212.

91 Memo by Salisbury, 7 Jan. 1902, *ibid.*, pp. 209–10.

92 *The Times*, 21 Oct. 1905. Grey had by this time reconciled himself to the Anglo-Japanese Alliance, which at first he had thought would obstruct an agreement with Russia.

93 *B.D.*, xi, nos. 426, 447.

94 Churchill to Balfour, 11 June 1912, Balfour MSS Add. MSS 49694; memo by

Balfour, 12 June 1912, see n. 24; Churchill to Grey and Asquith, 23 Aug. 1912, in R. S. Churchill, *Winston S. Churchill*, ii, companion part 3 (London, 1969), p. 1639; Grahame to Tyrrell, 27 May 1912, Grey MSS F.O. 800/53.

95 Esher to Fisher, 9 July 1912, in Brett and Esher, *Journals and Letters of Reginald, Viscount Esher*, iii, p. 101.

96 *Manchester Guardian*, 27 May, 5 July 1912; D. Ayerst, *The Manchester Guardian – Biography of a Newspaper* (New York, 1971), p. 369; *Westminster Gazette*, 30 May 1912.

97 C. P. Scott Diary, 1 Dec. 1911, 6, 22 Jan. 1912, Add. MSS 50901. The *Daily News* of 30 March 1911 said: 'Those who want Conscription want it as something which will enable them to intervene decisively in the affairs of the Continent.'

98 See n. 83.

99 Minute by Grey, 29 May 1908, F.O. 371/455/18454.

100 Metternich to Bulow, 11 Dec. 1908, *G.P.*, xxviii, no. 10237.

101 Metternich to Bulow, 1 Aug., 16 July 1908, *ibid.*, xxiv, nos. 8219, 8217.

102 Grahame to Tyrrell, 27 May, 5 Dec. 1912, Grey MSS F.O. 800/53.

103 Minute by Villiers, 29 May 1908, F.O. 371/455/18454.

104 Memo by Milner, 10 Apr. 1907 of conversation with Clemenceau, printed by R. B. Jones, 'Anglo-French Negotiations 1907: A Memorandum by Sir Alfred Milner', *B.I.H.R.*, xxxi (1958), pp. 224–7; memo by Haldane on Army Estimates, 23 Nov. 1907, CAB 37/90/103; H. Wilson Diary, 6 May 1912; *G.P.*, xxviii, no. 10237.

105 Memo by Bulow, 11 Feb. 1909, *G.P.*, xxviii, no. 10261; M. J. Allison, 'The National Service Issue 1899–1914' (D.Phil thesis, University of London, 1975), pp. 144–5.

106 Milner to Midleton, 27 July 1909, Midleton MSS P.R.O. 30/67/24.

107 *G.P.*, xxiv, no. 8219; Allison, 'The National Service Issue', p. 164.

108 Lord Riddell, *More Pages from My Diary 1908–14* (London, 1934), p. 140; R. J. Scally, *The Origins of the Lloyd George Coalition*, pp. 187–93, 232–3; Gwynne to Lady Bathurst, 30 Oct. 1911, 27 Feb. 1912, Glenesk-Bathurst MSS. 'The Writing on the Wall' was a series of articles commissioned by Gwynne from Roberts in September 1911.

109 Allison, 'The National Service Issue', pp. 150, 157, 215–22; Dawson to Saunders, 21 Feb., to Northcliffe, 8 Mar. 1913, in *The History of 'The Times'*, iv, part 1 (London, 1952), pp. 95–8.

110 C. P. Scott Diary, 7 Jan. 1912, Add. MSS 50901.

111 Runciman to Harcourt, 24 Aug. 1911, Runciman MSS. This elicited Harcourt's remark that the landing of British troops to assist a French Army on the Meuse would be 'a criminal folly': Harcourt to Runciman, 26 Aug. 1911, *ibid.*

112 Chamberlain to Lansdowne, 2 Aug. 1914, A. Chamberlain MSS AC14/2/11; see notes by Philip J. Baker and Charles Trevelyan, August 1914, Trevelyan MSS CPT 61.

113 Loreburn to Grey, 25 Aug. 1911, Grey MSS F.O. 800/99; Scott to Grey, 12 Jan. 1912, C. P. Scott MSS, uncat.

114 Cambon to Rouvier, 31 Jan. 1906, *D.D.F.*, 2nd Series, ix, no. 106; *B.D.*, iii, nos. 219, 220(b). See J. Wilson, *Campbell-Bannerman*, pp. 525–33.

115 An overture from Delcassé was ignored in April 1909: Bertie to Grey, 4 Apr. 1909, Grey MSS F.O. 800/51; in April 1911, Cruppi was forbidden to use in a speech words which 'would have been construed as if an offensive and defensive alliance were impending' – the fuss this would have created 'here' would have been greater than that created 'elsewhere': *B.D.*, vii, nos. 200, 201; Grey to Bertie, 8 Apr. 1911, Grey MSS F.O. 800/52.

116 Loreburn to Grey, 25 Aug. 1911, Grey MSS F.O. 800/99.

117 Chamberlain, *Politics from Inside*, p. 486, 4 May 1912; *Down the Years*, p. 68; H. Wilson Diary, 8 May 1912.

118 Memos by Bertie, 25 July 1912, 23 June 1913, Bertie MSS F.O. 800/165, /166.

119 Grey to Asquith, 26 Oct. 1910, Asquith MSS vol. 12; Esher to Harcourt, 29 Sept. 1912, Harcourt MSS; Riddell, *More Pages from My Diary*, p. 140, 19 Apr. 1913.

120 Harcourt to F. G. Thomas, 5 Aug. 1914, Harcourt MSS.

121 Bertie to Grey, 17 Apr. 1907, Grey MSS F.O. 800/50.

122 W. J. Mommsen, 'Domestic Factors in German Foreign Policy before 1914', *Central European History*, vi (1973), pp. 36–9; F. Stern, 'Bethmann-Hollweg and the War: The Limits of Responsibility', in F. Stern and L. Krieger (eds.), *The Responsibility of Power* (New York, 1967), p. 263.

4. The Dissimulation of the Balance of Power

1   *B.D.*, iii, p. 403.

2   Hansard, 4th Series, cxxxv, cols. 535–6, 1 June 1904.

3   C. P. Scott Diary, 6–8 Sept., 1 Dec. 1911, 29 Sept. 1912, Add. MSS 50901; Pease Diary, 20 July 1910, Gainford MSS.

4   Grey to Cartwright, 6 Jan. 1909, Grey MSS F.O. 800/41, to Goschen, 9 June 1909, *B.D.*, vi, no. 182.

5   Hansard, 5th Series, xxxii, col. 60, 27 Nov. 1911.

6   Lichnowsky to Bethmann-Hollweg, 3 Dec. 1912, *G.P.*, xxxix, no. 15612.

7   Memo by Crowe, 31 July 1914, *B.D.*, xi, no. 369.

8   Minute by Crowe, 14 May 1911, *B.D.*, vi, p. 628.

9   Note by Ommanney on memo by Grant-Duff, 4 Jan. 1907, W.O. 106/46.

10 Memo by Ewart, March 1909, W.O. 106/45 E1/1; Grey MSS F.O. 800/102; Ewart Diary, 12 July 1909, 21 Mar. 1910, Ewart MSS.

11 Memo by Wilson, 12 Aug. 1911, 'The Military Aspect of the Continental Problem', CAB 38/19/47.

12 Minutes of 114th meeting of C.I.D., 23 Aug. 1911, p. 5, CAB 2/2/2.

13 Notes by Wilson, 15 Aug. 1911, on memo by Churchill, 13 Aug. 1911, W.O. 106/47A, and CAB 38/19/50. Pellé to Berteaux, 7 Mar. 1911, *D.D.F.*, 2nd Series, xiii, no. 180.

14 Chirol to Hardinge, 1 Dec. 1910, Hardinge MSS vol. 19.

15 Wilson to Roberts, 17 Apr. 1910, Roberts MSS W.O. 105/45.

16 Memo by Gorton, 30 June 1911, D.M.O. to C.I.G.S., 3, 8 May 1911, W.O. 106/49C; Wilson Diary, 20 July, 9, 29 Sept. 1911.

17 Pease Diary, 8 Mar. 1911.

18 Minutes of 114th meeting of C.I.D., 23 Aug. 1911, p. 2, CAB 2/2/2; proceedings of first meeting of C.I.D. sub-committee on the Military Needs of the Empire, 3 Dec. 1908, CAB 16/5; see also CAB 38/16/9, and undated, uninitialled note on W.A./1 in W.O. 106/49C.

19 Minute by D.M.O., 26 Dec. 1911, W.O. 106/49.

20 Wilson Diary, 12 Nov. 1912; memo on the Development of the Expeditionary Force, unsigned, Sept. 1913, W.O. 106/49; notes of a conversation with Dewar, Assistant Chief of Staff, Admiralty, on the Recent Trend of Admiralty Policy, 11 Oct. 1913, *ibid.*

21 Minute by Hardinge, 29 May 1908: 'At best our army can never have more than a moral effect on the Continent since we could never send an expeditionary force of more than 150,000 men while continental armies are counted by millions.' F.O. 371/455/18454.

22 Grey to Bertie, 15 Jan. 1906, *B.D.*, iii, no. 216.

23 Memo by Churchill, 27 June 1908, CAB 37/94/89; for Lloyd George in similar vein see E. T. S. Dugdale (ed.), *German Diplomatic Documents 1871–1914* (London, 1930), iii, p. 286; minutes of 114th meeting of C.I.D., CAB 2/2/2; memo by Churchill, 16 Oct. 1911, ADM 116/3474.

24 *D.D.F.*, 2nd Series, vi, pp. 602–3; C. Andrew, *Théophile Delcassé and the Making of the Entente Cordiale* (London, 1968), p. 297; *B.D.*, iii, no. 98. See also Chirol to Steed, 2 June 1905, Chirol MSS.

25 ADM 116/3486, /1043b, part i; R. F. MacKay, *Fisher of Kilverstone* (Oxford, 1973), p. 370.

26 Marder, *From the Dreadnought to Scapa Flow*, i, p. 379.

27 Note by Esher, 14 Dec. 1908, App. VII to proceedings of sub-committee on the Military Needs of the Empire, CAB 16/5.

28 Memo by General Staff, 5 Mar. 1909, App. VIII (B), *ibid.*

29 Report of C.I.D. sub-committee on the Military Needs of the Empire, 24 July 1909, para. 13, *ibid.*, my italics.

30 CAB 17/8; MacKay, *Fisher of Kilverstone*, p. 375. The C.I.D. sub-committee appointed to enquire into Certain Questions of Naval Policy raised by Lord Charles Beresford, consisting of Asquith, Crewe, Morley, Grey and Haldane,which reported in August 1909, had not failed to remark on this: *ibid.*, p. 416.

31 Minute by Hardinge, 23 Feb. 1906, *B.D.*, iii, no. 299.

32 Memo by Hardinge, May 1909, *B.D.*, v, App. V.

33 Nicolson to Cartwright, 23 Jan. 1911, Carnock MSS F.O. 800/347.

34 Nicolson to Bertie, 17 May 1911, *ibid.* /348; minute by Nicolson, 10 May 1911, *B.D.*, vi, p. 623.

35 Wilson Diary, 11 Sept., 23 Nov. 1911, 11 Jan. 1912; Nicolson to Hardinge, 18 Apr. 1912, Hardinge MSS vol. 92.

36 Report by de Salis, Trench and Heath, forwarded by Goschen, 26 Mar. 1910, CAB 17/61; Goschen to Nicolson, 22 Oct. 1910, *B.D.*, vi, no. 405.

37 Goschen to Grey, 12 Mar. 1911, *B.D.*, vi, no. 446.

38 Goschen to Nicolson, 18 Aug. 1911, Carnock MSS F.O. 800/349.

39 Bulow, for instance, who in December 1904 did think that Germany would lose much in a purely Anglo-German war, believed that such losses could be more than made up if Germany involved France and the Low Countries in the war. Rich and Fisher, *The Holstein Papers*, iv, pp. 318–19.

40 Spring-Rice to Chirol, 13 Apr. 1905, Spring-Rice MSS 1/20; *D.D.F.*, 2nd Series, vi, Annex 1; minute by Spicer, 26 May 1908, F.O. 371/455/18033; memo by Bertie, 8 Mar. 1914, sent to Tyrrell, Grey MSS F.O. 800/55; Nicolson to Buchanan, 7 Apr. 1914, Carnock MSS F.O. 800/373. Langley may be considered an exception: in January 1911 he minuted on a report of the former Italian Prime Minister's remarks that Italy relied for the maintenance of her position on British naval forces in the Mediterranean: 'Signor Luzzatti did not explain how our naval preponderance was to be made effective against the great military strength of Austria mentioned in the last few lines of this despatch.' F.O. 371/1133/2007. For some reason, it was not perfectly obvious that this applied, *mutatis mutandis*, to France and Germany.

41 Chirol to Hardinge, 17 Feb. 1911, Hardinge MSS vol. 92; Bertie to Nicolson, 28 Nov. 1912, Carnock MSS F.O. 800/360; C. P. Scott Diary, 1 Dec. 1911, 6, 22 Jan. 1912, Add. MSS 50901.

42 Watson to Goschen, 12 May 1913, Carnock MSS F.O. 800/367.

43 Memos by Selborne, 17 Jan., 16 Nov. 1901, CAB 37/56/8, /59/118; Lansdowne to Lascelles, 22 Apr. 1902, Lascelles MSS F.O. 800/11; Lascelles to Lansdowne, 25 Apr. 1902, Lansdowne MSS F.O. 800/129. All Selborne's questions were first answered in the negative. Only in a postscript did Lascelles allow himself to be corrected by his Naval Attaché. Even so Lascelles still maintained that Germany would not actually join France and Russia in an attack on Britain – 'but she might dictate terms which would be advantageous to her and which we, weakened by war might be unable to resist'.

44 Memo by Selborne, 7 Dec. 1903, CAB 37/67/83, p. 4.

45 Balfour in the House of Commons, 1 Mar. 1904, Hansard, 4th Series, cxxx, col. 1410.

46 Balfour to the King, 26 Feb. 1902, Lansdowne MSS F.O. 800/145.

47 Arnold-Foster Diary, 20 Nov. 1903, Add. MSS 50335.

48 Memo by Balfour, 2 Jan. 1904, A. Chamberlain MSS AC17/1/30.

49 Hamilton to Curzon, 9 July 1903, I.O.L. MSS Eur. C. 126/5.

50 Memo by Lansdowne, 10 Sept. 1903, F.O. 27/3765; Lansdowne to Cromer, 7 Dec. 1903, Lansdowne MSS F.O. 800/124.

51 Memos by Selborne, 7 Dec. 1903, 26 Feb. 1904, CAB 37/67/83, /69/32.

52 Hansard, 4th Series, cxxx, cols. 1405–6, 1 Mar. 1904.

53 Minutes of 111th meeting of C.I.D., CAB 2/2/2; C. P. Scott Diary, 25 July 1911, Add. MSS 50901.

54 Minutes of 117th and 118th meetings of C.I.D., 4 and 11 July 1912, CAB 2/2/3.

55 Hansard, 5th Series, lix, cols. 2189–90, 18 Mar. 1914.

56 Note by Tweedmouth, 11 Nov. 1906, Campbell-Bannerman MSS Add. MSS 41231.

57 Haldane to Asquith, 1 Sept. 1922, Asquith MSS vol. 34; to Rosebery, 14 Aug. 1916, Rosebery MSS box 24.

58 Hansard, 4th Series, cxxx, col. 1412.

59 G. E. Buckle (ed.), *Letters of Queen Victoria*, 3rd Series (London, 1930–2), i, pp. 194–5, 29 Aug. 1886; Salisbury to Malet, 16 Feb. 1887, Salisbury Papers, Hatfield House MSS A/64; minute by Salisbury, Oct. 1895, para. 5, CAB 37/40/64.

60 Minute by Grey, 19 Feb. 1913, F.O. 371/1647/7737.

61 Lansdowne to Cromer, 10 Sept. 1905, Lansdowne MSS F.O. 800/124.

62 Grey to Brodrick, 11 Mar. 1899, Midleton MSS P.R.O. 30/67/4; Grey to Maxse, 20 Oct. 1902, 21 June 1904, Maxse MSS.

63 *The Times*, 21 Oct. 1905; *B.D.*, iii, no. 299.

64 *B.D.*, iii, nos. 90, 94, 95; Cromer to Balfour, 15 Oct. 1903, Cromer MSS F.O. 633/6; Chamberlain, *Politics from Inside*, p. 427.

65 Nish, *The Anglo-Japanese Alliance*, pp. 300–9.

66 *B.D.*, iv, no. 135; Minto to Morley, 12 June 1906, I.O.L. MSS Eur.D 573/8.

67 Morley recognised this when he wrote to Minto on 23 Mar. 1906: 'Suppose you were coming to some sort of understanding with Russia . . . and suppose even that we held the upper hand in the negotiations . . .'. J. Morley, *Recollections*, 2 vols. (London, 1917), ii, p. 167.

68 CAB 38/13/20; Morley to Minto, 19 Sept. 1907, I.O.L. MSS Eur.D 573/2. In April 1904, Balfour and Arnold-Foster had agreed that, as a military problem, the Indian Frontier Question was 'insoluble': 'Diplomacy rather than preparations on the Frontier, must come to our aid.' Arnold-Foster Diary, 28 Apr. 1904, Add. MSS 50337.

69 Nish, *The Anglo-Japanese Alliance*, pp. 354–8; B. Williams, 'The Strategic Background to the Anglo-Russian Entente of August 1907', *H.J.*, ix, no. 3 (1966), p. 365; minutes of 96th meeting of C.I.D., CAB 2/2/1; memo by General Staff, 19 Dec. 1906, CAB 38/12/60.

70 Minutes by Grey and Hardinge, 6 Aug. 1907, on Spring-Rice to Grey, 16 July 1907, F.O. 371/371/26042, my italics; see Grey to Spring-Rice, 30 Nov. 1906, Spring-Rice MSS F.O. 800/241; Morley to Minto, 16 Jan. 1906, I.O.L. MSS Eur.D. 573/1.

71 Morley to Minto, 20 Mar. 1908, I.O.L. MSS Eur.D 573/3; Grey to Campbell-Bannerman, 31 Aug. 1907, Grey MSS F.O. 800/100.

72 *B.D.*, iii, no. 299.

73 Grey to Nicolson, 26 Aug. 1907, F.O. 371/320/28370.

74 See D. Dakin, *The Greek Struggle in Macedonia 1897–1913* (Salonika, 1966), p. 349. In 1912, the Director of the Operations Division at the Admiralty was prepared, as Arnold-Foster had been in 1904, to contemplate a Russian naval presence in the eastern Mediterranean, partly because 'it would . . . divert Russian ambitions from the Persian Gulf': minute by Ballard, 20 July 1912, ADM 116/3109/0091; Arnold-Foster Diary, 21 Nov. 1904, Add. MSS 50340.

75 Hardinge to Nicolson, 25 Nov. 1907, 7 Jan. 1908, Carnock MSS F.O. 800/
    340, /341; minute by Hardinge, 28 Oct. 1907, *B.D.*, iv, no. 544.
76 B. Williams, 'Great Britain and Russia 1905–7', in F. H. Hinsley (ed.), *The
    Foreign Policy of Sir Edward Grey* (Cambridge, 1977), p. 135.
77 Hardinge to Nicolson, 4 Jan. 1909, *B.D.*, v, p. 550, to de Salis, 29 Dec. 1908,
    Hardinge MSS vol. 13.
78 Nicolson to Goschen, 15 Apr. 1912, *B.D.*, vi, no. 575, to Barclay, 24 Oct.
    1911, to Buchanan, 22 Oct. 1912, Carnock MSS F.O. 800/351, /359.
79 Nicolson to Buchanan, 22 Apr. 1913, Carnock MSS F.O. 800/365.
80 Hardinge to Nicolson, 16 May 1913, *ibid.* /367.
81 Nicolson to Townley, 7 Apr. 1914, *ibid.* /373.
82 Buchanan to Nicolson, 16 Apr. 1914, *B.D.*, x (ii), no. 538.
83 Grey to Goschen, 5 May 1910, *B.D.*, vi, no. 361.
84 Grey to Churchill, 22 Apr. 1909, Grey MSS F.O. 800/89.
85 Grey to Bertie, 7 Jan. 1909, Bertie MSS F.O. 800/171, to Bertie, 30 Aug.
    1909, Grey MSS F.O. 800/51, to Goschen, 26 Oct. 1910, *ibid.* /62, to Bertie,
    7 Feb. 1912, *ibid.* /53.
86 Pease Diary, 20 July 1910.
87 *B.D.*, x (i), no. 914; Goschen to Nicolson, late Jan. 1913, Carnock MSS F.O.
    800/363. See Selborne to Curzon, 19 Apr. 1901, in Monger, *The End of Iso-
    lation*, p. 7; Hamilton to Curzon, 8 Apr. 1903, *ibid.*, p. 109; Balfour to
    Selborne, 6 Apr. 1904, Selborne MSS 1.
88 C. P. Scott Diary, 25 July 1911, Add. MSS 50901.
89 Grey to Hardinge, 28 Jan. 1912, Hardinge MSS vol. 92.
90 *B.D.*, xi, no. 101.
91 *Ibid.*, no. 490. See K. M. Wilson, 'Imperial Interests in the British Decision for
    War, 1914: the Defence of India in Central Asia', *Review of International
    Studies*, x, no. 3 (1984).
92 This was embodied in a letter to Bertie which was clearly subsequent to the
    telegram sent at 8.20 p.m. It was probably after writing it that Grey retired to
    his club for dinner, in the course of which he indicated his intention to have
    it out with the Cabinet on the morrow, which he duly did, taking a much
    stronger line than hitherto. *B.D.*, xi, nos. 426, 447; and see chapter 8.
93 Note by Nicolson for Grey, 21 July 1911, Grey MSS F.O. 800/94; Nicolson
    to Goschen, 24 July 1911, Carnock MSS F.O. 800/349; note by Nicolson,
    3 Aug. 1911, F.O. 371/1123/32100.
94 Mallet to Short, 4 May 1912, Balfour MSS Add. MSS 49747, to Bryce,
    22 Dec. 1911, Bryce MSS USA vol. 32.
95 Memo by Grey, 28 Apr. 1908, Grey MSS F.O. 800/92; minute by Grey,
    29 May 1908, F.O. 371/455/18454.
96 Asquith to Grey, 7 Sept. 1908, Grey MSS F.O. 800/100.
97 Grey to Nicolson, 12 Feb. 1906, *B.D.*, iii, no. 278; to Bertie, 15 Mar. 1906,
    Bertie MSS F.O. 800/160.
98 Hardinge to Nicolson, 8 Feb. 1906, Carnock MSS F.O. 800/338; Sanderson
    to Spring-Rice, 20 Feb. 1906, Spring-Rice MSS F.O. 800/241; *B.D.*, iv, nos.
    544, 550.

99 Memo by Hardinge, May 1909, *B.D.*, v, App. V; Hardinge to Cartwright, 18 May, 4 Oct. 1909, Cartwright MSS.

100 Memo by Hardinge, 11 Nov. 1908, Grey MSS F.O. 800/92.

101 Wilson Diary, 9 Aug. 1911; minutes on Buchanan to Grey, 3 Sept. 1911, *B.D.*, vii, no. 501; memos by Wilson, 11, 13 Aug. 1911, W.O. 106/47A, CAB 38/19/47.

102 Minutes of 114th meeting of C.I.D., CAB 2/2/2.

103 Minute by Grey on letter of 9 Feb. 1912, Carnock MSS F.O. 800/353; minute by Parker on Buchanan to Grey, 3 Sept. 1911, F.O. 371/1164/34653; Nicolson to Grey, 15 Feb. 1912, Carnock MSS F.O. 800/353.

104 Nicolson to Goschen, 11 Mar. 1913, Carnock MSS F.O. 800/364.

105 Minute by Hardinge, 6 Aug. 1907, F.O. 371/371/26042.

106 *The Times*, 21 Oct. 1905; Grey to Spring-Rice, 22 Dec. 1905, Grey MSS F.O. 800/72; *B.D.*, iv, p. 623; Williams, 'The Strategic Background', p. 361 fn. 10.

107 D. W. Sweet and R. T. B. Langhorne, 'Great Britain and Russia 1907–14', in Hinsley, *The Foreign Policy of Sir Edward Grey*, p. 244.

108 Hardinge to Grey, 17 June 1908, Grey MSS F.O. 800/92.

109 Sweet and Langhorne, in Hinsley, *The Foreign Policy of Sir Edward Grey*, pp. 239–41; B. Williams, 'The Revolution of 1905 and Russian Foreign Policy', in C. Abramsky and B. Williams (eds.), *Essays in Honour of E. H. Carr* (London, 1974), pp. 115–17.

110 B. de Siebert, *Entente Diplomacy and the World* (New York, 1921), p. 99; F. Kazemdadeh, *Russia and Great Britain in Persia 1864–1914* (New Haven, Conn., 1968), p. 576.

111 *B.D.*, x (i), no. 914; Grey to Buchanan, 12 Feb. 1912, Grey MSS F.O. 800/74; de Siebert, *Entente Diplomacy*, pp. 113, 132–3.

112 I. Klein, 'The Anglo-Russian Convention and the Problem of Central Asia 1907–14', *J.B.S.*, xi, no. 1 (1971), pp. 140–3.

113 Tyrrell to Spring-Rice, 25 May 1907, Spring-Rice MSS F.O. 800/241.

114 Grey to Buchanan, 18 Mar. 1914, *B.D.*, x (ii), no. 535; to Crewe, 21 Mar. 1914, Crewe MSS C/17.

115 Klein, 'The Anglo-Russian Convention', pp. 144–5; Grey to Crewe, 11 May 1914, Crewe MSS C/17; *B.D.*, x (ii), nos. 547, 556, 561.

5. The Fiction of the Free Hand

1 Graham to Grey, 1 May 1913, Grey MSS P.R.O. F.O. 800/54.

2 Harcourt in *The Times*, 14 Apr. 1897; Asquith, 10 June 1898, Hansard, 4th Series, lviii, col. 1350; Campbell-Bannerman, 13 Feb. 1902, *ibid.*, cii, col. 1293.

3 111th meeting of C.I.D., CAB 2/2/2.

4 Hansard, 5th Series, lxv, col. 1814.

5 Minute by Nicolson, 6 Apr. 1912, *B.D.*, vi, p. 739; M. Paléologue, *Journal de 1913 et 1914* (Paris, 1947), p. 28, 4 Feb. 1913.

6 *B.D.*, iii, nos. 212, 213, 215, and p. 203; Grey to Asquith, 16 Apr. 1911, Grey

MSS F.O. 800/100; to Goschen, 15 Mar. 1912, *B.D.*, vi, no. 539; minute by Grey, 5 May 1912, *B.D.*, x (ii), no. 383.

7 Asquith to the King, 16 Nov. 1911, 16 July 1912, Asquith MSS vol. 6; *B.D.*, x (ii), nos. 400, 404, 416–17.

8 Asquith to the King, 14 May 1914, Asquith MSS vol. 7; Grey to Bertie, 1 May 1914, Grey MSS F.O. 800/94; minutes by Crowe and Nicolson on Buchanan to Grey, 3 Apr. 1914, F.O. 371/2092/15312.

9 Memo by Hardinge, May 1909, *B.D.*, vi, p. 311; Goschen to Hardinge, 28 May 1909, Hardinge MSS vol. 15; Nicolson to Goschen, 1 Apr. 1912, *B.D.*, vi, no. 562.

10 Memo by Grey, 24 Sept. 1912, Grey MSS F.O. 800/94.

11 *B.D.*, vii, nos. 433, 540; Grey to Nicolson, 13 Sept. 1911, Carnock MSS F.O. 800/350.

12 *B.D.*, vii, no. 617; see K. M. Wilson, 'Opposition and Crisis', pp. 399–413.

13 Nicolson to Hardinge, 29 Jan. 1908, Hardinge MSS vol. 12; Ripon to Grey, 15 Dec. 1907, Ripon MSS Add. MSS 43640.

14 Hansard, 5th Series, xxxii, cols. 57–8, 27 Nov. 1911.

15 Grey to Harcourt, 10 Jan. 1914, Grey MSS F.O. 800/91. On his copy of a despatch to Buchanan of 14 Nov. 1912 embodying the *official* line, Harcourt had underlined in red the words where Grey said he was speaking to show Benckendorff 'how impossible it was to give a reply in advance'. Harcourt MSS 590.

16 *B.D.*, iii, no. 439.

17 Hansard, 5th Series, xxxii, col. 5.

18 Mallet to Bertie, 11 Jan. 1906, Bertie MSS F.O. 800/164; *B.D.*, iii, nos. 213, 219.

19 T. Wilson, *The Political Diaries of C. P. Scott*, p. 51, 25 July 1911.

20 *B.D.*, vii, nos. 397, 403, 408; minute by Crowe, 21 July 1911, F.O. 371/1164/28529.

21 *B.D.*, vii, nos. 409, 417, 421, 425, 433, 532.

22 *G.P.*, xxix, p. 119; C. P. Scott Diary, 3 Nov. 1911, Add. MSS 50901.

23 Hansard, 5th Series (Lords), x, cols. 390–1, 28 Nov. 1911.

24 Pease Diary, 8 Mar. 1911, Gainford MSS; see *The Times*, 3 Feb. 1911, col. 8b.

25 *B.D.*, vii, no. 206; Hansard, 5th Series, xxiii, col. 1490.

26 Pease Diary, 1 Nov. 1911. Pease probably meant to write 'relations' for 'negotiations'.

27 Asquith MSS vol. 6, f. 81. The word 'previous' was insisted upon by the Radical section of the Cabinet: T. Wilson, *The Political Diaries of C. P. Scott*, p. 63.

28 Pease Diary, 15, 16 July 1912.

29 Trevelyan to Runciman, 4 Aug. 1914, Runciman MSS. Grey had made no effort to correct Barrington when in June 1906 the latter had written of 'our alliance with France'; in July 1905 Grey himself had written: 'Rosebery was striking high notes about the French alliance.' *B.D.*, iii, p. 360; Trevelyan,

Grey of Fallodon, p. 84. See also Ripon to Grey, 23 Jan. 1906, Grey MSS F.O. 800/99.

30 *B.D.*, vi, no. 195; Grey to Bertie, 7 Feb. 1912, Grey MSS F.O. 800/53.

31 Grey to Nicolson, 10 Nov. 1908, *B.D.*, v, no. 441; Hardinge to Nicolson, 11 Nov. 1908, Hardinge MSS vol. 13; Hardinge to Cartwright, 26 Jan., 6 Apr. 1909, Cartwright MSS.

32 Lascelles to Grey, 16 Feb. 1906, Grey MSS F.O. 800/61; to Knollys, 8 Feb. 1906, Lascelles MSS F.O. 800/19; memo by Hardinge, 25 Oct. 1906, ADM 1/7904; minutes by Spicer, Hardinge, Grey, 14 Jan. 1907, F.O. 371/257/ 1481.

33 *B.D.*, v, no. 441.

34 Brett and Esher, *Journals and Letters of Reginald, Viscount Esher*, ii, p. 359, 12 Nov. 1908.

35 Hardinge to Villiers, 19 Nov. 1908, Hardinge MSS vol. 13; see his remark on the small margin between peace and war over the Casablanca incident in a minute of 10 Nov. 1909, *B.D.*, vi, p. 311.

36 Hardinge to Bryce, 26 Mar., to Nicolson, 27 Apr. 1909, Hardinge MSS vol. 17.

37 *B.D.*, ix (ii), no. 328; *B.D.*, x (ii), no. 453; Goschen to Nicolson, 8 Dec. 1912, Carnock MSS F.O. 800/361; P. Cambon to Poincaré, 4 Dec. 1912, *D.D.F.*, 3rd Series, iv, no. 622; Prince Karl Max von Lichnowsky, *Heading for the Abyss* (New York, 1928), p. 167.

38 Sanderson to Lascelles, 9 Jan. 1906, Lascelles MSS F.O. 800/13.

39 Cartwright to Nicolson, 27 Aug. 1912, Cartwright MSS.

40 *B.D.*, ix (ii), no. 626.

41 T. Wilson, *The Political Diaries of C. P. Scott*, p. 49, 22 July 1911; minute by Nicolson, 21 July 1911, *B.D.*, vii, no. 409.

42 Nicolson·to Buchanan, 3, 31 Dec. 1912, Carnock MSS F.O. 800/360, /361; Grey to Cartwright, 1 May 1913, *B.D.*, ix (ii), no. 926.

43 Grey to Harcourt, 10 Jan. 1914, Grey MSS F.O. 800/99; Grey to Goschen, 2 Jan. 1914, *B.D.*, x (i), no. 457. On 6 January 1914, Sazonov threatened that if England failed to support Russia on this issue 'there would be an end to our understanding'. Buchanan's report of this (*B.D.*, x (i), no. 459) had caused Harcourt to write to Grey on 9 January.

44 Nicolson to Buchanan, 31 Dec. 1912, to Cartwright, 7 Jan. 1913, Carnock MSS F.O. 800/361, /362; Bertie to Nicolson, 28 Nov. 1912, *ibid.* /360.

45 Mallet to Grey, 26 Aug. 1909, *B.D.*, vi, no. 191, my italics.

46 *Ibid.*, no. 566; *B.D.*, x (ii), no. 385.

47 Minute by Grey on Kerr to Grey, 30 Mar. 1911, Grey MSS F.O. 800/108; see Pease Diary, 8 Mar. 1911, where Grey explained that he wanted 'not to take any course which might make Russia and France suspicious, lest we lose every friend we possessed in Europe'.

48 Grey to Lascelles, 18 Sept. 1907, Lascelles MSS F.O. 800/13.

49 Hardinge to de Salis, 29 Dec. 1908, Hardinge MSS vol. 13; Nicolson to Goschen, 15 Apr. 1912, *B.D.*, vi, no. 575.

50 Grey to Bertie, 9 Jan. 1912, Bertie MSS F.O. 800/161.

51 Goschen to Nicolson, undated, late Jan. 1913, Carnock MSS F.O. 800/363.
52 *B.D.*, iii, no. 299. Ripon had written on 11 Jan. 1906 to Grey's Parliamentary
   Under Secretary, Fitzmaurice, that if Britain declined to go further than diplomacy would reach, 'I cannot but fear a cry of "Perfide Albion" and a destruction of the present friendship between France and Britain.' Ripon MSS Add.
   MSS 43543.
53 Paget to Nicolson, 26 Nov. 1912, Carnock MSS F.O. 800/360. See *B.D.*, ix
   (ii), no. 920; and R. J. Crampton, 'The Balkans 1909–14', in Hinsley, *The
   Foreign Policy of Sir Edward Grey*, p. 264.
54 Chamberlain, *Down the Years*, pp. 97–8. And see Nicolson to Grey, 12 Sept.
   1911, on the 'extreme likelihood' of Britain's acting alongside of the French
   in the case of war: Grey MSS F.O. 800/93; *B.D.*, xi, no. 369.
55 *B.D.*, iii, nos. 219, 229.
56 *D.D.F.*, 2nd Series, xi, pp. 931, 933.
57 Memo by Bertie, 16 Feb. 1912, Bertie MSS F.O. 800/171; Graham to Tyrrell,
   5 Dec. 1912, 26 Jan. 1913, Grey MSS F.O. 800/53, /54; minute by Grey on
   Nicolson to Grey, 24 Feb. 1913, Carnock MSS F.O. 800/363; Grey to Bertie,
   4 Mar. 1913, Bertie MSS F.O. 800/166; *B.D.*, ix (ii), no. 660.
58 *B.D.*, vii, no. 617, my italics; David, *Inside Asquith's Cabinet*, p. 108;
   Nicolson to Goschen, 11 Mar. 1913, Carnock MSS F.O. 800/364.
59 *B.D.*, iii, no. 299; Grey to Haldane, 3 Sept. 1906, Haldane MSS 5907.
60 Loreburn to Grey, 27 July, 25 Aug. 1911, Grey MSS F.O. 800/99; T. Wilson,
   The Political Diaries of C. P. Scott, p. 48. On 1 August 1914, Loreburn wrote
   to Harcourt out of his retirement: 'I fear that the foolish coquetting with the
   French to which some of us so strongly objected has raised expectations in
   that quarter which it would be criminal for us to satisfy. And there will be no
   doubt recriminations and charges of perfidy if the thing comes to a point and
   France goes to war without our aid. But I cannot bring myself to believe any
   government will be capable of entering upon this war, especially on the side
   of Frenchmen and Russians who are wholly untrustworthy allies.' Harcourt
   MSS.
61 Grey to McKenna, 5 Nov. 1908, *B.D.*, vii, no. 132.
62 Hardinge to Lascelles, 26 Feb. 1906, Lascelles MSS F.O. 800/13; Cambon to
   Pichon, 18 Nov. 1908, *D.D.F.*, 2nd Series, xi, no. 558.
63 Grey had been apprised in a letter from Repington, military correspondent of
   The Times, of 3 Jan. 1906, of the vulnerability of the Low Countries and of
   the fears of the French authorities of 'a German irruption along the Meuse':
   Grey MSS F.O. 800/100. In August 1911 Grey remarked that any hasty or
   false move in Morocco 'might be followed by a mobilisation of German Army
   on French frontier': *B.D.*, vii, no. 475.
64 Memo by Loraine, 22 Aug. 1913, Grey MSS F.O. 800/54.
65 Bertie to Grey, 18 Feb. 1909, Bertie MSS F.O. 800/165.
66 Memo by Bertie of conversation with Wickham Steed, 8 Mar. 1914, forwarded to Tyrrell, Grey MSS F.O. 800/55; Isvolsky to Sazonov, 5 Dec. 1912,
   in Marchand, *Livre noir*, i, p. 362.
67 Sazonov to Benckendorff, 15 Apr., Benckendorff to Sazonov, 6 May

1914, Marchand, *Un Livre noir*, ii, pp. 314, 317. M. Paléologue, *La Russie des Tsars pendant la Grande Guerre*, 3 vols. (Paris, 1921), i, p. 23.

68 Tyrrell to Hardinge, 13 July 1911, Hardinge MSS vol. 92; memo by Bertie, 25 July 1911, Bertie MSS F.O. 800/160.

69 B.D., vii, ed. note, p. 545.

70 Bertie to Grey, 12 Feb., Grey to Bertie, 13 Feb., 4 Mar. 1914, Grey MSS F.O. 800/55.

71 Hardinge to Goschen, 3 Nov. 1908, to Gorst, 25 Feb. 1909, Hardinge MSS vols. 13, 17; Grey to Cartwright, 31 Dec. 1908, Cartwright MSS; Hardinge to the King, 26 Mar. 1909, Hardinge MSS vol. 18; Lichnowsky, *Heading for the Abyss*, p. 167; Nicholson to Cartwright, 30 Apr. 1913, Cartwright MSS.

72 Crewe, *Lord Rosebery*, ii, pp. 581–2.

73 Nicolson to Goschen, 3 Dec. 1912, Carnock MSS F.O. 800/360. See J. C. G. Rohl, 'Admiral von Muller and the Approach of War, 1911–14', *H.J.*, xii, no. 4 (1969), p. 663; Fischer, *War of Illusions*, p. 165; K. M. Wilson, 'The British Démarche of 3 and 4 December 1912: H. A. Gwynne's Note on Britain, Russia and the First Balkan War', *Slavonic and East European Review*, lxii, no. 4 (1984).

74 Fischer, *War of Illusions*, pp. 159–64, 179, 191; Rohl, 'Admiral von Muller', pp. 661–3.

75 Rohl, 'Admiral vonMuller', p. 665; note by Bethmann, 14 Dec. 1912, *G.P.*, xxxix, no. 15623; Fischer, *War of Illusions*, pp. 164, 166.

76 Rohl, 'Admiral von Muller', p. 661, my italics; Fischer, *War of Illusions*, pp. 168–9, 173; G. Ritter, *The Sword and the Sceptre*, 2 vols. (London, 1972), ii, pp. 202, 216–19; Ritter, *The Schlieffen Plan*, pp. 68–9.

6. The Invention of Germany

1 Memo by Hardinge, 25 Oct. 1906, ADM 1/7904; minute by Hardinge, 10 Nov. 1909, *B.D.*, vi, p. 311.

2 Minute by Hardinge, 4 May 1909, *B.D.*, vi, p. 312; de Salis to Hardinge, 12 Nov. 1909, Hardinge MSS vol. 16.

3 Nicolson to Grey, 24 Mar. 1909, *B.D.*, v, no. 764.

4 Tyrrell to Hardinge, 21 July 1911, Hardinge MSS vol. 92.

5 Minute by Crowe, 6 Apr. 1912, *B.D.*, vi, p. 738.

6 Minute by Crowe, 3 Mar. 1912, *ibid.*, p. 703.

7 Spring-Rice to Nicolson, 8 Nov. 1910, Spring-Rice MSS F.O. 800/241.

8 Minute by Crowe, 17 Mar. 1913, F.O. 371/1642/11813.

9 C. P. Scott Diary, 29 Sept. 1912, Add. MSS 50901.

10 Goschen to Lascelles, 16 June 1907, Lascelles MSS F.O. 800/13; Grey in the House of Commons, 29 Mar. 1909, Hansard, 5th Series, iii, cols. 57–8.

11 Hardinge to Goschen, 1 May 1911, Hardinge MSS vol. 92.

12 See K. M. Wilson, 'Sir Eyre Crowe on the Origin of the Crowe Memorandum of 1 January 1907', *B.I.H.R.*, lvi, no. 134 (1983), pp. 238–41.

13 See K. M. Wilson, 'The Question of Anti-Germanism at the British Foreign

Office before the First World War', *Canadian Journal of History*, xviii, no. 1 (1983), pp. 24–5.

14 *B.D.*, iii, p. 417.

15 *Ibid.*, pp. 414–15.

16 *Ibid.*, p. 416.

17 See above n. 13, pp. 25–6.

18 Hardinge to Chirol, 12 Mar. 1912, Hardinge MSS vol. 92.

19 Hardinge to Lascelles, 19 May 1908, *ibid.* vol. 13. I suggest he intended to write 'army'instead of 'fleet'.

20 Cartwright to Grey, 8 Jan. 1908, F.O. 371/457/1308, my italics, to Hardinge, 23 Dec. 1909, Hardinge MSS vol. 15, my italics.

21 Nicolson to Grey, 24 Mar., to Hardinge, 2 June 1909, Carnock MSS F.O. 800/337.

22 See above n. 13, p. 26.

23 Memo by Tilley, *B.D.*, i, pp. 328, 330; *ibid.*, iii, pp. 428–9. Grey had written on 24 Nov. 1901 to Leo Maxse that Britain's weakest point used to be Egypt, that 'some years ago Lord Cromer could not have got along there unless the dead weight of the Triple Alliance had been on the side of keeping things quiet'. Maxse MSS.

24 Spencer Wilkinson, *Britain at Bay* (London, 1909), pp. 77–8, 83–6, 101.

25 Lord Midleton, *Records and Reactions* (London, 1939), p. 176.

26 Spender, *Life, Journalism and Politics*, i, p. 244.

27 Spring-Rice to Spender, 14 Aug. 1905, Spender MSS Add. MSS 46391, to Lascelles, 2 May 1905, Lascelles MSS F.O. 800/12; memo by Hardinge, May 1909, *B.D.*, v, p. 824. See also *ibid.*, iii, no. 98, iv, p. 610.

28 R. J. Crampton, 'August Bebel and the British Foreign Office', *History*, lviii (1973), pp. 218–32. Cartwright to Grey, 10 Sept. 1911, and minutes by Villiers, Parker and Campbell, F.O. 371/1164/35571; memo by Oppenheimer, 21 Oct. 1911, section E no. 2, and minutes by Villiers and Crowe, *B.D.*, vii, pp. 803–5.

29 *B.D.*, iii, pp. 195–6; Chirol to Hardinge, 18 Apr. 1913, Hardinge MSS vol. 93.

30 *B.D.*, iii, pp. 405–6.

31 *Ibid.*, p. 418.

32 'After a big war a nation doesn't want another for a generation or more, but after 40 years of peace, if a nation is strong it begins spoiling for a fight. It was so with us between 40 and 50 years after the Crimean War, and it was so with Russia; and it was so with the United States nearly forty years after her Civil War. And now it is 38 years since Germany had her last war, and she is very strong and restless, like a person whose boots are too small for him. I don't think there will be war at present, but it will be difficult to keep the peace of Europe for another five years.' Grey to Ella Pease, 8 Nov. 1908, in Trevelyan, *Grey of Fallodon*, pp. 154–5. A variation on this is to be found in Grey to Roosevelt in December 1906, *ibid.*, p. 115.

33 Cited in E. R. May, *'Lessons' of the Past* (New York, 1973), p. 18.

34 Memo by Hardinge, 25 Oct. 1906, ADM 1/7904.

35 ADM 116/3486.

36 *B.D.*, vi, no. 73.

37 *Ibid.*, pp. 121, 132; and minute by Crowe, 5 Apr. 1909, *ibid.*, pp. 259–60.

38 Grey to Nicolson, 10 Nov. 1908, *ibid.*, no. 441; in January 1909 Mallet took the attacks of the Central Powers on Britain in the press, which they were flooding with 'the legend that Britain is desirous of a war in order to fight Germany whilst she is still vulnerable', as evidence 'of the strength of our position in Europe'. F.O. 371/599/497. A year before, when Aehrenthal declared that the British idea that the Sanjak railway project was inspired from Berlin indicated that 'England had Germany on the brain', Mallet commented: 'that is our own affair'. F. R. Bridge, *Great Britain and Austria-Hungary 1906–14* (London, 1972), pp. 86–7.

39 Minute by Grey, March 1908, *B.D.*, vi, p. 132; see also P. Schroeder, 'World War I as Galloping Gertie', *J.M.H.*, xliv, no. 3 (1972), p. 330; J. Steinberg, 'The Copenhagen Complex', *J.C.H.*, i, no. 3 (1966), pp. 23–46.

40 *B.D.*, vi, pp. 238, 240.

41 *Ibid.*, p. 117; Mackenzie King Diary, 9 Apr. 1908.

42 Grey to Asquith, 26 Aug., Asquith to Grey, 28 Aug. 1908, Grey MSS F.O. 800/100; *B.D.*, vi, no. 113.

43 Hardinge to Goschen, 27 July 1909, Hardinge MSS vol. 17.

44 Clarke to Balfour, 25 Aug. 1905, Balfour MSS Add. MSS 49702.

45 Spring-Rice to Chirol, 21 June 1907, in Gwynn, *Letters and Friendships of Sir Cecil Spring-Rice*, ii, p. 101.

46 *B.D.*, iii, p. 426.

47 Grey at 111th meeting of C.I.D., 26 May 1911, CAB 2/2/2, my italics; *B.D.*, vi, p. 266.

48 *B.D.*, vi, p. 275.

49 C. P. Scott Diary, 3 Nov. 1911, Add. MSS 50901; Pease Diary, 20 July 1910, Gainford MSS.

50 Grey to Maxse, 24 Nov. 1901, Maxse MSS.

51 Grey to Campbell-Bannerman, 4 Sept. 1907, Campbell-Bannerman MSS Add. MSS 52514.

52 Gwynn, *Letters and Friendships of Sir Cecil Spring-Rice*, i, p. 350; Brodrick to Maxse, 11 Apr. 1903, Maxse MSS; Arnold-Foster to Lansdowne, 25 Dec. 1903, A. Chamberlain MSS AC17/1/23.

53 Minute by Grey, 17 Sept. 1912, F.O. 371/1371/38804.

54 Gwynn, *Letters and Friendships of Sir Cecil Spring Rice*, i, p. 243; Z. S. Steiner, *Britain and the Origins of the First World War* (London, 1977), p. 31.

55 Kimberley to Sanderson, 20 Oct. 1894, Sanderson MSS F.O. 800/1.

56 Minute by Grey on Cartwright to Hardinge, 23 Dec. 1909, Hardinge MSS vol. 15; Hansard, 5th Series, xl, 10 July 1912, col. 1992; Trevelyan, *Grey of Fallodon*, pp. 219–20.

57 Memo by Selborne, 'England's position and Naval policy compared with foreign navies', late 1904, Selborne MSS 158; A. Chamberlain to Balfour and Lansdowne, 14 Jan. 1905, A. Chamberlain MSS AC17/1/59.

58 Bertie to Mallet, 11 June 1904, Bertie MSS F.O. 800/170, to Lansdowne, 1 Aug. 1905, Lansdowne MSS F.O. 800/127.
59 Hardinge to Goschen, 9 Dec. 1908, Hardinge MSS vol. 13; Nicolson to Hardinge, 9 Feb. 1910, *ibid.* vol. 20.
60 Cartwright to Hardinge, 23 Dec. 1909, *ibid.* vol. 15; minute by Grey, Feb. 1913, F.O. 371/1647/7737.
61 Minutes by Spicer, 30 Mar. 1909, *B.D.*, vi, p. 257; by Villiers, 26 Feb. 1913, F.O. 371/1647/7737.
62 Grey to Cartwright, 6 Jan. 1909, Cartwright MSS, to Rodd, 26 Jan. 1909, Grey MSS F.O. 800/64; minute by Grey on Findlay to Hardinge, 18 Feb. 1909, Hardinge MSS vol. 15.
63 Minutes by Spicer and Grey, 5 Aug. 1908, F.O. 371/399/27154; see K. M. Wilson, 'Isolating the Isolator: Cartwright, Grey and the Seduction of Austria-Hungary 1908–12', *Mitteilungen des Österreichischen Staatsarchivs*, xxxv (1982), pp. 169–98.
64 Minutes by Spicer and Grey, 8 Feb. 1909, F.O. 371/599/5138.
65 *B.D.*, vi, nos. 15, 16; minutes by Hardinge, Grey, Asquith on Rodd to Hardinge, 30 Apr. 1909, Hardinge MSS vol. 16.
66 Enclosure in Egerton to Grey, 12 Feb. 1907, F.O. 371/267/5107; Lister to Grey, 25 Feb. 1907, *ibid.* /6314.
67 Minute by Crowe, 2 Jan. 1909, F.O. 371/682/109; by Langley, 22 Oct. 1910, *ibid.* /917/38377; Rodd to Grey, 28 Feb., 16 Oct. 1911, Grey MSS F.O. 800/64.
68 Minute by Crowe, 24 Apr. 1909, F.O. 371/683/11613.
69 Hardinge to Bax-Ironside, 28 Oct. 1909, Hardinge MSS vol. 17.
70 Minute by Hardinge, 2 Jan. 1909, F.O. 371/682/109; Hardinge to Lowther, 18 May, to Rodd, 28 May 1909, Hardinge MSS vol. 17.
71 Hardinge to Bax-Ironside, 28 Oct. 1909, *ibid.*
72 P. Cambon to Bourgeois, 24 Oct. 1906, *D.D.F.*, 2nd Series, x, no. 241; minute by Hardinge, 24 Apr. 1909, F.O. 371/683/11613; Hardinge to the King, 31 Mar. 1909, Hardinge MSS vol. 18; minute by Hardinge, 20 Apr. 1909, *B.D.*, vi, p. 266.
73 See P. Schroeder, 'Munich and the British Tradition', *H.J.*, xix, no. 1 (1976), pp. 223–43.
74 Hardinge to Cartwright, 29 June 1909, Cartwright MSS.
75 Hardinge to Graham, 23 Oct. 1908, Hardinge MSS vol. 13.
76 Hardinge to Goschen, 25 May 1909, *ibid.* vol. 17.
77 *B.D.*, iv, p. 605.
78 Cartwright to Grey, 24 Dec. 1908, to Hardinge 24 June 1909, to Nicolson, 11 July 1911, Cartwright MSS; to Grey, 4 June 1910, F.O. 371/827/20925; minute by Crowe, 3 May 1909, *B.D.*, vi, p. 270.
79 Rodd to Grey, 16, 25 Oct., Grey to Rodd, 14 Nov. 1911, Grey MSS F.O. 800/64; minute by Grey on Russell to Nicolson, 21 Nov. 1913, Carnock MSS F.O. 800/371.
80 *B.D.*, vi, pp. 266, 310, 312; Nicolson to Hardinge, 9 Feb. 1910, Hardinge MSS vol. 20; memo by Crowe, 14 Jan. 1912, *B.D.*, vii, p. 824.

81 *B.D.*, vi, p. 312; Nicolson to Goschen, 24 July 1911, Carnock MSS F.O. 800/349.
82 Minute by Nicolson, 3 Jan. 1913, F.O. 371/1647/140; Tyrrell to Hardinge, 21 July 1911, Hardinge MSS vol. 92.
83 Nicolson to Goschen, 28 Feb. 1911, Carnock MSS F.O. 800/347.
84 *B.D.*, vi, p. 461.
85 Grey in the House of Commons, 29 Mar. 1909, Hansard, 5th Series, iii, col. 58; minute by Nicolson, March 1911, *B.D.*, vi, p. 595.
86 *B.D.*, vi, p. 266; Lansdowne to Lascelles, 13 Aug., 31 Oct., to Tower, 20 Aug. 1905, Lansdowne MSS F.O. 800/130. Spring-Rice to Chirol, 12 Jan. 1898, Spring-Rice MSS 1/18.
87 Memo by Mallet, 13 July 1905, Lansdowne MSS F.O. 800/145; memo by Grey, 28 Apr. 1908, Bertie MSS F.O. 800/170; minute by Crowe, 16 Apr. 1907, F.O. 371/253/12179; Bertie to Nicolson, 15 Mar. 1911, Bertie MSS F.O. 800/186; Grey to Bertie, 31 May 1913, Grey MSS F.O. 800/54.
88 *B.D.*, v, p. 825; Hardinge to Bryce, 4 June 1909, Hardinge MSS vol. 17.
89 Nicolson to Hardinge, 9 Feb. 1910, Hardinge MSS vol. 20.
90 Hardinge to Goschen, 30 Mar. 1909, *ibid.* vol. 17; *B.D.*, v, p. 824; *ibid.* vi, p. 311; minute by Crowe, 26 Apr. 1909, F.O. 371/704/15557; minute by Drummond, 27 Nov. 1911, *ibid.* /1127/47197; Bertie to Grey, 4 Nov. 1911, *ibid.* /1168/45309.
91 *B.D.*, vi, p. 266; Grey to Nicolson, 5 Apr. 1912, Grey MSS F.O. 800/94; C. P. Scott Diary, 1 Dec. 1911, 29 Sept. 1912, Add. MSS 50901.
92 Hardinge to Chirol and to Nicolson, 12 Mar. 1912, Hardinge MSS vol. 92.
93 Nicolson to Hardinge, 9 Feb. 1910, *ibid.* vol. 20.
94 Spender, *Life, Journalism and Politics*, i, p. 244.
95 P. M. Kennedy, 'The Development of German Naval Operations Plans against England 1896–1914', *E.H.R.*, lxxxix (1974), pp. 59–63; F. Fischer, 'Recent Work on German Naval Policy', *E.S.R.*, v, no. 4 (1975), p. 460. Bertie to Grey, 20 Jan. 1913, Grey MSS F.O. 800/54; Russell to Goschen, 3 Mar. 1911, forwarded to Grey, *B.D.*, vi, no. 442.
96 Sanderson to Lansdowne, 20 Jan. 1905, Lansdowne MSS F.O. 800/145; see also Lascelles to Lansdowne, 25 Apr. 1902, *ibid.* /129.
97 *B.D.*, ii, no. 91.
98 Memos by Selborne, 7 Dec. 1903, 26 Feb. 1904, CAB 37/67/83, /69/32. Only after the Balkan War of 1912 did the Germans challenge their assumption that their continental position was strong enough to allow them to pursue a World Policy. The German Navy was planned, initiated and fixed at a time when Franco-Russian enmity to Britain was assumed to be permanent and something of which the Germans could begin to take advantage once they had a Fleet, in order to conduct 'a great overseas policy'. See V. R. Berghahn, *Germany and the Approach of War in 1914* (London, 1973), pp. 35–40, 115; Fischer, *War of Illusions*, pp. 90, 185, 197; Rich and Fisher, *The Holstein Papers*, ii, pp. 630–1, 674–5; J. Steinberg, *Yesterday's Deterrent* (London, 1965).
99 K. Jarausch, *The Enigmatic Chancellor* (New Haven, Conn., 1973), p. 113.

100 Hardinge to Grey, 3 Mar. 1915, Hardinge MSS vol. 93.

101 Memo by Bertie, 9 Nov. 1901, *B.D.*, ii, p. 76; Bertie to Spring-Rice, 26 Dec. 1902, Spring-Rice MSS 1/2.

102 Chirol to Hardinge, 10 Apr. 1913, Hardinge MSS vol. 93; Tyrrell to Spring-Rice, 25 May 1907, Spring-Rice MSS F.O. 800/241.

103 *B.D.*, vi, p. 311, my italics. In May 1909, he had written of Britain as the one Power capable of offering then, 'as in the past', effectual resistance: *ibid.*, v, p. 824.

104 Note by Nicolson of conversation with Metternich, 12 Aug. 1911, F.O. 371/1123/32100.

105 *B.D.*, xi, no. 369.

106 Memo by Hardinge, 1 Oct. 1906, Grey MSS F.O. 800/92; P. Mackesy, *The Strategy of Overthrow 1798–99* (London, 1974), pp. 3–4. See Nicolson's reaction to British naval reductions in the Mediterranean in letters to Goschen, 21 May, 18 July 1912, Carnock MSS F.O. 800/355, /357.

107 Hansard, 5th Series, xxxii, cols. 121–2; CAB 2/2/2; Morley, *Memorandum on Resignation*, p. 3. During the Agadir crisis Lloyd George had told C. P. Scott that 'there was a real danger that Prussia should seek a European pre-dominance not far removed from the Napoleonic': C. P. Scott Diary, 22 July 1911, Add. MSS 50901.

7. The Military Entente with France

1 See N. d'Ombrain, *War Machinery and High Policy* (Oxford, 1973), pp. 113–14.

2 J. Terraine, *Douglas Haig – the Educated Soldier* (London, 1963), p. 72.

3 P. Guinn, *British Strategy and Politics 1914–18* (Oxford, 1965), pp. 24–5; S. Williamson, *The Politics of Grand Strategy* (Cambridge, Mass., 1969), pp. 200, 361.

4 d'Ombrain, *War Machinery and High Policy*, p. 102.

5 Grey to Asquith, 16 Apr. 1911, Viscount Grey of Fallodon, *Twenty-Five Years 1892–1916*, 2 vols. (London, 1925), i, p. 94; *B.D.*, vii, no. 207. Bertie to Grey, 17 Apr. 1907, Grey MSS F.O. 800/50.

6 *B.D.*, iii, nos. 210, 216.

7 Proceedings and report in CAB 16/5.

8 Asquith to the King, 2, 16 Nov. 1911, CAB 41/33, Asquith MSS vol. 6.

9 Asquith to the King, 1, 21 Nov. 1912, *ibid.*; *B.D.*, x (ii), nos. 414–16; minute by Grey on Nicolson to Grey, 4 May 1912, Grey MSS F.O. 800/94.

10 Hansard, 5th Series, i, cols. 42–3, 10 Mar. 1913; Asquith to Grey, 14 Mar. 1913, Grey MSS F.O. 800/100; *B.D.*, vi, no. 467.

11 *B.D.*, x (ii), no. 466.

12 H. Wilson Diary, 11 Mar. 1913.

13 Isvolsky to Sazonov, 5 Dec. 1912, Marchand, *Livre noir*, i, p. 362; memo by Bertie, 23 June 1913, Bertie MSS F.O. 800/166.

14 Esher MSS, journal, 4 Oct. 1911, to Brett 12 Mar. 1913, Brett and Esher, *Journals and Letters of Reginald, Viscount Esher*, iii, pp. 61, 122.

15 Notes by McKenna of conversation with Asquith, 20 Oct. 1911, McKenna MSS 4/2.

16 Nicholson to Haldane, 16 Dec., to Churchill 2 Sept. 1911, ADM 116/3474.

17 Grey to Asquith, 8 Sept. 1911, Grey MSS F.O. 800/100.

18 David, *Inside Asquith's Cabinet*, p. 108.

19 C. P. Scott Diary, 23–4 Oct. 1914, Add. MSS 50901.

20 H. Wilson Diary, 2 Aug. 1914. According to Sazonov, Poincaré told him during a visit to St Petersburg in the summer of 1912 of 'une convention verbale en vertu de laquelle l'Angleterre s'est déclarée prête à porter secours à la France par ses forces de terre comme par ses forces de mer, dans le cas d'une attaque de la part de l'Allemagne'. Marchand, *Livre noir*, ii, p. 339.

21 David, *Inside Asquith's Cabinet*, p. 108; and see Marder, *From the Dreadnought to Scapa Flow*, i, pp. 250–1.

22 Lord Newton, *Lord Lansdowne* (London, 1929), p. 441, my italics; Major Grant-Duff of the General Staff also disputed Esher's view that Britain was 'absolutely compromised': he noted in his diary on 6 November 1911: 'the understanding has always been absolutely clear that the negotiations committed no one to anything'. Grant-Duff MSS 2/1. The Grant-Duff Diary is quoted by kind permission of Mrs S. S. Grant.

23 See Williamson, *The Politics of Grand Strategy*, p. 309.

24 *Ibid.*, p. 222; see also *B.D.*, ix (ii), no. 656; Bertie to Tyrrell, 8 Mar. 1914, Grey MSS F.O. 800/55.

25 David, *Inside Asquith's Cabinet*, pp. 108, 124; Pease Diary, 1 Nov. 1911, Gainford MSS; Morley, *Memorandum on Resignation*, p. 18.

26 *B.D.*, iii, no. 299.

27 Memo by Ewart, 8 Mar. 1909, 'The Value to a Foreign Power of an Alliance with the British Empire', W.O. 106/45 E1/1.

28 Memo by Wilson, 11 Aug. 1911, W.O. 106/47A E2/23; see also Appendix A to General Staff memo 'The Military Aspect of the Continental Problem', 12 Aug. 1911, para. 15, CAB 38/19/47; Grant-Duff Diary, 17, 25 Aug. 1911.

29 Memo by Churchill, 16 Oct. 1911, ADM 116/3474. This and other documents from this file are printed in my article 'The War Office, Churchill and the Belgian Option: August to December 1911', *B.I.H.R.*, l, no. 122 (1977), pp. 218–28.

30 Memo by Wilson, 'Appreciation of the Political and Military Situation in Europe', 20 Sept. 1911, para. 25, W.O. 106/47A E2/26.

31 CAB 42/1/2.

32 This was composed of Asquith (Chairman), Crewe, McKenna, Haldane, Hardinge, Esher, Fisher, French, Nicholson, Ewart and Slade (replaced as D.N.I. by Bethell in March 1909).

33 R. H. S. Bacon, *Life of Lord Fisher of Kilverstone*, 2 vols. (London, 1929), ii, pp. 182–3.

34 A. J. Marder (ed.), *Fear God and Dread Nought* (London, 1952–9), ii, pp. 232–3.

35 Sub-committee of the C.I.D. on the Military Needs of the Empire, report

24 July 1909, CAB 16/5; McKenna, 'Remarks by the Admiralty on Proposal (B) of Memo by the General Staff 130B', Aug. 1911, CAB 38/19/48.

36 Grant-Duff Diary, 17 Aug. 1911, Grant-Duff MSS 2/1; minutes of 114th meeting of C.I.D., CAB 2/2/2.

37 CAB 2/2/2; Marder, *From the Dreadnought to Scapa Flow*, i, p. 387; Fisher's views were unchanged: see his notes for Churchill, 30 Oct. 1911, in Churchill, *Winston S. Churchill*, ii, companion part 2, p. 1303.

38 Asquith to Haldane, 31 Aug. 1911, Haldane MSS 5909; also 9 Sept.: 'The arguments as put in the W.O. letters are, of course, conclusive as against Sir A.W.'s scheme.' *ibid.*

39 d'Ombrain, *War Machinery and High Policy*, pp. 255–8; Sir F. Maurice, *Haldane*, 2 vols. (London, 1937), i, pp. 283–4.

40 H. Wilson Diary, 21 Nov. 1911.

41 Churchill to Haldane, 8 Jan. 1912, Haldane MSS 5909.

42 Marder, *From the Dreadnought to Scapa Flow*, i, pp. 367–77.

43 Esher MSS, journal, 4 Oct. 1911.

44 CAB 16/5, report and App. IV.

45 d'Ombrain, *War Machinery and High Policy*, p. 97; W.O. 106/49C, WS5(1).

46 d'Ombrain, *War Machinery and High Policy*, p. 89; W.O. 106/49C, W4/1.

47 Only one memorandum went to the heart of the matter. Colonel Adye, in a long note on a memo by Grant-Duff of January 1907, wrote: 'In discussing possible British military operations in Belgium we need consider one situation only, that which would be brought about by a conflict between France and Germany in which the latter, for strategic reasons, decides to violate Belgian territory . . . If Germany decides to violate neutral territory it may be that she will not confine that violation to Belgium, but, by moving north of the Meuse, force the line of that river and obtain the advantage of the superior railway facilities north of Cologne without increasing the risk of British intervention . . . It may be assumed that the initiative will rest with Germany, and, had she a Napoleon to inspire her policy and direct her armies in the field, there is little doubt that an advance through Belgium . . . would be undertaken.' Grant-Duff's memo of 4 Jan. 1907, 'A War with Germany in the Defence of the Neutrality of Belgium', and Adye's note, are in W.O. 106/46. Contrast memo by Grant-Duff, 'Military Policy in a War with Germany', July 1908, *ibid.*; General Staff memo, 23 Sept. 1905, 'The Violation of the Neutrality of Belgium during a Franco-German War', pp. 1, 3: CAB 38/10.

48 Report, para. 5, CAB 16/5. The attitude of the Foreign Office was best revealed by Hardinge in a minute in November 1908: 'Supposing that France violated the neutrality of Belgium in a war against Germany, it is, under present circumstances, doubtful whether England or Russia would move a finger to maintain Belgian neutrality, which [*sic*] if the neutrality of Belgium were violated by Germany it is probable that the converse would be the case.' *B.D.*, viii, no. 311.

49 Notes by Ommanney on Grant-Duff memo, 4 Jan. 1907, W.O. 106/46. These are taken by d'Ombrain (*War Machinery and High Policy*, p. 104) to have

been made in September, but may well have been made later. The dating reads 'Sept/10'. Adye's notes are undated.

50 Memo by Grant-Duff, July 1908, W.O. 106/46.

51 See memo by Wilson, 12 Aug. 1911, W.O. 106/47A E2/25; Wilson at 114th meeting of C.I.D., p. 5, CAB 2/2/2; memo by Wilson, 20 Sept. 1911, W.O. 106/47A E2/26. This became the accepted orthodoxy. Not even Kitchener could shift it well into August 1914. Sir George Arthur, *Life of Lord Kitchener* (London, 1920), iii, pp. 22–3.

52 C.I.D. sub-committee on the Military Needs of the Empire, App. IV, para. 4, CAB 16/5.

53 Memo by General Staff, 8 Apr. 1907, 'Our Position as regards the Low Countries', CAB 18/24.

54 *Ibid.*; memo by Grierson, 1 Jan. 1906, W.O. 106/44; memo by Grant-Duff and Adye notes, Jan. 1907, W.O. 106/46; sub-committee report, para. 19, and App. IV, CAB 16/5.

55 Pellé to Berteaux, 7 Mar. 1911, *D.D.F.*, 2nd Series, xiii, no. 180.

56 Note by Wilson, 24 Apr. 1911, W.O. 106/47A E2/21; *B.D.*, vi, no. 460.

57 H. Wilson Diary, 28 Aug. 1911; Wilson to Churchill, 29 Aug. 1911, ADM 116/3474.

58 H. Wilson Diary, 29, 31 Aug. 1911; Nicholson to Wilson, 1 Sept., to Churchill, 2 Sept. 1911, ADM 116/3474. This point had not been neglected by Churchill when he followed up his original questions with a note to the D.M.O. on 30 Aug. 1911: 'If the withdrawal of 2 divisions from the decisive centre led to the utilisation of the Belgian Army, would it not mean a far larger subtraction from German strength at the decisive point? If Belgium were our ally wd it not be better to send the whole army to Antwerp and act against the German flank than simply to take posts on the left of the French?' *Ibid.* In conversation with Churchill on 31 Aug. Wilson had mentioned the figure of 10 or 12 German divisions being subtracted from the decisive battle by Anglo-Belgian cooperation on the German flank. Churchill to Lloyd George, 31 Aug. 1911, Churchill, *Winston S. Churchill*, ii, companion part 2, pp. 1118–19.

59 H. Wilson Diary, 4, 9 Sept. 1911; Williamson, *The Politics of Grand Strategy*, p. 179 fn. 36.

60 H. Wilson Diary, 5, 10 Sept. 1911; Wilson memo, 20 Sept. 1911, W.O. 106/47A E2/26, my italics.

61 H. Wilson Diary, 20, 21 Sept. 1911. Macleay was able to report that no secret agreement had been made between Belgium and Germany such as would allow the passage of troops by the latter through Belgian territory and more especially through the south-eastern corner of Belgium, and that in his opinion the Belgian reaction to any such German action would in great measure be governed by the assurances of support she may receive from Great Britain. Grey congratulated him on exploring 'this delicate ground with promptness, ability and discretion'. Macleay to Nicolson and minute by Grey, 29 Sept. 1911, F.O. 371/1050/39992.

62 H. Wilson Diary, 24, 27 Oct. 1911; Macleay to Nicolson, 7, 28 Oct. 1911, Carnock MSS F.O. 800/351.

63 Williamson, *The Politics of Grand Strategy*, p. 180 fn. 40; Gwynne to Lady Bathurst, 14, 17 Sept. 1911, Glenesk-Bathurst MSS.

64 H. Wilson Diary, 29 Sept. 1911.

65 Churchill in a memo of 16 October 1911 considered that 'the strategic advantage of placing the British Army behind the line of the Belgian Meuse wd appear to exceed any that can be obtained from prolonging the French left on the Verdun-Maubeuge front'. ADM 116/3474. See Williamson, *The Politics of Grand Strategy*, p. 179 fn. 36; *B.D.*, vii, no. 640.

66 Note by Wilson, 30 Oct. 1911, W.O. 106/47A, my italics in A.1. This was elaborated by Wilson in November and finally initialled by Nicholson in December 1911. To Answer 1 was added:'The area of detraining and of concentration would alone be altered.' The estimate of the number of German divisions detached from the decisive point became '10 to 15'. It was agreed that 'in the opening stages of the war the British Force ought never to lose touch with the French Army if the latter has to fall back'. Note by Wilson, 21 Nov. 1911, *ibid.*, and enclosure in Nicholson to Haldane, 16 Dec. 1911, ADM 116/3474.

67 'Attitude of Great Britain towards Belgium in the event of the violation of the neutrality of the latter Power by Germany', Apr. 1912,W.O. 106/48 E2/27.

68 H. Wilson Diary, 7 Apr. 1912; J. E. Helmreich, 'Belgian Concern over Neutrality and British Intentions 1906–14', *J.M.H.*, xxxvi (1964), pp. 423–4.

69 H. Wilson Diary, 22 Oct. 1912; note by Wilson, 21 Oct. 1912, W.O. 106/48.

70 H. Wilson Diary, 18 Nov. 1912; Nicolson, *Lord Carnock*, pp. 398–400; *B.D.*, viii, no. 330. Sir J. French was much more in harmony with Wilson's views on Belgium than Sir W. Nicholson had been. Wilson had come to consider the latter 'hopeless' (H. Wilson Diary, 6 Sept., 31 Dec. 1911, 7 Jan. 1912). He believed Nicholson did not even read his long paper of 20 Sept. 1911 and that he refused to allow it to be circulated. French, on the other hand, was highly complimentary about it and arranged for it to be printed for the C.I.D. (*ibid.*, 28 Oct. 1911, 20 Mar., 12, 17, 19 Apr. 1912). He also supported at the C.I.D. in April 1912 the idea that the attitude of the Belgians would make an immense difference to a British Army employed on the continent (minutes of the 116th meeting, 25 Apr. 1912, CAB 2/2/3).

71 Williamson, *The Politics of Grand Strategy*, pp. 217–18.

72 CAB 42/1/2.

73 H. Wilson Diary, 17 Nov. 1912. French, who in March 1911 had the idea of having flat-bottomed boats full of troops towed up the Rhine to form a *point d'appui*, aptly described by Wilson as 'AMAZING' (*ibid.*, 20 Mar. 1911), revived in August 1914 an idea for landing at Antwerp. This was not possible then because naval protection did not extend so far north (*ibid.*, 3 Aug. 1914; CAB 42/1/2). Both Haig, especially, and French were not absolutely convinced that Britain should not wait for some months before crossing to the continent. H. Wilson Diary, 5 Aug. 1914.

74 See Wilson questioned by Churchill at 116th meeting of C.I.D. sub-committee on Invasion, 12 Nov. 1913, CAB 16/28A, and Wilson note, 17 Oct. 1912, on his paper of 20 Sept. 1911 in C. Hazlehurst, *Politicians at War* (London, 1971), p. 319.

75 Wilson to Seely, 21 Oct. 1912, W.O. 106/48.

76 Hazlehurst, *Politicians at War*, p. 87, my italics.

77 Pease to Mrs Pease, 2, 3 Aug. 1914, Gainford MSS 521.

78 CAB 42/1/2, /3. Also R. Blake (ed.), *The Private Papers of Douglas Haig 1914–19* (London, 1952), pp. 68–70. On 12 August, Wilson claimed that Maubeuge had been agreed upon as concentration area. This was not so. H. Wilson Diary, 5, 12 Aug. 1914.

79 CAB 42/1/2; Wilson at 114th meeting of C.I.D., 23 Aug. 1911, p. 9, CAB 2/2/2; enclosure in Nicholson to Haldane, 16 Dec. 1911, ADM 116/3474.

80 Memo by Grant-Duff, July 1908, W.O. 106/46; sub-committee of C.I.D. on the Military Needs of the Empire, Apps. IV, VI, and minutes of meeting of 23 Mar. 1909, CAB 16/5.

81 114th meeting of C.I.D., p. 5, CAB 2/2/2. Also memo by Churchill, 13 Aug. 1911, CAB 38/19/50.

82 *B.D.*, xi, no. 487; and see memo by Major Ollivant, 1 Aug. 1914, in Hazlehurst, *Politicians at War*, p. 326.

83 Brett and Esher, *Journals and Letters of Reginald, Viscount Esher*, iii, pp. 175, 178: 6, 14 Aug. 1914; *B.D.*, vi, nos. 10, 14; Balfour to Haldane, 4 Aug. 1914, Balfour MSS Add. MSS 49724.

84 Asquith's announcement to the Cabinet, moreover, was couched in very reassuring terms, according to the Pease Diary of 6 Aug. 1914: 'the big experts . . . all urged an expeditionary force should be landed and kept on our right hand of naval force – not on left hand of French force necessary – they would not be wiped out as they could always retire to the sea, even in the event of France being overwhelmed'. See also note by Kitchener, 31 May 1915, CAB 37/128/30.

85 Lord Hankey, *The Supreme Command 1914–18* (London, 1961), i, pp. 170–1.

86 Brett and Esher, *Journals and Letters of Reginald, Viscount Esher*, ii, p. 359; *D.D.F.*, 2nd Series, xi, no. 558; Hardinge to Nicolson, 11 Nov. 1908, Hardinge MSS vol. 13.

87 Williamson, *The Politics of Grand Strategy*, p. 367; Hardinge at meeting on 23 Mar. 1909 of sub-committee on the Military Needs of the Empire, CAB 16/5.

88 *B.D.*, vii, no. 197, my italics.

89 *Ibid.*, no. 206; see note by Nicolson, 2 Nov. 1911, and minute by Grey, *ibid.*, no. 617.

90 *B.D.*, x (ii), nos. 400, 415.

8. The Cabinet's Decision for War, 1914

1 Grey, *Twenty-Five Years*, ii, pp. 10–11; R. Blake, *The Unknown Prime Minister* (London, 1955), pp. 222–3.

2 D. Lammers, 'Arno Mayer and the British Decision for War: 1914', *J.B.S.*, xii, no. 2 (1973), pp. 137–65.

3 D. C. Watt, 'The British Reactions to the Assassination at Sarajevo', *E.S.R.*, i, no. 3 (1971), p. 247; Ritter, *The Sword and the Sceptre*, ii, pp. 62–3.

4 Churchill to Lloyd George, ?2 Aug. 1914, Churchill, *Winston S. Churchill*, ii, companion part 3, p. 1996.

5 Asquith to the King, 30 July, Crewe to the King, 2 Aug. 1914, Spender and Asquith, *Life of Asquith*, ii, pp. 81–2; CAB 37/120/95; Pease Diary, 29 July 1914; K. Kautsky, *Outbreak of the World War: German Documents* (New York, 1924), no. 676; Blake, *The Unknown Prime Minister*, p. 224.

6 Burns Diary, 29 July 1914, Add. MSS 46336.

7 Pease Diary, 31 July 1914, Gainford MSS.

8 Hazlehurst, *Politicians at War*, pp. 88–90; H. Wilson Diary, 1 Aug. 1914; H. F. Young, 'The Misunderstanding of August 1, 1914', *J.M.H.*, xlviii (1976), pp. 644–63.

9 Morley, *Memorandum on Resignation*, p. 5.

10 Burns Diary, 1 Aug. 1914, Add. MSS 46336.

11 Note by Runciman, Runciman MSS; Masterman later described the day as 'the Fateful Sunday': Masterman to Runciman, 14 Feb. 1915, *ibid.*

12 *B.D.*, xi, no. 487; Pease Diary, 2 Aug. 1914.

13 Spender and Asquith, *Life of Asquith*, ii, p. 82; Pease Diary, 2 Aug. 1914; Morley, *Memorandum on Resignation*, p. 21; Burns' letter of resignation is dated 2 August: Burns MSS Add. MSS 46282; Burns Diary 2, 3 Aug. 1914, *ibid.* 46336.

14 Simon to Asquith, 2 Aug. 1914, Simon MSS 2.

15 A. Murray's Diary, 1 Aug. 1914, in Hazelburst, *Politicians at War*, p. 91; *D.D.F.*, 3rd Series, xi, no. 532; see chapter 4, nn. 93, 94.

16 Pease Diary, 2 Aug. 1914.

17 Lord Riddell, *War Diary* (London, 1933), p. 6.

18 Memo by Runciman, 2 Aug. 1914, Runciman MSS.

19 Chamberlain, *Down the Years*, p. 99; I. Colvin, *Life of Lord Carson* (London, 1936), iii, p. 19; Pease Diary, 2 Aug. 1914.

20 Chamberlain, *Down the Years*, p. 97; Colvin, *Life of Lord Carson*, p. 15; L. S. Amery, *My Political Life*, 3 vols. (London, 1953), ii, p. 17.

21 Riddell, *War Diary*, p. 3; Viscount Samuel, *Memoirs* (London, 1945), p. 104.

22 Samuel to his wife, 2 Aug. 1914, in C. J. Lowe and M. L. Dockrill, *The Mirage of Power*, 3 vols. (London, 1972), iii, pp. 489–91, and i, pp. 150–1; Hazlehurst, *Politicians at War*, pp. 93–7; Kautsky, *Outbreak of the World War*, no. 764.

23 R. I. Lovell, 'England is Drawn in – July and August 1914', in D. C. McKay (ed.), *Essays in the History of Modern Europe* (New York, 1936), pp. 149–67.

24 B.D., xi, nos. 521, 525, 547.

25 Ibid., no. 523.

26 Pease Diary, 2, 3 Aug. 1914; Samuel, Memoirs, p. 104.

27 Hazlehurst, Politicians at War, p. 101; Morley, Memorandum on Resignation, pp. 27–8; Asquith to Simon, 3 Aug., Simon to Asquith, 4 Aug. 1914, Simon MSS 2.

28 T. Wilson, The Political Diaries of C. P. Scott, p. 96.

29 Memo by Runciman, 2 Aug. 1914, Runciman MSS.

30 Memo by Haldane, Apr. 1916, pp. 153–4, Haldane MSS 5919; Hobhouse to Burns, 7 Aug. 1914, Burns MSS Add. MSS 46303, f. 72.

31 Pease Diary, 2 Aug. 1914.

32 L. Masterman, C. F. G. Masterman (London, 1939), p. 265; F. Owen, Tempestuous Journey (London, 1954), p. 265; Riddell, War Diary, pp. 5–6.

33 Robbins, Sir Edward Grey, fn. 67 to chapter 14, pp. 402–3; Spender and Asquith, Life of Asquith, ii, pp. 85, 101; Dawson Diary, 1, 2 Aug. 1914, and Dawson to Maxse, 13 Aug. 1918, Dawson MSS 20, 67.

34 Pease Diary, 2 Aug. 1914.

35 B.D., xi, nos. 297, 303.

36 Ibid., nos. 348, 382–3.

37 Minute by Crowe, ibid. no. 293; H. Wilson Diary, 1 Aug. 1914; Chamberlain, Down the Years, p. 97.

38 B.D., xi, nos. 465, 468, 473, 476, 486.

39 Spender and Asquith, Life of Asquith, ii, p. 84; Lord Birkenhead, F.E. (London, 1959), p. 241. Churchill had also established that Balfour's attitude was 'splendid': J. E. Wrench, Geoffrey Dawson and our Times (London, 1955), p. 105.

40 Riddell, War Diary, p. 3; Morley, Memorandum on Resignation, p. 20. Morley also remembered that on the morning of 3 August Asquith started the proceedings of the Cabinet by saying 'with some emphasis that nothing would induce him to separate from Grey': Morley, Memorandum on Resignation, pp. 26–7.

41 Riddell, War Diary, p. 6.

42 Owen, Tempestuous Journey, pp. 264–5; Asquith, Memories and Reflections, ii, p. 20.

43 Pease Diary, 2 Aug. 1914.

44 Morley, Memorandum on Resignation, p. 25; Pease to his wife, 3 Aug. 1914, Gainford MSS box 521; Chirol of The Times recounted to Hardinge on 4 August a story that the King had told Asquith, on being informed that in view of dissensions in the Cabinet ministers might have to resign collectively, that in that case he would send for Asquith and Lansdowne and charge them with the formation of a National Defence Government. Hardinge MSS vol. 93.

45 C. Addison, Four and a Half Years (London, 1934), i, p. 35.

46 Pease to Trevelyan, 5 Aug. 1914, Trevelyan MSS 59.

47 Runciman to Trevelyan, 4 Aug. 1914, ibid. 33.

48 J. Pope-Hennessy, Lord Crewe (London, 1955), p. 144; Lloyd George to Churchill, 13 Sept. 1911, Churchill, Winston S. Churchill, ii, companion part

2, pp. 1125–6; T. Wilson, *Political Diaries of C. P. Scott*, p. 92; Churchill to Smith, 1 Aug. 1914, Birkenhead, *F.E.*, p. 241.

49 Morley, *Memorandum on Resignation*, pp. 10, 15. Pease's Diary confirms Morley's impression that the neutrality of Belgium 'was secondary to the question of our neutrality in the struggle between Germany and France; and to our liability to France under the Entente': see K. M. Wilson (ed.), 'The Cabinet Diary of J. A. Pease 24 July to 5 August 1915', *Proceedings of the Leeds Philosophical and Literary Society*, xix, part 3 (1983).

50 Burns Diary, 2 Aug. 1914, Add. MSS 46336; memo by Burns, *ibid.* 46308, f. 163.

51 David, *Inside Asquith's Cabinet*, p. 179; Pease Diary, 2 Aug. 1914.

52 Burns Diary, 3 Aug. 1914, Add. MSS 46336. This was a note drawn up by Loreburn and Harcourt dated 29 Nov. 1911 and shown by Morley to Asquith, Grey and Haldane. It ran: '1. That at no time has the Cabinet decided whether or not to give either military or naval assistance to France in the event of her being at war with Germany. 2. That at no time has the British Government given any promise of such assistance to France. 3. That the Cabinet was not informed til the end of October of any naval and military preparations being made to meet the contingency of war this summer or autumn, nor was any plan for a landing of troops on the Continent at any time communicated to or approved by the Cabinet.' See *ibid.*, 46308, ff. 163–4.

53 In Morley's recollection, this letter had been 'extorted' from Grey. Morley, *Memorandum on Resignation*, p. 18.

54 Pease Diary, 2 Aug. 1914.

55 Churchill, *Winston S. Churchill*, ii, companion part 3, pp. 1638–9.

56 *B.D.*, x (ii), nos. 399, 404, 410.

57 *Ibid.*, nos. 413–16.

58 Nicolson to Hardinge, 5 Sept. 1914, Hardinge MSS vol. 93.

59 *B.D.*, xi, no. 424; *D.D.F.*, 3rd Series, xi, no. 532.

60 Gwynne to Tyrrell, 1 Aug. 1914, Glenesk-Bathurst MSS.

61 Cambon's letter in reply contained no sentence corresponding to this. *B.D.*, x (ii), nos. 416, 417.

62 *Ibid.*, no. 404; Hansard, 5th Series, lxv, cols. 1815–17.

63 *D.D.F.*, 2nd Series, xi, pp. 931, 933. See reports of Churchill's Parliamentary Private Secretary F. A. Whyte on Liberal opinion between 31 July and 2 August, Trevelyan MSS 59; Ponsonby to Churchill, 31 July 1914, Churchill, *Winston S. Churchill*, ii, companion part 3, pp. 1990–1.

64 F. W. Hirst Diary, 3 Aug. 1914, in *Common Sense*, vii, no. 5, 2 Aug. 1919.

65 David, *Inside Asquith's Cabinet*, p. 179.

66 Hazlehurst, *Politicians at War*, p. 52; Morley, *Memorandum on Resignation*, p. 26; Pease Diary, 3 Aug. 1914: 'Grey said he felt some responsibility for the resignations and felt it acutely . . .'.

67 Lowe and Dockrill, *The Mirage of Power*, iii, pp. 489–90.

68 It reveals much of the previous day's discussions and of the thinking of the Cabinet that Pease, in his first attempt to expand and clarify his account, inserted the word 'alleged' before 'moral obligation', then crossed it out and

ended with 'our moral obligation justifying our giving support to France ...'.
Pease Diary, 3 Aug. 1914. Similarly, when on 4 August the Cabinet discussed
what the Blue Book should contain, Pease recorded urging that as much as
possible should be conveyed 'so that those who were hesitating to come to the
support of the Government should not make up their minds and take a hostile
view now, without a full understanding of the German intention to force war
on Belgium and run the risk of our internal differences preventing our support
being given to France and in the interest of small independent States'.

69 Addison, *Four and a Half Years*, i, p. 35; B.D., xi, no. 293 is no. 85 in the Blue
    Book.
70 Hazlehurst, *Politicians at War*, p. 98.
71 Lammers, 'Arno Mayer', p. 161; T. Wilson, *Political Diaries of C. P. Scott*,
    pp. 96–8.
72 Morley, *Memorandum on Resignation*, p. 23; on Harcourt see Hazlehurst,
    Politicians at War, p. 114.
73 Morley, *Memorandum on Resignation*, p. 14; Morley to Spender, 6 Aug.
    1914, Spender MSS Add. MSS 46392.
74 Trevelyan's memo of events leading to his resignation, Trevelyan MSS 59.
75 Hazlehurst, *Politicians at War*, p. 112 fn. 3; Morley, *Memorandum on Resig-
    nation*, p. 20.
76 Grey to Runciman, 2 Oct. 1911, Runciman MSS; Pease to his wife, 2, 3 Aug.,
    Mrs Pease to J. A. Pease, 4 Aug. 1914, Gainford MSS boxes 521, 91.
77 Lowe and Dockrill, *The Mirage of Power*, iii, p. 489.
78 Lammers, 'Arno Mayer', p. 158.
79 He wrote, in pencil, at the top of his diary entry for 2 August: 'See B.L.'s letter
    to P.M.' Add. MSS 46336.
80 Memo by Runciman, 2 Aug. 1914, Runciman MSS.
81 Masterman, *C. F. G. Masterman*, p. 265.
82 Morley told Almeric Fitzroy on 2 August that 'the high-handed action of
    Germany was weakening the efforts of the peacemakers in the Cabinet';
    Bryce did not deny that 'Germany has played her cards badly'; Gilbert
    Murray was reported as feeling it 'very difficult to oppose Government action
    when the German Government has plainly run amok'. Sir A. Fitzroy,
    Memoirs (London, 1925), ii, pp. 559–60; Bryce to C. P. Scott, 3 Aug. 1914,
    Bryce MSS E31; Mair to Scott, 4 Aug. 1914, T. Wilson, *Political Diaries of
    C. P. Scott*, p. 95.
83 T. Wilson, *Political Diaries of C. P. Scott*, p. 106; Loreburn to Scott, 2 Sept.
    1914, E. Montagu to Scott, 11 Aug. 1914, C. P. Scott MSS uncat.

Bibliography

Primary sources

a. Private papers
Arnold-Foster MSS: Bodleian Library, Oxford
Asquith MSS: Bodleian Library, Oxford
Balcarres MSS: University Library, Bristol
Balfour MSS: British Library, London
Bertie MSS: Public Record Office, London
Bonar Law MSS: House of Lords Record Office, London
Bryce MSS: Bodleian Library, Oxford
Burns MSS: British Library, London
Campbell-Bannerman MSS: British Library, London
Carnock MSS: Public Record Office, London
Carrington MSS: Bodleian Library, Oxford
Cartwright MSS: County Record Office, Northampton
A. Chamberlain MSS: University Library, Birmingham
Chirol MSS: archives of *The Times*, London
Crewe MSS: University Library, Cambridge
Cromer MSS: Public Record Office, London
Curzon MSS: India Office Library, London
Dawson MSS: Bodleian Library, Oxford
Elibank MSS: National Library of Scotland, Edinburgh
Gainford MSS: Nuffield College, Oxford
Glenesk-Bathurst MSS: University Library, Leeds
Grant-Duff MSS: Churchill College, Cambridge
Grey MSS: Public Record Office, London
Gwynne MSS: Bodleian Library, Oxford
Haldane MSS: National Library of Scotland, Edinburgh
Harcourt MSS: Bodleian Library, Oxford
Hardinge MSS: University Library, Cambridge
Lansdowne MSS: Public Record Office, London
Lascelles MSS: Public Record Office, London
Lloyd George MSS: House of Lords Record Office, London
Lowther MSS: Public Record Office, London

McKenna MSS: Churchill College, Cambridge
Maxse MSS: West Sussex County Record Office, Chichester
Midleton MSS: Public Record Office, London
Morley MSS: India Office Library, London
Ripon MSS: British Library, London
Roberts MSS: Public Record Office, London
Rosebery MSS: National Library of Scotland, Edinburgh
Runciman MSS: University Library, Newcastle
Salisbury MSS: Hatfield House, Hertfordshire
Samuel MSS: House of Lords Record Office, London
Sandars MSS: Bodleian Library, Oxford
Sanderson MSS: Public Record Office, London
C. P. Scott MSS: British Library, London, and *Manchester Guardian* archives,
     Manchester
Selborne MSS: Bodleian Library, Oxford
Simon MSS: Bodleian Library, Oxford
Spender MSS: British Library, London
Spring-Rice MSS: Public Record Office, London, and Churchill College,
     Cambridge
Sydenham MSS: British Library, London
Trevelyan MSS: University Library, Newcastle
Villiers MSS: Public Record Office, London
H. Wilson MSS: Imperial War Museum, London

b. Official papers

In the Public Record Office, London, the files of the following Departments of
Government:
Cabinet
Foreign Office
India Office
Admiralty
War Office
Committee of Imperial Defence

c. Published documents and correspondence

Churchill, R. S., *Winston S. Churchill*, ii, companion parts 1, 2, 3 (London, 1969).
Documents diplomatiques français 1871–1914, Ministère des Affaires Étrangères,
     Commission de publication des documents relatifs aux origines de la guerre
     de 1914 (Paris, 1929–62).
Geiss, I., *July 1914* (London, 1957).
Gooch, G. P., and Temperley, H. W. V. (eds.), *British Documents on the Origins
     of the War, 1898–1914* (London, 1926–38).
Kautsky, K., *Outbreak of the World War: German Documents* (New York, 1924).
Lepsius, J., Mendelssohn-Bartholdy, A., and Thimme, F. (eds.), *Die Grosse Politik
     der Europäischen Kabinette 1871–1914* (Berlin, 1922–7).
Lichnowsky, Prince Karl Max von, *Heading for the Abyss* (New York, 1928).

Lumby, E. W. R. (ed.), *Policy and Operations in the Mediterranean 1912–14*, Navy Records Society, cxv (London, 1970).

Marchand, R. (ed.), *Un Livre noir: diplomatie d'avant-guerre d'après les documents des archives russes*, 2 vols. (Paris, 1922–3).

Rich, N., and Fisher, M. H., *The Holstein Papers*, 4 vols. (Cambridge, 1955–63).

Siebert, B. de, *Entente Diplomacy and the World* (New York, 1921).

d. Hansard's *Parliamentary Debates*, 3rd, 4th, 5th Series.

e. Diaries, memoirs, biographies

Addison, C., *Politics from Within 1911–28*, 2 vols. (London, 1924).

Amery, L. S., *My Political Life*, 3 vols. (London, 1953).

Asquith, H. H., Earl of Oxford and Asquith, *Memories and Reflections*, 2 vols. (London, 1928).

Asquith, M., Countess of Oxford and Asquith, *Autobiography*, 2 vols. (London, 1920–2).

Bacon, R. H. S., *Life of Lord Fisher of Kilverstone*, 2 vols. (London, 1929).

Bertie of Thame, *The Diary of Lord Bertie 1914–18*, ed. Lady A. G. Lennox, 2 vols. (London, 1924).

Birkenhead, Lord, *F.E.* (London, 1959).

Blake, R., *The Unknown Prime Minister: The Life and Times of Andrew Bonar Law 1858–1923* (London, 1955).

(ed.), *The Private Papers of Douglas Haig 1914–19* (London, 1952).

Blunt, W. S., *My Diaries, being a Personal Narrative of Events 1888–1914*, 2 vols. (London, 1919–20).

Brett, M. V., and Esher, Reginald, Viscount, *Journals and Letters of Reginald, Viscount Esher*, 4 vols. (London, 1934–8).

Buchanan, Sir G., *My Mission to Russia and Other Diplomatic Memories*, 2 vols. (London, 1923).

Callwell, Sir C. W., *Field-Marshal Sir Henry Wilson*, 2 vols. (London, 1927).

Chamberlain, A., *Down the Years* (London, 1935).

Politics from Inside (London, 1936).

Churchill, W. S., *The World Crisis 1911–28*, 2 vols. (London, 1923).

Conwell-Evans, T. P., *Foreign Policy from a Back-Bench 1904–18* (Oxford, 1932).

Crewe, Lord, *Lord Rosebery*, 2 vols. (London, 1931).

David, E. (ed.), *Inside Asquith's Cabinet: From the Diaries of Charles Hobhouse* (London, 1977).

Fitzroy, Sir A., *Memoirs*, 2 vols. (London, 1925).

Grey of Fallodon, Viscount, *Twenty-Five Years 1892–1916*, 2 vols. (London, 1925).

Gwynn, S. (ed.), *The Letters and Friendships of Sir Cecil Spring-Rice*, 2 vols. (London, 1929).

Hamer, D. A., *John Morley* (Oxford, 1968).

Hardinge of Penshurst, *Old Diplomacy* (London, 1947).

Howard, C. H. D. (ed.), *The Diary of Edward Goschen 1900–14* (London, 1980).

Kent, W., *John Burns* (London, 1950).

Loreburn, Earl, *How the War Came* (London, 1919).

McKenna, S., *Reginald McKenna* (London, 1948).

Masterman, L., *C. F. G. Masterman* (London, 1939).

Maurice, Sir F., *Haldane*, 2 vols. (London, 1937).

Midleton, Lord, *Records and Reactions* (London, 1939).

Morley, J. *Recollections*, 2 vols. (London, 1917).

   Memorandum on Resignation (London, 1928).

Murray, A. C., *Master and Brother* (London, 1945).

Newton, Lord, *Lord Lansdowne* (London, 1929).

Nicolson, H., *Lord Carnock: A Study in the Old Diplomacy* (London, 1930).

Owen, F., *Tempestuous Journey: Lloyd George, His Life and Times* (London, 1954).

Paléologue, M., *La Russie des Tsars pendant la Grande Guerre*, 3 vols. (Paris, 1921).

   Journal de 1913 et 1914 (Paris, 1947).

Pope-Hennessy, J., *Lord Crewe* (London, 1955).

Riddell, Lord, *War Diary* (London, 1933).

   More Pages from My Diary 1908–14 (London, 1934).

Robbins, K., *Sir Edward Grey – a Biography* (London, 1971).

Samuel, Viscount, *Memoirs* (London, 1945).

Spender, J. A., *The Life of the Right Hon. Sir Henry Campbell-Bannerman*, 2 vols. (London, 1923).

   Life, Journalism and Politics, 2 vols. (London, 1927).

Spender, J. A., and Asquith, C., *Life of H. H. Asquith Lord Oxford and Asquith*, 2 vols. (London, 1932).

Trevelyan, G. M., *Grey of Fallodon* (London, 1937).

Wilson, J., *CB: A Life of Sir Henry Campbell-Bannerman* (London, 1973).

Wilson, T. (ed.), *The Political Diaries of C. P. Scott 1911–28* (London, 1970).

Wolf, L., *Life of the First Marquess of Ripon*, 2 vols. (London, 1921).

Wrench, J. E., *Geoffrey Dawson and Our Times* (London, 1955).

Secondary works

a. Books

Andrew, C., *Théophile Delcassé and the Making of the Entente Cordiale* (London, 1968).

Barnett, C., *The Collapse of British Power* (London, 1972).

Berghahn, V. R., *Germany and the Approach of War in 1914* (London, 1973).

Bridge, F. R., *Great Britain and Austria-Hungary 1906–14* (London, 1972).

Busch, B. C., *Great Britain and the Persian Gulf 1894–1914* (Berkeley, 1967).

Campbell, A. E., *Great Britain and the United States 1895–1903* (London, 1960).

Crampton, R. J., *The Hollow Détente: Anglo-German Relations in the Balkans 1911–14* (London, 1980).

d'Ombrain, N., *War Machinery and High Policy* (Oxford, 1973).

Fischer, F., *War of Illusions: German Policies from 1911 to 1914* (New York, 1975).

Fry, M., *Lloyd George and Foreign Policy 1890–1916* (Montreal, 1977).

Gooch, J., *The Plans of War* (London, 1974).

Grenville, J. A. S., *Lord Salisbury and Foreign Policy: The Close of the Nineteenth Century* (London, 1964).

Hale, O. J., *Publicity and Diplomacy: England and Germany 1890–1914* (New York, 1940).

Hazlehurst, C., *Politicians at War* (London, 1971).

Hinsley, F. H. (ed.), *The Foreign Policy of Sir Edward Grey* (Cambridge, 1977).

Howard, C. H. D., *Britain and the Casus Belli 1822–1902* (London, 1974).

Jarausch, K., *The Enigmatic Chancellor: Bethmann-Hollweg and the Hubris of Imperial Germany* (New Haven, Conn., 1973).

Jones, R., *The Nineteenth Century Foreign Office: An Administrative History* (London, 1971).

Kazemdadeh, F., *Russia and Great Britain in Persia 1864–1914* (New Haven, Conn., 1968).

Kehr, E., *Economic Interest, Militarism and Foreign Policy: Essays on German History*, ed. G. A. Craig (London, 1977).

Kennedy, P. M., *The Rise of the Anglo-German Antagonism 1860–1914* (London, 1980).

Lowe, C. J., and Dockrill, M. L., *The Mirage of Power: British Foreign Policy 1902–14*, 3 vols. (London, 1972).

Lowe, P., *Great Britain and Japan 1911–1915: A Study of British Far Eastern Policy* (London, 1969).

MacKay, R.F., *Fisher of Kilverstone* (Oxford, 1973).

McLean, D., *Britain and Her Buffer-State: The Collapse of the Persian Empire 1890–1914* (London, 1979).

Marder, A. J., *From the Dreadnought to Scapa Flow: The Royal Navy in the Fisher Era 1904–19*, i (Oxford, 1961).

Monger, G. W., *The End of Isolation: British Foreign Policy 1900–1907* (London, 1963).

Morris, A. J. A., *Radicalism against War 1906–14* (London, 1972).

Nish, I., *The Anglo-Japanese Alliance: The Diplomacy of Two Island Empires 1894–1907* (London, 1966).

Rich, N., *Friedrich von Holstein*, 2 vols. (Cambridge, 1965).

Ritter, G., *The Schlieffen Plan* (New York, 1958).

The Sword and the Sceptre: The Problem of Militarism in Germany, ii (London, 1972).

Rolo, P. G. V., *Entente Cordiale: The Origins and Negotiation of the Anglo-French Agreements of 8 April 1904* (London, 1969).

Scally, R. J., *The Origins of the Lloyd George Coalition: The Politics of Social-Imperialism, 1900–18* (Princeton, N.J., 1975).

Searle, G. R., *The Quest for National Efficiency* (Oxford, 1971).

Steinberg, J., *Yesterday's Deterrent: Tirpitz and the Birth of the German Battle Fleet* (London, 1965).

Steiner, Z. S., *The Foreign Office and Foreign Policy 1898–1914* (Cambridge, 1969).
  Britain and the Origins of the First World War (London, 1977).
Taylor, A. J. P., *The Struggle for Mastery in Europe 1848–1918* (Oxford, 1954).
  The Troublemakers (London, 1957).
Terraine, J., *The Western Front 1914–1918* (London, 1964).
The Times, The History of 'The Times', iii (London, 1947), iv, part 1 (London, 1952).
Williamson, S. R., *The Politics of Grand Strategy: Britain and France Prepare for War 1904–14* (Cambridge, Mass., 1969).
Woodward, E. L., *Great Britain and the German Navy* (Oxford, 1935).
Young, H. F., *Prince Lichnowsky and the Great War* (Athens, Georgia, 1977).

b. Articles

Andrew, C., 'The Entente Cordiale from its Origins to 1914', in Waites, N. (ed.), *Troubled Neighbours: Franco-British Relations in the Twentieth Century* (London, 1971).
Berghahn, V. R., 'Naval Armaments and Social Crisis: Germany before 1914', in Best, G., and Wheatcroft, A. (eds.), *War, Economy and the Military Mind* (London, 1976).
Boyle, T., 'The Formation of Campbell-Bannerman's Government in December 1905: A Memorandum by J. A. Spender', *B.I.H.R.*, xlv (1972).
Butterfield, H., 'Sir Edward Grey in July 1914', *Historical Studies*, v (1965).
Cairns, J. C., 'International Politics and the Military Mind: The Case of the French Republic 1911–14', *J.M.H.*, xxv, no. 3 (1953).
Cohen, S. A., 'Sir Arthur Nicolson and Russia: The Case of the Baghdad Railway', *H.J.*, xviii, no. 4 (1975).
  'The Genesis of the British Campaign in Mesopotamia, 1914', *Middle Eastern Studies*, xii (1976).
  'Mesopotamia in British Strategy 1903–1914', *International Journal of Middle East Studies*, ix (1978).
Cooper, M. B., 'British Policy in the Balkans 1908–9', *H.J.*, vii, no. 2 (1964).
Crampton, R. J., 'August Bebel and the British Foreign Office', *History*, lviii (1973).
  'The Decline of the Concert of Europe in the Balkans 1913–14', *Slavonic and East European Review*, lii (1974).
Dockrill, M. L., 'David Lloyd George and Foreign Policy before 1914', in Taylor, A. J. P. (ed.), *Lloyd George: Twelve Essays* (London, 1971).
Edwards, E. W., 'The Far Eastern Agreements of 1907', *J.M.H.*, xxvi, no. 4 (1954).
  'The Japanese Alliance and the Anglo-French Agreement of 1904', *History*, xlii (1957).
  'The Franco-German Agreement on Morocco, 1909', *E.H.R.*, lxxviii (1963).
  'Great Britain and the Manchurian Railways Question, 1909–10', *E.H.R.*, lxxxi (1966).
  'The Prime Minister and Foreign Policy: The Balfour Government 1902–5', in

Hearder, H., and Loyn, H.R., *British Government and Administration: Studies Presented to S. B. Chrimes* (Cardiff, 1974).

Fischer, F., 'Recent Work on German Naval Policy', *E.S.R.*, v, no. 4 (1975).

Francis, R. M., 'The British Withdrawal from the Baghdad Railway project in April 1903', *H.J.*, xvi, no. 1 (1973).

French, D., 'Spy Fever in Britain 1900–1915', *H.J.*, xxi, no. 2 (1978).

Gooch, J., 'Sir George Clarke's Career at the Committee of Imperial Defence 1904–1907', *H.J.*, xviii, no. 3 (1975).

Gowen, R. J., 'British Legerdemain at the 1911 Imperial Conference: The Dominions, Defense Planning, and the Renewal of the Anglo-Japanese Alliance', *J.M.H.*, lii (Sept. 1980).

Greaves, R. L., 'British Policy in Persia 1892–1903', *Bulletin of the School of Oriental and African Studies*, xxviii (1965).

'Some Aspects of the Anglo-Russian Convention and its working in Persia 1907–14', *ibid.*, xxxi (1968).

Haggie, P., 'The Royal Navy and War Planning in the Fisher Era', *J.C.H.*, viii (1971).

Hatton, P. H. S., 'Harcourt and Solf: The Search for an Anglo-German Understanding through Africa 1912–14', *E.S.R.*, i, no. 2 (1971).

Ingram, E., 'A Strategic Dilemma: The Defence of India 1874–1914', *Militärgeschichtliche Mitteilungen*, xiv (1974).

'Great Britain's Great Game: An Introduction', *International History Review*, ii, no. 1 (1980).

Jarausch, K., 'The Illusion of Limited War: Chancellor Bethmann-Hollweg's Calculated Risk, July 1914', *Central European History*, ii (1969).

Jones, R. B., 'Anglo-French Negotiations 1907: A Memorandum by Sir Alfred Milner', *B.I.H.R.*, xxxi (1958).

Kennedy, P. M., 'German World Policy and the Alliance Negotiations with England 1897–1900', *J.M.H.*, xlv, no. 4 (1973).

'The Development of German Naval Operations Plans Against England 1896–1914', *E.H.R.*, lxxxix (1974).

'Fisher and Tirpitz: Political Admirals in the Age of Imperialism', in Jordan, G. (ed.), *Naval Warfare in the Twentieth Century* (London, 1977).

Klein, I., 'The Anglo-Russian Convention and the Problem of Central Asia 1907–14', *J.B.S.*, xi, no. 1 (1971).

Kumar, R., 'The Records of the Government of India on the Berlin–Baghdad Railway Question', *H.J.*, v, no. 1 (1962).

Lammers, D., 'Arno Mayer and the British Decision for War: 1914', *J.B.S.*, xii, no. 2 (1973).

Langhorne, R. T. B., 'Anglo-German Negotiations Concerning the Future of the Portuguese Colonies 1911–14', *H.J.*, xvi, no. 2 (1973).

Leaman, B. R., 'The Influence of Domestic Policy on Foreign Affairs in France 1898–1905', *J.M.H.*, xiv, no. 4 (1942).

Lee, H. I., 'Mediterranean Strategy and Anglo-French Relations 1908–12', *Mariner's Mirror*, lvii (1971).

'The Grey–Cambon Exchange of 22 November 1912: A Note on the Documents', *B.I.H.R.*, xlvi (1973).

McDermott, J., 'The Revolution in British Military Thinking from the Boer War to the Moroccan Crisis', *Canadian Journal of History*, ix, no. 2 (1974).

MacKay, R. F., 'The Admiralty, the German Navy, and the Redistribution of the British Fleet, 1904–5', *Mariner's Mirror*, lvi (1970.

'Historical Reinterpretations of the Anglo-German Naval Rivalry, 1897–1914', in Jordan, G. (ed.), *Naval Warfare in the Twentieth Century* (London, 1977).

Maehl, W., 'Bebel's Fight against the Schlachtflotte, Nemesis of the Primacy of Foreign Policy', *Proceedings of the American Philosophical Society*, cxxi (1977).

Mahajan, S., 'The Defence of India and the End of Isolation: A Study in the Foreign Policy of the Conservative Government 1900–1905', *Journal of Imperial and Commonwealth History*, x, no. 2 (1982).

Mommsen, W. J., 'Domestic Factors in German Foreign Policy before 1914', *Central European History*, vi (1973).

'The Topos of Inevitable War in Germany in the Decade before 1914', in Berghahn, V. R., and Kitchen, M. (eds.), *Germany in the Age of Total War* (London, 1981).

Morris, A. J. A., 'Charles Trevelyan and Two Views of "Revolution" ', in Morris, A. J. A. (ed.), *Edwardian Radicalism* (London, 1974).

Murray, J. A., 'Foreign Policy Debated: Sir Edward Grey and his Critics 1911–12', in Askew, W. C., and Wallace, L. P., *Power, Public Opinion and Diplomacy, Essays in Honour of E. M. Carroll* (Durham, North Carolina, 1959).

Palmer, A. W., 'Lord Salisbury's Approach to Russia, 1898', *Oxford Slavonic Papers*, vi (1955).

Robbins, K., 'Sir Edward Grey and the British Empire', *Journal of Imperial and Commonwealth History*, i (1972–3).

Rohl, J. C. G., 'Admiral von Muller and the Approach of War, 1911–14', *H.J.*, xii, no. 4 (1969).

Schroeder, P., 'World War I as Galloping Gertie', *J.M.H.*, xliv, no. 3 (1972).

'Munich and the British Tradition', *H.J.*, xix, no. 1 (1976).

Searle, G. R., 'The "Revolt from the Right" in Edwardian Britain', in Kennedy, P. M., and Nicholls, A. (eds.), *Nationalist and Racialist Movements in Britain and Germany before 1914* (London, 1981).

Silberstein, G. E., 'Germany, France and the Casablanca Incident 1908–9: An Investigation of a Forgotten Crisis', *Canadian Journal of History*, xi (1976).

Spring, D. W., 'The Trans-Persian Railway project and Anglo-Russian Relations 1909–14', *Slavonic and East European Review*, liv (1976).

Steiner, Z. S., 'Grey, Hardinge and the Foreign Office 1906–10', *H.J.*, x, no. 3 (1967).

Steiner, Z. S., and Cromwell, V., 'The Foreign Office before 1914: A Study in Resistance', in Sutherland, G. (ed.), *Studies in the Growth of Nineteenth Century Government* (London, 1972).

Summers, A., 'Militarism in Britain before the Great War', *History Workshop*, no. 2 (1976).

'The Character of Edwardian Nationalism: Three Popular Leagues', in Berghahn, V. R., and Kitchen, M. (eds.), *Germany in the Age of Total War* (London, 1981).

Thomas, M. E., 'Anglo-Belgian Military Relations and the Congo Question 1911–13', *J.M.H.*, xxv, no. 2 (1953).

Towle, P., 'The Russo-Japanese War and the Defence of India', *Military Affairs* (October 1980).

Vincent-Smith, J. D., 'The Anglo-German Negotiations over the Portuguese Colonies in Africa, 1911–14', *H.J.*, xvii, no. 3 (1974).

Watt, D. C., 'The British Reactions to the Assassination at Sarajevo', *E.S.R.*, i, no. 3 (1971).

Weinroth, H., 'The British Radicals and the Balance of Power 1902–14', *H.J.*, xiii, no. 4 (1970).

'Left-Wing Opposition to Naval Armaments in Britain before 1914', *J.C.H.*, vi, no. 4 (1971).

Williams, B., 'The Strategic Background to the Anglo-Russian Entente of August 1907', *H.J.*, ix, no. 3 (1966).

'The Revolution of 1905 and Russian Foreign Policy', in Abramsky, C., and Williams, B., *Essays in Honour of E. H. Carr* (London, 1974).

Wilson, K.M., 'The Agadir Crisis, the Mansion House Speech and the Double-Edgedness of Agreements', *H.J.*, xv, no. 3 (1972).

'The War Office, Churchill and the Belgian Option: August to December 1911', *B.I.H.R.*, l, no. 122 (1977).

'The Opposition and the Crisis in the Liberal Cabinet over Foreign Policy in November 1911', *International History Review*, iii, no. 3 (1981).

'Isolating the Isolator: Cartwright, Grey and the Seduction of Austria-Hungary 1908–12', *Mitteilungen des Österreichischen Staatsarchivs*, xxxv (1982).

'The Cabinet Diary of J. A. Pease 24 July to 5 August 1914', *Proceedings of the Leeds Philosophical and Literary Society*, xix, part 3 (1983).

'Sir Eyre Crowe on the Origin of the Crowe Memorandum of 1 January 1907', *B.I.H.R.*, lvi, no. 134 (1983).

'The Foreign Office and the "Education" of Public Opinion before the First World War', *H.J.*, xxvi, no. 2 (1983).

'The Question of Anti-Germanism at the British Foreign Office before the First World War', *Canadian Journal of History*, xviii, no. 1 (1983).

'Imperial Interests in the British Decision for War, 1914: the Defence of India in Central Asia', *Review of International Studies*, x, no. 3 (1984).

'The British Démarche of 3 and 4 December 1912: H. A. Gwynne's Note on Britain, Russia and the First Balkan War', *Slavonic and East European Review*, lxii, no. 4 (1984).

Winzen, P., 'Prince Bulow's Weltmachtpolitik', *Australian Journal of Politics and History*, xxii, no. 2 (1976).

Young, H. F., 'The Misunderstanding of August 1, 1914', *J.M.H.*, xlviii (1976).

Index

Acland, A., 22, 88
Admiralty, 7, 8, 63–4, 125, 127
Aehrenthal, Count A. L. von, 113
Algeciras Conference, 74, 94
Anglo-French Agreement, (1904), 71–2, 75, 87–8, 96
Anglo-German Agreements, (1898) 97, (Oct. 1900) 5; negotiations,(1901) 5, 6, (1909–12) 12, 26–7, 34, 86–7, (1912–14) 10, 28–9
Anglo-Japanese Alliance, (1902) 42–5, 52, 71, 74, (1905) 75
Anglo-Russian Conventions, (1907) 6, 74–7, 82–3; negotiations, (1914) 48, 58, 84, 85
Arnold-Foster, H. O., 71, 109
Asquith, H. H., 4, 14–15, 20–2, 28, 32–4, 92, 107, 122, 127, 141
Austria-Hungary, 78, 98, 103, 104, 111, 113

Balcarres, Lord, 32
Balfour, A. J., 15, 29, 32, 41, 43, 48–9, 71, 73
Balkan War (1912), 60, 92
Ballard, Admiral G. A., 67
Beauchamp, Lord, 138–9, 146
Bebel, A., 105
Belgium, 10, 127ff, 135, 136, 142; neutrality of, 96, 99, 107, 127ff, 140
Benckendorff, A., 41, 97
Bentinck, H., 31
Bertie, Sir F., 38, 41, 46, 88–9, 116–17
Bethell, Admiral, 63, 64
Bethmann-Hollweg, T. von, 29, 34, 48, 58, 99, 113, 140
Birrell, A., 139
Boer War, 4, 11, 20, 109
Bosnia–Hercegovina, 103, 104
Briand, A., 8
Bridges, G. T. M., 132

British Empire, 7, 8, 15, 80, 84, 108, 115
British Expeditionary Force, 33, 51, 62–3, 92, 121ff
Brodrick, St J. (Midleton), 55, 109
Buchanan, Sir G. W., 40, 78
Buckmaster, S., 146
Bulow, Prince von, 103
Bunsen, Sir M. de, 52
Burns, J., 51, 96, 136–7, 141, 147
Buxton, N., 119

Cabinet, Committee on Anglo-German negotiations, 27; resolutions of November 1911, 28, 86, 90, 122, 124, 136, 142
Caillaux, J., 89, 116
Cambon, P., 23, 56, 78–9, 87, 92, 96, 122, 133, 134, 142, 144
Campbell-Bannerman, Sir H., 17, 22, 23, 51, 54
Canning, G., 42, 85
Cartwright, Sir F., 9, 113
Castlereagh, Viscount, 42
Chamberlain, Sir A., 30, 110
Chamberlain, J., 4, 5
Chirol, V., 18, 23, 30, 63, 118
Churchill, W. S., 24, 32, 33, 53, 96, 123, 125, 130–1, 139, 143, 145
Clarke, Sir G., 6, 107
Clemenceau, G., 58, 114
Committee of Imperial Defence, 21, 72, 84, 85, 121; sub-committees of, on the Military Needs of the Empire, 66, 81, 116, 121, 125–6, 129, 133, on the Military Requirements of the Empire as affected by the Defence of India, 75–6, on Invasion, (1909) 54, (1913) 14; 114th meeting, 27, 62–3, 81, 124, 125–6, 133
conscription, 25, 53–5
Corbett, J., 121

197